MURDEROUS MANCHESTER

The executed of the Twentieth Century

MURDEROUS MANCHESTER

The executed of the Twentieth Century

JOHN J. EDDLESTON

First published in Great Britain by The Breedon Books Publishing Company Limited, Breedon House, 44 Friar Gate, Derby, DE1 1DA. 1997

Paperback edition published in Great Britain in 2011 by The Derby Books Publishing Company Limited, 3 The Parker Centre, Derby, DE21 4SZ.

ISBN 978-1-85983-939-3

Printed and bound by CPI Anthony Rowe, Chippenham

CONTENTS

ACKNOWLEDGEMENTS

First and foremost, I would like to offer my sincere thanks to Yvonne Berger who has helped a great deal in the production of this book. In addition to assisting with my research, she has sourced photographs, proof read the entire volume and helped me with the index. Without her assistance, my task in preparing this book would have been immeasurably more difficult.

My thanks, too, must go to the staff at the Public Record Office, whom I have always found helpful, courteous, efficient and professional. I would also like to mention the staff of Colindale Newspaper Library for their assistance.

Finally, a special mention must go to Ms Kath Lapsley of the Central Library in Manchester for helping with some of the case histories.

INTRODUCTION

THIS book tells the story of every murder which took place in Manchester this century and which ended in the execution of the person found guilty of the crime and who went on to pay the ultimate penalty of death by hanging at the end of a rope.

Some cases are well-known, such as those of George Rice, William Burtoft and Walter Graham Rowland – who was reprieved for a murder he did commit but was later hanged for one which he may not have committed – but any of the lesser known murders have equally absorbing stories of love, jealousy and lust. Readers will discover child killers such as John Horner, wife killers such as Frederick Ballington, and those who killed out of rage or for revenge, such as James Ryder. And then there was James Henry Corbitt, where the hangman was someone he had known as a friend.

All manner of motives are shown, all sorts of weapons are used, but in the final analysis each story represents a human tragedy in which at least two people lost their lives. Read these stories and then decide for yourselves whether or not every one was guilty as charged.

Note: The story of Jan Mohamed, referred to on the dust jacket, has been omitted as its connection with Manchester is tenuous.

John J. Eddleston
Sussex
Summer 1997

CHAPTER ONE

A WOMAN OF IMTEMPERATE HABITS

ELIZA Range had led a chequered life. Married three times, her last husband was William Range, a railway worker for the Lancashire and Yorkshire Railway Company. In all they had been married for 18 years, but in reality the relationship between them had been over for most of that time. Indeed, after a couple of years, Eliza had walked out on William but had returned five or six years later with a son in tow. After his estranged wife promised to mend her ways, William Range allowed her to move back into his house at 99 Husband Street, Collyhurst, but they were to have separate lives, separate rooms, and each was free to enjoy other relationships.

For her part, Eliza sought comfort in the company of 43-year-old Charles Whittaker, a bacon roller, and by August 1903 he had known Eliza for some two and a half years. For the last six months of that period, Whittaker had been visiting Eliza at Husband Street, and was known to her son, Arthur, who was by now 15 years old, as 'Charlie'.

It was quite early on the morning of Saturday, August 8th, 1903, when William Range went to work as usual on the railway. When he left, Eliza and Arthur – who had taken to using the name Range, even though he was not William's son – were still in bed. Eliza eventually got up, but it was not until 10.50am that Arthur found his way downstairs for breakfast. His mother was already in the front room, sitting at the table, drinking with Charles Whittaker.

As Arthur sat down, Eliza handed Whittaker a glass of beer before declaring, "This won't do, I shall have to get me washed," whereupon she walked into the scullery, took off her bodice and drew some water. Without a word, Whittaker got to his feet and followed her, drawing a knife from his pocket as he went. Young Arthur Range watched as Whittaker pushed his mother into the far corner of the scullery, where she was out of his view, and then heard words spoken, although he was unable to hear clearly what they were.

Suddenly, Eliza cried, "Arthur! Murder!" Arthur dashed into the scullery in time to see Whittaker running out into the yard. His mother, meanwhile, was sitting on a stool, bleeding profusely from a wound in the left side of her neck. Terrified, the young lad ran to a neighbour's house to get help.

Mary Whiitaker lived at number 103, but was no relation to Charles. She was expecting the doctor to call to see her sick child and after hearing what had happened she went back to 99 Husband Street with Arthur. By now, Eliza was standing at the slopstone, bathing her neck but was able to speak to Mary. Moments later, Arthur went back outside to wait for Dr Southam. Once that gentleman had arrived, Arthur had rushed off to fetch the police.

It was 11.10am by the time Sergeant John Richard Pope arrived at Husband Street. Dr Southam was still tending his patient, who by now was lying on the sofa in the front room. Four minutes later, Constable Charles Neville arrived and these officers were present when Eliza Range succumbed to her injuries and breathed her last.

A search of the premises was organised and in the yard at the back, Constable Neville found the shaft of a knife which corresponded with a blade which Arthur had found in the scullery and handed over to Sergeant Pope. Eliza's body was taken to the mortuary and a full scale search for her assailant was launched.

In fact, it was not the result of the police investigation which led to the apprehension of Charles Whittaker. Constable John Maxwell was on duty in the Albert Street police station at 1.15pm on Sunday, August 9th, when Whittaker walked in and told the officer, "I believe you want me." Constable Maxwell asked why that should be, to which Whittaker replied, "For that murder yesterday. Haven't you heard of it?" He was taken into the charge office where he was seen by Inspector Daniel Oakden, to whom Whittaker announced, "I am the man who committed that murder yesterday. I have come to give myself up." Whittaker gave the inspector his full name and was cautioned. Oakden then referred to a written description of the wanted man, in order to make sure that Whittaker was indeed who he claimed to be, but the prisoner noticed this and added, "Oh it's all right, you need not look at that – it's me all right. I should have come before only I wanted some drink." He was then charged with the murder of Eliza Range.

There were three appearances at the police court, the first taking place on August 10th. Other hearings followed on August 13th, and again on August 20th when the evidence was heard before the stipendiary magistrate, Mr F.J. Headlum. The case for the

Director of Public Prosecutions was given by Mr Bell, but Whittaker had no legal representation. At the end of the proceedings, the police court returned the same verdict as the inquest had done and Whittaker was sent for trial on the capital charge.

The case of the Crown versus Charles Whittaker was heard at Manchester on November 13th, 1903, before Mr Justice Ridley. Whittaker was by now represented by Mr J.B. Sandbach, while the prosecution evidence was put by Mr Ambrose Jones and Mr Pope.

William Range told the court that his wife was either 43 or 44 years old, he was not sure which. She had earned her living as a laundress but had been addicted to drink and often used to go out at nights, many times not returning until well after 11.00pm. He claimed that he did not know that his wife was entertaining other men at his house. The meetings with Whittaker had been kept from him and the prisoner had been careful to leave before William Range returned home. On the night before her death, Eliza had been at home at 6.00pm when William got back from work, but by 8.00pm when he went to bed, she had gone out. William was not sure what time she returned, but at 4.15am on August 8th, when he got up to go to work, Eliza was in bed with her son, Arthur. That was the last he knew until the police told him what had happened when he returned home at 2.00pm to find that his wife's body had already been removed to the mortuary.

Arthur Range was an important witness for the prosecution, since he had witnessed at least some of the attack upon his mother. He confirmed that he slept in the same bed as his mother and had done so on the night of August 7th. Arthur went on to explain the events leading up to his mother going into the scullery on August 8th, and of her being followed by Whittaker who he knew only as Charlie. At the time, Whittaker had his back to Arthur as his mother was washing in order to go to a cleaning job she had on Saturday mornings. After the attack, Whittaker had run off and Arthur had found part of a knife blade between the stool and the wall in the scullery. He had then run out of the back, to a neighbour's house where he had seen Mrs Mary Whittaker. Mrs Whittaker had gone back to the house with Arthur and mentioned that she was expecting Dr Southam to call as her child had measles. He had then gone outside to wait for the doctor, so that he could tell him what had taken place and ask him to treat his mother's injuries. Finally, Arthur confirmed that he had been told by his mother not to let William Range know of the visits Whittaker paid to the house.

Mary Catherine Whittaker lived at 103 Husband Street and she reported that it was around 11.00am when Arthur came to fetch her. When she got to the scullery of number 99, Eliza Range was bathing her neck and when Mary asked her what had happened, Eliza said that a man named Charles had done it. After hearing this, Mary left to see if

Arthur had found the doctor yet. She also told the court that Eliza was fond of drink and that she had seen her very drunk, on two or three occasions.

Emily Saunders lived next door to Eliza, at number 101. She said that some time between 11.00am and noon she had heard the sound of a scream coming from number 99 but that there had been no audible argument before. Emily recognised Eliza's voice but did not go into the house next door as she did not know her neighbour well enough.

Harriett Rothwell, who also lived in Husband Street and was the wife of a beerhouse keeper, said that Eliza, who was a regular customer, came in at some time between 10.00am and 10.15am on August 8th to buy a gill of beer to take away. In her opinion, Eliza was sober at the time.

Sergeant Pope said that when he arrived at Husband Street, he found Eliza lying semi-conscious on the sofa, still being attended to by the doctor. There was a large pool of blood on the scullery floor and, returning to the front room, Pope asked Eliza several times if she could tell him who had done this to her. Finally she managed to say, "Yes, I will tell you, look what he's done. Charlie Whittaker." Soon after this, Eliza had died. The next day, Sergeant Pope had received Whittaker into custody. There were obvious bloodstains on his coat and handkerchief and in Whittaker's pocket, Pope found a key to a locker at 232 Great Ancoats Street. The prisoner admitted that this was where he had been staying but said that he had not slept there since the night of August 6th.

Dr Stanley Southam gave evidence that when he first arrived at Husband Street, he had plugged a large hole in Eliza's neck. After she had passed away, he examined the wounds more closely and saw a deep stab wound in the left side of her neck, just above the collarbone. There were also three wounds, two of which were superficial, on her forearm and these had almost certainly been defence wounds. Dr Southam had conducted a post-mortem on August 11th and he confirmed that death was due to syncope and haemorrhage. He said that there was no sign of alcohol in the dead woman's blood.

Charles Whittaker gave evidence on his own behalf. He said that the cause of the trouble between Eliza and himself was due to the fact that she had, of late, been going into a neighbour's house to clean for him and he suspected that she might be having an affair. On the morning in question, he had had two noggins of whisky at her house, followed by two pints of beer.

When Eliza went into the scullery, Whittaker had followed her and asked if she would stop seeing the neighbour. She told him that she would continue to go next door as long as she liked. She then made a personal remark against him and he remembered nothing more until the next day when he read a report of the crime in the newspaper and realised that Eliza was dead.

In his closing speech, Mr Sandbach for the defence claimed that Whittaker was so mad with drink and rage that he had no proper idea of the nature of what he was doing. The judge, though, destroyed any lingering hopes which Whittaker might have held by saying that he saw no evidence of any provocation which could reduce the charge to one of manslaughter. The judge added, "On his own confession, he is guilty." The jury did not even bother to leave the box, conferring for only a few minutes before returning their guilty verdict. Whittaker heard the sentence of death without betraying any sign of emotion and then, in a firm voice, said, "Thank you my Lord."

Less than three weeks after the trial, on Wednesday, December 2nd, 1903, Charles Whittaker was hanged at Strangeways prison by John Billington and John Ellis. The year saw a total of 27 executions in the prisons of England and Wales, the most this century. Whittaker's was the 19th, and seven more men and one woman would follow him to the gallows before 1903 was over.

CHAPTER TWO

PROVOCATION

I T WAS an innocent enough question. A neighbour had asked 58-year-old Edward Hartigan, a hod-carrier, why he had not gone to work, but the reply was filled with anger and venom.

"How can I work without grub?" spat Hartigan, who then began to speak about his wife, Catherine. It was her fault, he raged, that he had not had enough to eat. Hartigan ended his tirade, "I will make her remember. She will not leave me without grub again, I will disable her for life." It was a threat which Hartigan, a powerfully-built man, feared in his neighbourhood, was to make good that very day, Tuesday, August 7th, 1906.

Both Edward and Catherine Hartigan were known to be fond of a drink and soon after making these comments to his neighbour, Hartigan took himself off to his local pub, the Railway Inn, where he downed several pints before walking home with Nellie, the eldest of his four children. Although Hartigan could not be described as drunk and incapable, he was certainly under the influence and it was clear that drink was still on his mind, for as soon as he and Nellie reached their home at 31 Peter Street, Stockport, Hartigan sent his daughter out to buy him another gill of beer. By the time Nellie returned it was 6.30pm and as Hartigan swallowed yet more alcohol, he told Nellie to go upstairs and make sure that the beds were made.

She did as she was ordered and found her mother lying on the bed in the front bedroom, apparently asleep and in all probability having already taken a few drinks herself. Nellie went back downstairs and asked her father to be quiet, if and when he went upstairs, as her mother was asleep.

But far from ensuring Catherine Hartigan's continued slumber, this had the effect of sending Edward Hartigan into another rage. He jumped to his feet, shouted, "Is she?" and ran upstairs. Nellie followed but her father pushed her back out of the room and although she could not see what was happening, the sounds that came from the front bedroom left her in no doubt that Catherine Hartigan was being subjected to yet another beating. Nellie heard her mother cry out, "What do you mean you fool?" And moments later, as the beating continued, she shouted, "I don't deserve it, I've done nothing."

Poor Nellie Hartigan could do nothing to help and ran back down the stairs and into the street, looking for a neighbour, anyone, to come to her mother's aid. As Nellie fell to her knees on the pavement, her cries brought a number of neighbours running, including Elizabeth Bramhall who bravely crept upstairs at number 31 in time to see Hartigan, who was wearing heavy clogs, still kicking at his wife, who by now was half-in and half-out of the bed. Somehow, Mrs Bramhall managed to calm the situation before leaving the house as Hartigan followed her downstairs.

Hartigan, though, was still in a fury. By now a small crowd had gathered in Peter Street and he went out to face them, threatening to shoot any man, woman or child who came near him. No one dared approach and Hartigan, who had blood on his hands, walked back inside his house.

Less than 20 minutes later, Hartigan reappeared at his front door and, without a word, set off up the street, heading back in the direction of the Railway Inn. Seeing that the coast was clear, Elizabeth Bramhall and another neighbour, Mary Leonard, entered number 31 and ran upstairs to the front bedroom. The sight which met their eyes almost made them physically sick. Catherine Hartigan lay on the floor in a large pool of blood, her skull caved in. Nearby was a heavy hammer which had apparently been used to inflict the terrible injuries she bore.

As word spread of the awful events at 31 Peter Street, Edward Hartigan reached the corner of the street where he was met yet another neighbour, Mrs Tratten. She knew nothing of what had taken place, but was aware that there had been many arguments between Hartigan and his wife. She asked him, "Why don't you be good?" Hartigan grasped Mrs Tratten's hand, shook it vigorously and announced, "It's, too, late, I've done it." Mrs Tratten asked, "Have you killed her?" and Hartigan, by now continuing on his way, called back, "Yes, I've done it."

By now, a crowd of neighbours were following Hartigan and Mrs Bramhall, seeing a policeman in the distance, called out, "You murderer, the bobbies are coming." Hartigan, though, seemed unconcerned. Arriving at the Railway Inn, he asked for a gill of beer but the landlord refused to serve him, saying that he had had enough. Hartigan was not dismayed and as he walked out of the pub he waved his hand and shouted to everyone present, "Goodbye lads, you won't see me again."

The knot of neighbours had approached the policeman, Sergeant Brierley, and told him what had taken place at 31 Peter Street. He dashed to the house, went up to the front bedroom and saw Catherine Hartigan on the floor. Brierley made a quick examination and found that, although deeply unconscious, Mrs Hartigan was still alive. He summoned a doctor and a police ambulance and then, after speaking to Mrs Bramhall and the others, went in search of Edward Hartigan.

In fact, Hartigan was already on his way to the police station, so when Sergeant Brierley found him, close to Howard Street, he offered no resistance and walked calmly to the station where he saw Inspector Marshall and greeted him with, "Mr Marshall, I have come to give myself up for the wilful murder of my wife." Hartigan, who was still heavily bloodstained, made a full statement outlining what he had done. At one stage he jumped to his feet and shouted, "I've bashed her brains out with the hammer. I've made a mistake this time."

Edward Hartigan made his first appearance before the magistrates at Stockport police court on August 8th. Only the most basic evidence of arrest was given, Sergeant Brierley telling the court that he had seen a crowd gathering in Peter Street and had gone to investigate and found the unconscious Catherine Hartigan. He had soon found Hartigan and taken him to the police station, where the prisoner had at first been charged with attempted murder, but when Catherine had succumbed to her injuries, the charge had been altered to one of murder. After hearing these details, the magistrates remanded Hartigan for a week.

His second court appearance took place on August 15th, by which time the prosecution had been taken over by Mr Dobson. The family history was now given. Hartigan was known to be a man of intemperate habits and had frequently argued with his wife, who was also fond of alcohol. There were four children from the marriage: Nellie who was 16; Annie at 14; Edward 12; and George, the youngest at nine. The only member of the family who had witnessed any of the attack was, of course, Nellie and she told the court that the hammer used to kill her mother had been taken upstairs by Hartigan on Sunday, August 5th, to knock some nails in. She went on to detail what she had seen and heard and was then cross-examined by her father, who had no legal representation.

Hartigan asked Nellie if she knew that her mother was constantly drunk and unable to cook for him and, consequently, he had gone without food. Nellie replied that she knew of only one occasion when this had been the case but after being pressed by Hartigan, admitted that her mother had been noisy and quarrelsome when she had taken drink, and that once, Catherine had been locked up for assaulting a policeman.

Elizabeth Bramhall agreed that Catherine had been drunk from time to time and the last occasion she had seen the deceased under the influence was on the Sunday before she died. She went on to describe seeing Nellie, obviously deeply distressed, in the street, shouting, "He is going to kill mama," over and over again. Later she heard Hartigan threaten his neighbours by saying, "If anyone comes here I will put a bullet through them."

Mrs Tratten was the neighbour to whom Hartigan had made his comments about not having any food when she asked him why he had not gone to work. This was early in the afternoon of August 7th and the next time she saw him, he was walking down Peter Street, heading for the Railway Inn. It was then that he admitted killing Catherine.

Having heard all the evidence, the magistrates had no difficulty in sending Hartigan for trial. Those proceedings took place on November 6th, at Chester, before Mr Justice Walton, Hartigan, who was rather deaf, having to be asked how he pleaded by the prison guard standing next to him. The prosecution case was led by Mr Ellis J. Griffith MP, who was assisted by Mr Ambrose Jones. Hartigan's defence rested in the hands of Mr T.E. Morris and that defence was that the prisoner had been sorely provoked and was so drunk at the time that he did not know what he was doing.

In addition to the witnesses already mentioned, Dr Russell Rew, the assistant house surgeon at Stockport Infirmary, testified that he had found 19 distinct lacerated wounds on Catherine Hartigan's head. Her skull was badly crushed and her brain was protruding from an area above her right ear. She had never regained consciousness and had died just before midnight on August 7th, the cause of death being haemorrhage and laceration of the brain. Further, Dr Rew confirmed that there was absolutely no sign of alcohol in the woman's system at the time she was admitted to hospital.

In addition to giving details of Hartigan's statements at the police station, Inspector Marshall told the court that he had seen the prisoner in King Street East before the attack on Catherine had taken place. Hartigan was drunk and Marshall had told him to go home. However, Inspector Marshall was at least able to show that Hartigan had some-times been sorely provoked by his wife. He stated that in 1894, an incident had taken place during which Catherine Hartigan had thrown a lighted paraffin lamp at her husband. He had been engulfed in flames and needed three months' treatment for burns at the local infirmary.

In the event, none of these details saved Hartigan from his fate and the jury returned a guilty verdict. Precisely three weeks later, on Tuesday, November 27th, 1906, Edward Hartigan was hanged at Knutsford jail by Henry Pierrepoint and William Willis.

At the inquest afterwards, the prison governor, Major Nelson, stated that Hartigan had been a model prisoner since his trial. He had risen at 6.00am and attended mass in his cell but had subsequently refused breakfast. During his stay in the condemned cell, Hartigan had caused no problems for his guards and had made a full confession of guilt to the chaplain. It was, however, also shown that Hartigan had been a violent man with a long police record dating back to 1871. In March 1883 he had received a sentence of 12 months' hard labour for breaking the jaw of the licensee of the Oddfellow's Arms on Heaton Lane. A six-month sentence had followed in 1884, for an assault upon his sister, and no sooner had he been released than he was given a further month for another assault. There had also been convictions for stealing and Hartigan had been well-known in his area as a man not to argue with.

The execution of Edward Hartigan was the second to take place at Knutsford this century, and the sixth in all. Only two more men would face a similar fate on those same gallows.

CHAPTER THREE

JUSTICE?

IN 1894, Arthur Charlton, a Manchester bookkeeper, and his wife, Lilian Jane Charlton, separated and Mrs Charlton took their three children, Joseph, George and Tellie, to live at 86 Crondall Street, Moss Side. For a time, mother and children lived alone but at the beginning of 1906, a new man, Charles Paterson, a sailor of mixed race who hailed from St Vincent in the West Indies, came into Lilian's life and soon moved in with her and the three children.

Unfortunately for Lilian there were soon major problems with the new man in her life. Paterson, who was unemployed, had a short fuse and much of his anger was directed towards Lilian, who soon began to sport bruises and other marks of physical violence. On several occasions she went to the police to complain about her ill-treatment, and more than once she spoke to Acting Sergeant David Shorthouse at Raby, on one occasion showing him a fresh bruise close to her eye. But while Sergeant Shorthouse sympathised with the woman, it was a domestic problem and he advised her that her best course of action was to apply to the local magistrates for a summons against the man who was subjecting her to this abuse.

Lilian Charlton acted on that advice and during the first week of June went to court in order to take out a warrant for Paterson's arrest. Lilian, though, had been supporting Paterson for the past year, and to add to her other worries also had financial problems and was unable to pay for the warrant. It was within the power of the magistrates to issue a free warrant, but it appeared to them that Lilian Charlton's fear of being assaulted was of lesser concern than the fact that she was unable to pay. The free warrant was refused and

Lilian, no doubt with a fresh opinion of British justice, returned to her home and the constant abuse she was suffering from the man she had taken as her lover.

At 1.15pm on Saturday, June 29th, 1907, Charles Paterson walked into the house at Crondall Street and Lilian, short of money as usual, asked if he had any cash to give her. Paterson claimed he had none and Lilian was now at her wit's end. She had supported this man for a year now and her own finances were stretched so far that she was finding it impossible to cope. Her 19-year-old son, George, heard his mother ask despairingly, "What am I going to do?" Paterson, though, seemed to care little for her troubles. It was Saturday, he declared, and so he was going out again for a few drinks. Lilian asked only that he should go out quietly, without causing trouble, and five minutes later he left the house.

When Paterson returned once more at 5.35pm, Lilian was surprised to see him, telling him, "Now Charlie, I thought you had gone." Paterson sat down in a chair and told her, "I'm not going away till I'm ready. You can go and get a policeman if you like and have me put out." Lilian Charlton said that she didn't want Paterson to get in trouble with the police, she just wanted him to leave her and her family in peace. Once again she begged him to leave but Paterson was adamant. He would go in his own good time.

For a few minutes, silence reigned and Lilian, who had by now also sat down, was clearly upset. Eventually she threw back her head and shouted, "What a fool I've been. To think I should waste my body on a man like you. I ought to be burnt for being such a fool. If you won't go, I'll make a start first." She turned to her son. "George, I leave the house to you." Then she pulled on her boots and went upstairs to the bathroom. It was clear that if Paterson would not leave, then she would. Things had finally come to a head.

Resigning himself to the fact that there was nothing he could do, George Charlton went into the yard to clean his boots, but he had not been there long when a terrible scream filled the air. He dropped the shoe brush and dashed upstairs to where the scream had come from.

The bathroom door was closed but George did not hesitate and kicked it open. There on the floor lay his mother, blood pouring from a wound to her throat, and standing near the bath was Charles Paterson, a razor in his hand. Paterson rushed at George, who ran back downstairs, out into the street and into a shop owned by Joseph Henry Hutchinson. He told Mr Hutchinson what had taken place and the shop owner rushed to number 86, while George ran on to fetch a policeman. He soon found Constable Harry Meeks and took him back to Crondall Street.

It was around 6.45pm when Joseph Hutchinson arrived at number 86 to find Paterson in the yard. He wasted no time in telling Hutchinson that he had 'done it on her' and then calmly asked for a chew of tobacco. He told the shopkeeper that it was no use going upstairs as the woman was dead. When Hutchinson asked why he had done it, he replied, "It was my temper."

Hutchinson called for help from a man named James Bootherstone and while Paterson remained in the kitchen, Hutchinson and Bootherstone went upstairs to investigate further. There they found the body of Lilian Charlton lying behind the bathroom door. Seeing that there was nothing they could do to help the poor woman, the two men went back downstairs where Bootherstone asked Paterson why on earth he had done such a terrible thing.

Paterson shrugged his shoulders and replied, "In passion I've had my revenge, and I'm waiting here till they fetch me." Hutchinson left the house to summon a doctor while Bootherstone waited in the passageway, near the kitchen, for the police to arrive.

By the time Constable Meeks arrived, Hutchinson had returned with Dr Garrett who pronounced life to be extinct. Meeks went upstairs to view the body where it lay and then went back downstairs to interview Paterson. The first question Meeks asked was, "Who has done this?" to which Paterson said, "I have done it. I have done it." At 6.50pm Constable William Wedge arrived and Meeks left him with the body while he took Paterson to Moss Lane East police station where he was searched and a bloodstained handkerchief and matchbox found on his person. In addition, a cut was noted on Paterson's right thumb and this was still bleeding. He was formally charged with murder at 11.50pm and made no response.

On July 1st, Paterson appeared at the Minshull Street police court where he was remanded in custody until July 3rd. On that day, too, no evidence was heard as the inquest had been fixed for that afternoon. As a result, the police court hearing was adjourned until the following day but at the inquest, a verdict of wilful murder was returned against Paterson.

On July 4th, the police court reconvened and all the evidence against Paterson was heard. George Charlton told the court what he had seen and heard up to the moment that he ran out of the house to get assistance. When he returned with Constable Meeks, Paterson was sitting on a sofa and admitted that he was responsible for what had taken place. George went on to give details of the financial problems Lilian had suffered due to Paterson's inability or reluctance to help her with money. Only a fortnight before, Paterson had pawned many of the family's clothes in order to raise a few shillings. Lilian had, of course, found out about this and confronted Paterson with it. He had picked up a poker and threatened Lilian, saying, "I'll smash everything in the house and kill you." George had gone to fetch Mr Hutchinson and he had managed to calm things down.

Joseph Charlton was Lilian's second son and he worked as a tramcar trolley boy for the Manchester Corporation. He reported that there had been many arguments between the accused and his mother, especially over the last five or six months. Joseph had been with his mother four times when she went to the police station to complain about the ill-treatment she was receiving at Paterson's hands and had been to court with her when the magistrates refused to grant her a free warrant.

Joseph Hutchinson, who ran his shop from 82 Crondall Street, said that he had known Lilian for around 18 months and in his experience, she was a sober and respectable woman. Although he had known Paterson by sight for some time, Hutchinson had only ever spoken to him once and that had been when George came to fetch him when Paterson threatened Lilian with the poker. At the time, George had asked him to go to number 86 as his mother and Paterson were, 'falling out.' On June 29th, George had come to his shop again and Hutchinson then went on to tell the court what he found when he went to the Charlton house.

James Bootherstone said that he first went into the middle bedroom and found no sign of a disturbance. He walked back out on to the landing and stood on a man's tobacco pipe lying on the floor. Going to the top of the stairs, he called down to Paterson, "Where is she?" Paterson had shouted back that she was in the bathroom. There, Bootherstone saw Lilian on the left hand side of the room. She was lying on her left side with her head towards the door and Bootherstone lifted her hand to see if there was response. But she was obviously dead and after going back downstairs, he stayed a little longer before his wife called and asked him to come out.

Constable Meeks told how, on the way to the police station, Paterson had said, "I am ready, I will swing." And then, "It's too late now." After staying with Paterson at the police station for some time, Meeks had returned to 86 Crondall Street and searched the premises. He found the tobacco pipe on the landing and also two bloodstained roller towels on the bathroom floor. Other police officers were there and Inspector Watson handed him a bloodstained razor which he had discovered. Later still, Constable Meeks accompanied Lilian's body to the Moss Lane East mortuary where Dr Heslop performed the post-mortem.

Constable John William Dawson was at the police station when Paterson was brought in and after the prisoner was charged, Dawson escorted him down to the cells. On the way, Dawson did not speak but Paterson volunteered, "I have done it. It is too late now. She was not my wife."

Dr William John Heslop, a police surgeon, had been called to the house at 8.30pm on June 29th. The body of Lilian Charlton was in a sitting position in the bathroom, with her head turned to the left. There was a single large wound on the left side of the neck and a large pool of blood had formed beneath and around the body. Dr Heslop ordered Lilian's body to be moved to the passageway so that a proper search of the bathroom could be conducted by the police, but no razor was discovered. Later, Dr Heslop helped to search the bedrooms and in the middle room he found a razor, wet with blood, on some paper in the fire grate. He handed the weapon over to Inspector Watson.

Dr Heslop was asked to go to the police station to examine Paterson. There was a small wound on Paterson's right thumb and bloodstains on his shirt cuffs but his mental condition appeared to be normal. The next day, Dr Heslop performed a post-mortem and found that the wound in the throat extended from slightly over the middle line of the neck backwards for five inches on the left side. It had divided the windpipe and the large blood vessels of the neck, reaching down to the spinal column. In his opinion, the wound had been inflicted from behind and great force must have been used. The cause of death was shock and haemorrhage due to the throat wound.

Having heard all the evidence, the magistrates had no doubt that Paterson should be sent for trial at the assizes. Under normal circumstances, of course, that trial would have taken place at Manchester, but those assizes were some time away and so that Paterson should be dealt with more quickly, the case was sent to Liverpool, where it was heard before Mr Justice Channell on July 16th.

As the case opened and the charge was read out, Paterson, who was not legally represented in court, stated that he wished to plead guilty. Faced with such a plea, the trial judge asked Paterson if he fully understood the charge and reminded him that this was not a question of manslaughter, but of murder. Paterson replied that he quite understood and did not wish to change his plea. Next, Mr Justice Channell called the medical officer of Walton prison, Dr Price, and asked him if he had made an examination of the prisoner and if he had formed any opinion as to his sanity. Dr Price told the court that Paterson was perfectly sane and responsible for his actions.

Turning back to Paterson, the judge told the prisoner that he had made extensive inquiries before accepting the plea, in order to see if there might be any mitigating circumstances which might reduce the charge to one of manslaughter. Having found no such circumstances, and knowing that Paterson had been adjudged to be responsible for his actions, he now had no alternative but to accept the plea and return the only sentence that the law allowed. Paterson listened impassionately as he was told he would be hanged by the neck until he was dead.

On the night before his execution, Paterson slept well. He rose early and ate a hearty breakfast. Then, at 8.00am on the morning of Wednesday, August 7th, 1907, Charles Paterson was hanged at Liverpool by Henry Pierrepoint and his brother, Thomas Pierrepoint. The drop was reported to be 7ft 2ins. Few people bothered to gather outside the gates to see the notices of execution posted.

CHAPTER FOUR

—⁕—

EIGHTEEN PENCE FOR
BLACKPOOL

—⁕—

FREDERICK Ballington had a drink problem that had cost him his home and his family life. A butcher by trade, 41-year-old Ballington had, at least until fairly recently, lived with his wife, Ellen Ann, and their son, Samuel William Ballington, at 143 Gladstone Street in Glossop from where Ellen ran the family shop. By May 1908, though, Ballington's drinking had become so bad that he had been forced out of his home and now lodged with Elizabeth Palin at 7 White Street, Hulme, Manchester.

Ellen Ballington still had a business to run and every Monday, she caught the train into Manchester, visited the abattoir and ordered her meat supplies for the coming week. She still remained on reasonably good terms with her estranged husband and on these Monday trips, she usually met him close to his lodgings and they spent the afternoon together. Things were no different on Monday, May 25th, 1908.

It was 2.00pm when, by arrangement, Ballington met Ellen at London Road railway station. The train from Glossop was on time and Ballington was friendly enough when they first met, asking after the family. The two then went into Manchester, calling at the Ellesmere Hotel on the way where they each enjoyed a beer. During the course of the afternoon, Ballington mentioned that he wanted to go to Blackpool to look for work. Unfortunately, though, he did not have the train fare and asked his wife if she could let him have the three shillings he needed. Ellen refused, but she did give Ballington some hope by saying that she would meet him back at the station later, after she had finished her business, and would then see what she could do.

It was 5.00pm when Ballington again met his wife. She paid for some meat and they walked on to the station at London Road together. Ellen's train was not due to leave until 5.20pm, so she felt she had time to go into the refreshment room. Ballington, concerned perhaps over his lack of cash, remained outside and waited for his wife to return.

The train was waiting at the platform now and Ballington walked with Ellen to the furthest carriage. As they walked, Ballington again asked for three shillings but Ellen, it seemed, had made her mind up not to help after all. She refused his request, climbing into the carriage as she turned him down. Ballington had seen that there was already a man sitting in the compartment and asked his wife to go to a different compartment but Ellen, as unmoveable as ever, simply sat down and waited for the train to depart.

Although he was not due to travel, Ballington also got into the carriage and again asked Ellen if she would help him financially. Yet again she said no, but then reached into her purse, took out some coins and placed them in Ballington's hand. He looked down, counted the coins and saw that she had given him just half of the money he needed. Turning to his wife, Ballington muttered, "Eighteen pence is no good to me."

As if she had not already treated Ballington badly enough, Ellen now accused him of being lazy. An argument followed and Ellen said that she was sorry now that she had given him any money at all. Ballington sighed heavily and announced that he would say goodbye, leaning forward as he spoke and adding, "We'll have a kiss." So saying, Ballington placed his arms around Ellen's neck and made as if to pull her towards him. Ellen, though, pushed him away, her hat being dislodged in the process, and refused to allow him near her. Reluctantly Ballington released his grip and, after a few seconds' silence, bade her farewell and started for the door, but turned back when Ellen insulted him once more. Then, in full view of the other people in the carriage, Frederick Ballington took out a knife and stabbed at his wife's throat.

Still the horror was not over. As Ellen fell to the floor of the carriage, Ballington took a step backwards and drew the blade across his own throat. As the knife fell from his hand, people alerted by the screams rushed to the scene. Both Ellen Ballington and her husband were rushed to the Royal Infirmary but she soon died from her injuries, leaving Frederick Ballington to face a charge of murder.

Ballington was not badly injured and after his wound had been stitched he was escorted to Whitworth Street police station where he was charged with murder and attempted suicide. He made his first appearance at the police court on May 26th where it was revealed that in reply to the charge of murder, Ballington had said, "Murder? Is she dead?" Told that this was indeed the case, Ballington remained silent for a few minutes and then continued, "The sooner they hang me the better. Then I shall follow her and be with her." Only evidence of arrest was given before Ballington was remanded to Friday, May 29th, when the inquest, too, was due to open.

The inquest on May 29th was before Mr Ernest Austin Gibson and all the evidence having been heard both there and at the police court, Ballington was committed for trial. Those proceedings took place at Manchester on July 7th, before Mr Justice Bucknill. Ballington was defended by Mr Gilbert Jordan while the case for the prosecution was led by Mr Spencer Hogg, who was assisted by Mr Rathbone. Surprisingly perhaps, there were a large number of witnesses to be heard.

Elizabeth Palin was Ballington's landlady and she testified that he had come to live at her house on May 3rd. He had remained there until the day of his arrest, May 25th, and had spent every night there except for one, May 19th. During his stay, Elizabeth had never seen Ballington drunk, although she was aware that he had taken alcohol from time to time. She went on to describe her lodger as 'quiet, rational and sensible'.

Samuel William Ballington, was Ellen's son and he also worked in the butcher's shop. He told the court that his mother had been 43 years old at the time of her death. Samuel said that on May 25th, she had left home to catch the 1.20pm train from Glossop to Manchester, as she did almost every Monday. Samuel had lived with his parents at 143 Gladstone Street for the past five and a half years and he reported that during that time there had been constant rows between his mother and father, due mainly to Ballington's drinking habits. Frederick could not be described as a habitual drunk, for he often went months without touching a drop, but these periods of sobriety would be followed by bouts of extreme drunkenness during which Ballington sometimes left home. The latest of these drinking sessions had started at the beginning of May and Ballington had been told to leave the house until he sorted himself out.

Ballington had returned to Glossop on May 19th and asked Ellen if he could stay the night. She refused and Samuel had no idea where his father had ended up on that occasion. The next time he had seen his father was on May 21st when he met him at the abattoir in Manchester. Ballington asked Samuel to intercede with Ellen and to ask if he could have some money to get to Blackpool where he might find work.

Walter Clitheroe Smith had climbed on to the train at London Road at 5.20pm on May 25th. At the time he was the only occupant of the last carriage but after a few minutes he heard voices at the door and looked up to see Frederick Ballington and his wife. The first thing Smith heard was Ballington saying, "Don't get in there, there's a gentleman in." Ellen had replied, "Yes I shall." Ballington replied to this remark, but Smith was unable to distinguish his words. He did hear Ellen repeat her previous statement, though, as she got in and sat on the same side as himself, facing the engine.

Smith saw that Ballington was half in and half out of the carriage door. He had one foot on the platform and the other on the footboard of the carriage, and it was from that position that he again asked Ellen for a few shillings. She turned him down, once more, telling him that she had worked hard for her money, but Ballington kept on asking until Smith saw Ellen take out her purse and hand over some coins. Smith then heard Ballington say, "Eighteen pence is no good to me," adding that he needed more. At this point, two more men got into the carriage, one sitting opposite him and the other sitting opposite Ellen, so that now all four corners were occupied. No sooner had they sat down than Ballington climbed in and asked Ellen for a kiss. She pushed him off, to which Ballington said, "Now it's goodbye and goodbye for ever." He then made to leave but Ellen called him 'a scamp'. Smith saw Ballington turn and was convinced that a full-scale argument was about to break out, so he left the carriage, jumping down on to the rails, intending to get into the next carriage. He had no sooner reached the ground than a terrible scream rang out. Looking back through the window, Smith saw Ballington take a step back and start hacking at his throat with a knife.

The two men who had climbed into the carriage where Smith and Ellen sat were Frank Margrave and Reginald Shaw. Margrave had sat down opposite Ellen while Shaw had occupied the seat opposite Walter Smith. Margrave said he had not heard any of what passed between Frederick Ballington and his wife but he saw him get into the compartment and attempt to kiss her. At the time, Margrave was reading a newspaper and he did not look up again until he heard Ellen scream. He saw to his horror that blood was pouring down her cheek and immediately ran from the train to summon help.

Reginald Shaw had heard Ballington ask Ellen for another eighteen pence and her reply that she had given him all she had. Shaw saw Ballington move to kiss Ellen but she turned her head away. Suddenly her hat was pushed off and she screamed, at which point another gentleman, which was of course Walter Smith, got up and left the carriage. Looking back on to the platform, Shaw saw Ballington with something in his hand which he at first thought might be a pistol so he ducked down, afraid that Ballington might be about to fire. Now Shaw left the compartment himself and got into another which was full of ladies. He heard someone say, "That's the man." Soon afterwards, the train pulled out.

Charles William Chorlton was about to get into the compartment at the far end of the platform when someone rushed out. Chorlton looked into the carriage and saw Frederick Ballington half sitting with his right hand to his head. The hand then dropped to his side and a knife fell to the floor. Chorlton picked up the weapon and handed it to a gentleman who he believed to be a railway company official.

George Ogden was a commercial traveller and he was in the compartment next to the one occupied by Ellen Ballington. He heard none of the conversation between Frederick

Ballington and his wife, but he did hear the scream and got out of his carriage to see if he could offer any assistance. Going to the next compartment, Ogden saw a woman on a seat. She was saturated with blood from a wound in her throat. Ballington was also there and was trying to get out on to the platform, his hands and his collar covered in blood. George Ogden put his hand on Ballington's shoulder and asked, "What has that got to do with you?" but received no reply. He stayed with Ballington until the police arrived to take him into custody. Ogden also saw the woman lifted gently out on to the platform and watched as Ballington bent forward, kissed her twice and said, "Goodbye." Later, Ballington also said, "All through eighteen pence for Blackpool."

Irvine Bramhall and Arthur Ashton were two more witnesses who were on the Glossop train on May 25th. Bramhall was in the next carriage and he heard some sort of disturbance which culminated in a scream. Soon afterwards a small crowd gathered around the door of the next compartment and Bramhall got out to see what was going on. Ellen was still on the seat, her lips covered in blood, and he helped lift her out on to the platform. Arthur Ashton also saw Ellen being taken off the train and heard someone ask who had done this. Ballington had replied, "Me," and when asked why, had added, "It's what I've intended doing for some time. I should have done it sooner." Ashton was later handed a bloody knife which he passed to a railway porter.

That porter was Josiah Charles Gregory who had heard Ellen scream and ran to the carriage to see what was going on. Ellen Ballington was raising herself from a stooping position and was bleeding badly from her face and neck. Gregory saw Ballington sitting opposite to her. As he watched, he saw Ballington drop the knife and one of the passengers picked it up. The knife was passed on to Gregory who later handed it to Ernest Bamford who administered medical aid to the stricken woman.

William Barratt was a porter and guard on the Glossop train and he testified that shortly before it was due to leave, he saw Ballington and his wife walk past as he was putting some luggage into the guard's van. Later he saw Ballington half standing on the train and later still, he was called to the compartment by a member of the public. There he saw Ellen sitting on a seat, her cheek cut and the carriage floor covered in blood. Barratt was the other man who helped carry Ellen out on to the platform before returning to his duties. Despite what had taken place, William Barratt was on the Glossop train when it pulled out just a moment or two later.

Alfred Milnes was also a guard for the Great Central Railway and on May 25th, he was an acting inspector on London Road station. At 5.10pm he was standing on platform 'A' waiting to see the Glossop train out and it was then that he saw Ballington and Ellen pass him. Milnes knew both of them quite well and said that he thought Frederick was looking white faced and excited. Soon afterwards, William Barrett approached him and told him that something had happened to a woman in the last carriage. He went to investigate and saw that a woman was bleeding from a wound to her neck. It was Milnes who sent for an ambulance and went to fetch the police.

George Hebden was a constable for the Great Central Railway and at the time of the attack upon Ellen, he was near the entrance to the platforms. He, too, knew the Ballingtons and saw them pass on to platform 'A'. Hebden said that Ballington seemed to be threatening his wife but that she looked defiant. Just a few minutes later, he received a message telling him to go to the far end of platform 'A' and was told by a member of a small crowd that a man had stabbed a woman. Someone else then pointed out Frederick Ballington and Hebden took him into custody, later escorting him to Whitworth Street police station. Later still he accompanied him to the Royal Infirmary to have his wounds dressed before handing him over to Constable Manley.

Ernest Victor Bamford was also a porter on the station but he possessed a St John's Ambulance certificate and for that reason, was called to platform 'A' to render aid to Ellen Ballington. By then, Ellen was lying on the platform and Bamford saw that she had wounds to her throat and scratches on her face. In addition to administering first aid, Bamford accompanied Ellen to the hospital. Before that, Josiah Gregory handed Bamford a blood stained knife which he later gave to Constable Lane.

Constable James William Lane was on duty outside the railway station when he was called inside. He saw Ellen being taken to the infirmary, accompanied by some of the railway employees, and went with them. Later he was handed a knife by Ernest Bamford. The blade was smeared with blood and it appeared that the weapon had been recently sharpened.

Herbert Manley was a police constable on duty at Whitworth Street station when Hebden brought Ballington in. Manley saw that the prisoner was bleeding from three wounds in his throat and although they did not appear serious, it was obvious that he would require medical attention. Constable Manley, together with Hebden, took Ballington to the infirmary and later accompanied him back to the police station where he was handed over to Inspector Thomas. During the time that Ballington was in his custody, though, he had announced, "This is all through her not giving me eighteen pence so as I could go to Blackpool and get work, and her having all that money on her." The final police witness was Detective Inspector Richard Thomas, who charged Ballington with murder. It was to him that Ballington made the remark about wanting to be hanged as soon as possible.

Medical evidence was given by Dr Herbert Henry Rayner, the resident surgical officer at the Royal Infirmary. He said that it was around 5.30pm when Ellen was brought in and that she was already dead. He had performed a post-mortem and revealed that there was a four-inch lacerated wound, close to her mouth on the right side of her face. This was half an inch deep and was consistent with a knife being used in a downward direction. On the left side of the neck, four inches below the ear, there was a stab wound which had passed inwards for two and a half inches and penetrated the internal jugular vein. Finally, Doctor Rayner was able to state that at the time of her death, Ellen was three weeks pregnant.

One of the final witnesses was Ernest Gibson, the coroner. During the inquest, Ballington had made a statement which had a direct bearing on the case and Mr Gibson now read this out in court. According to this statement, Ballington had met his wife and they had walked together to Oldham Street where she went into a shop and made a purchase. During this time, he waited outside, doing the same when she went into Lord's restaurant and the fishmarket. Walking on to Deansgate, he asked her for the first time if she would give him the three shillings he needed to get to Blackpool, but she had refused.

From Deansgate, Ballington and his wife travelled by tram to Water Street, visiting the abattoir on the way. They then found themselves at the Ellesmere public house where Ellen said she wanted a drink. They went in together but bought their own drinks and he again brought up the matter of the three shillings he needed. Ellen refused at first but later told him to meet her near the railway station. This he did at around 5.00pm, when Ellen went into the refreshment room and he again waited outside. From there, they walked up platform 'A' together and he asked once more for three shillings. The statement ended where Ballington had said, "She got into the railway carriage and then you know what happened. I did it on the spur of the moment in a moment of mad passion."

There could be no doubt that Frederick Ballington was responsible for the death of his wife, but in his summing up, Mr Jordan, for the defence, claimed that there was no evidence of the malice aforethought which was essential for a crime of murder. He asked the jury to return a verdict of manslaughter but after 15 minutes, they filed back into court to announce that Ballington was guilty as charged. As the sentence of death was passed, Mr Justice Bucknill seemed deeply affected and almost broke down a number of times.

Exactly three weeks after the trial had ended, on Tuesday, July 28th, 1908, Frederick Ballington, a native of Derby, was executed at Manchester by Henry Pierrepoint who was assisted by William Willis. As he approached the scaffold, Ballington made a comment but no one present could distinguish what he said. Meanwhile, a crowd estimated at 200 strong had gathered outside the prison to see the notices pinned to the gates.

CHAPTER FIVE

STRANGE BEHAVIOUR

EVEN from its beginning, the relationship between John Ramsbottom and Charlotte MacCraw was not a happy one. In 1907, Charlotte lived with her two brothers, James and William, and their mother, Elizabeth Ann MacCraw, at the Prince of Wales public house situated at 45 Abbey Hey Lane, Gorton, where Elizabeth was landlady. Towards the beginning of that summer, Charlotte discovered that she was pregnant and since 34-year-old Ramsbottom was the only man she had been involved with, arrangements were made for a wedding to take place. Thus, on October 1st, 1907, Charlotte MacCraw married John Ramsbottom and they went to live with his mother, Dora, at 98 Lees Street, also in Gorton.

Although there was no trouble between Charlotte and her mother-in-law, the arrangement could only be temporary and after about a month, Ramsbottom took the tenancy of a house further down the same street. The newly-weds duly moved in and on December 12th, 1907, at 45 Lees Street, Charlotte Ramsbottom, as she now was, gave birth to a son.

John Ramsbottom liked a drink and there were three occasions during the next couple of months when he came home drunk and threatened Charlotte with violence. Once, he even went so far as to admit to his wife that he had behaved improperly with another woman. Charlotte weathered all this until February 3rd, 1908, when, on a visit to the Prince of Wales, she told her mother about the problems she was having at home. Elizabeth MacCraw did not hesitate in telling Charlotte that she should return to Abbey Hey Lane and the bosom of her family. Charlotte agreed, but when Ramsbottom called at the pub some time before 11.00pm that night and asked her to return home, Charlotte went with him.

On February 4th, Charlotte was back at the pub where she spent the entire day. Once again Ramsbottom arrived, but when he announced that he was going home to his bed, this time Charlotte did not go with him. Over the next five days, Ramsbottom came to the pub as often as he could, but Charlotte showed no inclination to return with him to 45 Lees Street.

On February 8th, Ramsbottom appeared at the pub after 10.00pm and yet again asked Charlotte to return home with him, saying, "I am not going to stop by myself." Charlotte would not be persuaded, but then Ramsbottom came up with a new idea, saying, "If she stops here, I will stop too." Elizabeth MacCraw reluctantly agreed, but stressed that if Ramsbottom did stay, he would have to behave himself. Ramsbottom agreed and for a time at least, he and Charlotte lived happily enough.

Every day, John Ramsbottom went off to work at Craven Brothers' factory, returning to the pub at night but then, on February 17th, his behaviour changed.

On that date, he went to work as normal, but at lunchtime told his employers that he had an appointment and needed to take the afternoon off. He was granted permission, providing he returned to work as usual the following day.

On February 18th, Ramsbottom left the pub at 5.30am, ostensibly to go to work, but he did not arrive at Craven Brothers, nor did he return to the Prince of Wales that night. No one saw him again until the morning of February 19th, when he went into work, only to be told that since he had broken his agreement, he had been dismissed. Ramsbottom did not return to the Prince of Wales again that night, and it was not until 6.30pm on Thursday, February 20th, that he finally walked into the pub, as though nothing had happened.

Naturally, Ramsbottom was questioned as to his whereabouts, but his answers were non-committal. Charlotte seemed happy enough to accept this state of affairs, though, and was friendly enough towards her husband. The same could not be said for Elizabeth MacCraw, however, for when she saw Ramsbottom in her kitchen, at 7.00pm she told him he was not welcome and must leave the pub.

John Ramsbottom ignored her demand and remained in the bar, even enjoying a drink with 22-year-old James MacCraw, his brother-in-law. Elizabeth saw Ramsbottom sitting at the bar at 9.00pm. He asked, "Can I stay?" but his mother-in-law told him, "No, I don't want you here." Again, Ramsbottom ignored this and at some time after 9.00pm he went upstairs to the bedroom he shared with Charlotte, asking her to bring him a warm drink when she retired for the night.

At 11.00pm Charlotte was in the kitchen where she enjoyed some supper with her mother. Half an hour later, she went up to bed, taking Ramsbottom some rather unappetising warmed beer. The pub closed, the MacCraw family settled down for the night, Elizabeth going to her room and her two sons going to the bedroom they shared.

It was 20 minutes past midnight when Elizabeth MacCraw heard a loud report, followed by her daughter calling for her. She ran into the couple's bedroom to see Charlotte sitting up in bed while Ramsbottom, wearing nothing but his shirt, stood by the bed on the opposite side to the door. To her horror, Elizabeth saw that he was holding a revolver in his right hand.

Charlotte climbed out of the bed and, picking up her son, made to leave the room as her brother James entered. Crying out, "Don't hurt my mother," Charlotte fled the room and Elizabeth saw that there was blood on her nightdress. Before she could determine exactly what had taken place, Ramsbottom raised the gun, aimed at the far corner and fired a bullet which struck a lead pipe, causing water to flood into the room.

Elizabeth MacCraw heard her son say something, but even as the words left his lips, Ramsbottom turned and aimed the gun directly at James. A shot was fired and as the bullet bit into James' arm, he cried out, "Mother, he's shot me." A second shot was fired, this time hitting James in the stomach. He staggered out of the bedroom and made to walk down the hallway but collapsed at the door to his mother's room. As William MacCraw, entered the bedroom, Ramsbottom, still wearing nothing but his shirt, pushed past him and ran out of the pub and into the cold night air. Charlotte Ramsbottom had also run out of the pub and dashed to her married sister's house at 65 Abbey Hey Lane.

Lily Sumner was just going to bed at 12.30am on February 21st when she heard someone hammering on her front door. Going to see who it was, Lily found her sister bleeding from an area around her right breast and in some distress. Before Charlotte could tell her what had happened, Elizabeth MacCraw appeared on the doorstep and asked Lily and her husband, George, to summon a doctor and the police. By the time Elizabeth returned to the Prince of Wales, the police were already there.

The doctor who attended, Dr Gunn, saw that although Charlotte had been shot close to the right breast, the wound was not life threatening and she received treatment at her sister's house. James MacCraw's stomach wound was much more serious, though, and he was rushed to Ancoats Hospital, being admitted there at 2.40am.

Constable Teddy Benson had arrived at the scene of the double shooting at 12.45am. By then, James had been put into his bed but Constable Benson later helped carry him into the police ambulance. Soon afterwards, Constable William Dunbar arrived and having interviewed the family, discovered that the man who had fired the shots was John Ramsbottom.

Constables Benson and Dunbar called at 45 Lees Street, Ramsbottom's home, to find no one there. They had also been told that the wanted man's mother lived just up the street, at number 98, so that was their next port of call. Here, the door was opened by

Dora Ramsbottom who said that her son was not there. The officers insisted on taking a look for themselves and as they entered the house, they saw Ramsbottom, still wearing only his shirt, standing at the top of the stairs, the revolver clasped in his hand. Luckily for the policemen, he offered no resistance and was disarmed with ease. Ramsbottom, too indecently dressed to be escorted to the police station, was told to lie on a sofa where he was covered with blankets until some of his clothes were brought from the Prince of Wales. Soon afterwards, Ramsbottom was charged with two counts of attempted murder.

Back at the hospital, James MacCraw was not responding to medical treatment. For this reason, Ramsbottom was placed under guard and taken to the hospital where in his presence, Richard Muscott, the clerk to the Manchester County Justices, took MacCraw's deposition. A few hours later, at 8.15am, James MacCraw died from his injuries and Ramsbottom was charged with murder. He made his first appearance at the police court that same day, when he was remanded until February 24th.

On February 24th, many of the details of the crime were heard but, due to her injuries, Charlotte Ramsbottom was unable to attend and so another remand was necessary, this time until March 3rd. On that date it was stated that although Charlotte had largely recovered, she had now fallen victim to influenza and so Ramsbottom was remanded until March 18th. On that date, Charlotte Ramsbottom finally gave her evidence but one further remand was necessary and so, it was not until March 26th that Ramsbottom was finally sent to the next assizes.

The trial of John Ramsbottom took place at Manchester on April 23rd, 1908, before Mr Justice Coleridge. Mr Spencer Hogg and Mr Bigham appeared for the prosecution and Ramsbottom was defended by Mr Merriman.

Charlotte Ramsbottom told the court what had taken place after she had taken the warmed beer up to her husband on the night of February 20th. After Ramsbottom had finished his drink, she had again returned to the subject of where he had been over the past day or so. Ramsbottom had tried to avoid the question, telling her to get into bed and 'never mind'. Charlotte, however, did mind very much and said that she was going to sleep with her mother instead. Ramsbottom had exclaimed, "Now Lottie, if you're not going to sleep with me, you're not going to sleep with anybody else."

In order to avoid further unpleasantness Charlotte had climbed into bed beside Ramsbottom, but had put their baby son between them. Ramsbottom had complained that he wanted Charlotte beside him, but before she could answer, he changed the subject and asked her who had taken some of his furniture out of 45 Lees Street. Charlotte told her husband that this had been done by some of the neighbours at her request, to which Ramsbottom remarked, "The neighbours might think they'll have a laugh at me but I'll take good care they won't tomorrow."

Charlotte had made no reply to this comment and lay silent, with her face towards her husband, the baby still between them. A hand reached out and Charlotte felt Ramsbottom touch her body. Thinking that this might be a prelude to sex, she pulled away, telling him, "I want none of that", and pushed his hand away as she made to get out of bed. Ramsbottom was out of bed first, though, and stood at the foot of the bed, a gun in his hand. Charlotte called for her mother, but as she did, a shot rang out and she felt a searing pain in her right breast. Despite the wound, she managed to get out of the room a minute or so after her mother had come in.

William MacCraw said that he had seen Ramsbottom drinking with James in the bar on the night of February 20th. At 11.30pm William had gone to bed. He shared a bedroom with James but by the time he had come to bed, William must have already been asleep as the next thing he knew, it was after midnight and he was woken by two shots. James, who was now in the bedroom, gave William a push and whispered, "Bill, get up, there's two shots gone." William began to dress but James ran out of the room wearing only a nightshirt.

By the time William got to the hallway, he saw Charlotte running out of her bedroom. Going into that room, William was just in time to catch his brother as he fell, and as he carried his wounded brother into his mother's room, Ramsbottom dashed out past him. Later he went looking for Ramsbottom, but found no sign of him.

There was evidence that Ramsbottom had deliberately planned to do some harm to his in-laws, or his wife, for the purchase of the revolver had only recently taken place. George Smith, a salesman for Edward Briggs, a pawnbroker of 16 Piccadilly, testified that on February 19th, Ramsbottom had come into his shop and asked to purchase a revolver. Mr Briggs asked to see Ramsbottom's gun licence and when he said he did not have one, the sale was refused. The next day, though, at 4.00pm, Ramsbottom was back in the shop and now produced a valid licence which he had taken out at Ardwick at 3.04pm that day. Ramsbottom selected a weapon, saying that he wanted it to send to a friend in South Africa. The cost, recorded in the sales book, was 8s 6d.

Alfred Ormond was also a salesman, for Robert Ramsbottom's sportsman's outfitters shop at 81 Market Street, Manchester. He testified that Ramsbottom, who was no relation to the shop owner, had come in at 5.00pm on February 20th and asked for a box of rim-fire cartridges. Ormond sold him a box of 25 for one shilling.

In addition to giving details of the arrest, Constable Dunbar also stated that after Ramsbottom had been taken to the police station, he (Dunbar) had made a search of the premises at 98 Lees Street, where he had found four rim-fire cartridges on the settee where Ramsbottom had lain prior to the arrival of his clothes.

Dora Ramsbottom, the prisoner's mother, testified that at 1.00am on February 21st, she had been woken by a knock at the front door. Going down she had called through the door, "Who's there?" and her son had replied, "It's me mother, open the door." To Dora's surprise, her son was wearing only a shirt and she exclaimed, "Oh Jack, whatever is to do that you have run out like that?" Ramsbottom had replied, "They've been on to me and I cannot stand it. I shan't live there anymore." Dora covered her son with a blanket and returned to her bed, only to be disturbed soon afterwards by yet another knock at the door. This time it was the police and she had told them that her son was not there but they had demanded entry anyway.

Dr William John Heslop had performed the post-mortem on James MacCraw. Dr Heslop reported that there was a wound in MacCraw's left arm. The bullet which caused it had passed completely through the arm, grazing the left side of the chest as it made its exit. There was another wound in the abdomen and here the bullet had passed through the colon and damaged the inner surface of the ileum, causing a large quantity of blood to collect in the abdominal cavity.

The final piece of evidence was, of course, James MacCraw's deposition. This read, "I live at Gorton and am a turner. I was going into the bedroom separating Jack Ramsbottom from my sister. Jack Ramsbottom shot twice at me, once in the arm and in the stomach. He had a revolver. I have had no quarrel with him. I live there and he does also. It was about 12.30 this morning.

"I had had drink but not much, about three or four glasses of beer. I was talking to him at tea time, about dogs, and one thing and another. I went to separate them as I heard my sister scream. She must have run out. I jumped out of bed. I was in my shirt and he was undressed also. I did not know he had a revolver. I am quite sure he shot me. I can't say how he was for drink."

The only defence possible could be one of insanity. In her testimony, Ramsbottom's mother had said that her brother and an uncle had both died in mental asylums and that Ramsbottom had often behaved strangely, sometimes walking on his toes and muttering to himself. None of this convinced the jury, however, and they concluded that Ramsbottom was guilty of wilful murder. A petition for a reprieve collected over 25,000 signatures, but even this did nothing to save Ramsbottom's life.

On the day before he was due to die, the condemned man was visited in prison by his mother, his wife, and his mother-in-law, all united in grief at what had taken place and what was about to happen. At 8.00am the next day, Tuesday, May 12th, 1908, an almost unprecedented crowd estimated at 2,000 strong, gathered in the streets outside Strangeways prison as John Ramsbottom was hanged by Henry Pierrepoint, who gave him a drop of 7ft.

CHAPTER SIX

THE LETTER WRITER

AT 5.30am on Thursday, May 13th, 1909, Frank Corrie was walking across fields at the back of the sewage works on Pink Bank Lane at Gorton, on the way to his work, when he came across the body of a young woman lying on the grass about four yards from some wooden boards which ran alongside the footpath. Taking a closer look, Corrie saw that the woman was lying face down and there was some frothing around her mouth and nose. He ran to find a policeman.

Constable Arthur Fisher was on duty in Hyde Road at 5.45am when he was approached by a breathless Corrie, who told him of his grim discovery. Constable Fisher accompanied Corrie back to the scene and there turned over the body. The woman's flesh was cold, her face swollen and the left cheek mottled. Her tongue protruded from between her lips and there were scratches on her left elbow. A handkerchief had been tied tightly around her neck and knotted underneath her right ear. Marks on the cinder path showed that she had been attacked a few yards away and dragged to where she now lay. Fisher summoned medical assistance and once life had been officially pronounced to be extinct, he accompanied the body to the local mortuary, were it was carefully searched but no trace of any identification could be found.

In fact, it was not long before a number of people came forward to report that a member of their family had gone out on the evening of May 12th and not returned home. That in turn led to the identification of the dead woman as 26-year-old Emily Ramsbottom who had lived with her mother, Annie Stephens, at 6 Ellesmere Street, Gorton.

Mrs Stephens explained that her daughter was a married woman but had been separated from her husband for a number of years. Emily had given birth to three children but once her husband had left her, she had returned home. For the last three or four years she had been keeping company with 32-year-old Mark Shawcross and had lived with him at various addresses, one of which had been a house in Herbert Street. That relationship had been quite serious at one time, for Emily had given birth to two more children, both by Shawcross, and had even followed him when he moved briefly to Sheffield. For the last 16 months, however, she had lived at Ellesmere Street. Shawcross had spent much of that time trying to get her to return to him. He called at her home and regularly waited outside her place of work so that he could talk to her and try to persuade her to go back to live with him.

Although Emily still saw Shawcross on a regular basis, there had been some trouble of late. Only ten weeks before, Shawcross had called at the house in Ellesmere Street and after further discussion about Emily not returning to him, he had lost his temper, picked up a poker and struck her on the head. All this made Annie Stephens wary about the relationship and she did her best to protect her daughter from Shawcross and his unwanted attentions.

The last time Annie had seen Emily alive was at around 7.50pm on Wednesday, May 12th. Emily had left the house, saying that she was going to the King's Theatre at Longsight. Concerned that Shawcross might be waiting for Emily, Annie sent another of her daughters, Eliza, to follow her sister and try to bring her back home. Eliza, who was just 17 years old, had seen Emily meet up with Shawcross and the two had walked together down Church Lane. Eliza followed as far as Taylor Street, where she lost sight of Emily. At the time, she and Shawcross seemed to be friendly enough, but bearing in mind the history of the relationship and the fact that Shawcross had now vanished from his lodgings at his sister's house at 148 Taylor Street, details of the missing man were published in the newspapers, along with the comment that the police wished to interview him. Part of the report was a full description of Shawcross which read: 'A labourer, 32 years of age, height 6ft 5ins, slender build, dark brown hair and moustache, long face, thin features, blue eyes and dressed in a brown jacket and vest, navy blue trousers, green cap, blue spotted muffler and laced black boots."

On the same day that Emily's body had been found, the inquest on her death opened at the Gorton Town Hall before the county coroner, Mr J.F. Price. Only the most basic evidence was heard before matters were adjourned until May 19th. Well before that, though, on May 15th, the case took a dramatic turn.

It was around noon on that day when Sergeant William Davies opened a letter delivered to the police station. Postmarked Todmorden, this missive appeared to be a letter from the man the police were searching for and showed that he, too, had seen the reports of the crime in the papers. The letter read, 'Dear Sir, When I first saw the report in the evening paper, I thought very little of their opinions. I killed her with my bare hands, and as quickly as possible. She was almost dead when I tied the handkerchief round her neck, and the piece of linen that was found was off her own body not mine. I am trying hard to get a job for a day or two so to buy a revolver to shoot a certain man who is nothing but a slave driver. And if I get it, it will be a more sure thing than any other. I will cheat all the police, while I do not mean to harm any of them. I have been very cunning all my life. You must think I should go for a ship like some fools would do, but not me. It is dropping right into a police trap when anyone does that, and I also warn other people that speaks, too, freely against me. This is not a letter, it is a note, it's to be noted.'

At the time of the fatal attack upon Emily Ramsbottom, Shawcross had been working as a stoker on the *SS Manchester City*, which was tied up in the docks, but he had previously worked at a factory owned by Kendall & Ghents, tool makers of Hyde Road, Gorton. His letter to the police had mentioned that he wished to kill someone who he referred to as a slave driver and soon another letter was delivered which made this somewhat clearer. The letter was delivered on May 19th, but had been posted in Oldham at 1.00pm on May 18th. It was addressed to Mr Thomas Horsfield, a foreman at Kendall & Ghents from where Shawcross had been sacked. It read in part, 'Just a line to warn you that your time is very short indeed. You played the game with me too far when I was working at Kendall & Ghents, but all men is not going to stand your slave driving.' The letter went on, 'There will be very little of you, Horsfield, this time next week. I might as well die for two as well as one, so you can expect a visit.' It ended, 'I am very cunning and very sure, so be prepared for the worst,' and was signed, 'M Shawcross'.

The same day that this letter was received, the inquest reopened and returned a verdict of murder against the missing man. In fact Mark Shawcross was not as cunning as he sought to make out. As a matter of course, the police had maintained a watch on his lodgings at 148 Taylor Street. Mary Shawcross, the wanted man's sister, rented the house and had already been interviewed by the police. She told the officers that she had not seen her brother since the evening of May 12th. Shawcross left the house at around 6.30pm, saying that he was going to walk to Yorkshire to try to find work. For that reason she had not been surprised when he did not come home that night.

It was 12.15am on the morning of May 20th when Mark Shawcross emerged from the back of the house and gave a low knock on the front door of 148 Taylor Street. He was admitted by Mary, but the visit had been witnessed by Constable Frank Capstick who was waiting outside the house for just such an occurrence. Even as Shawcross was let into the house, another police officer, Constable Bamford Hawkwood, arrived and Capstick told him what had just taken place. Constable Hawkwood knocked on the front door while Capstick went around to the back. In due course, both officers were admitted and quickly searched the downstairs of the house. They found nothing, but on going upstairs they saw Shawcross at the top of the stairs. Hawkwood demanded, "Where are you going?" Shawcross replied, "It's all over, it's alright."

Shawcross was escorted to the police station and on the way commented, "If you had been five minutes later there would have been another murder in the morning." Charged with murder, he replied, "That's right," and was remanded in custody. That afternoon, Shawcross appeared at the police court where it was explained that the dead woman had left him some 16 months earlier and gone to stay with her mother. Annie Jones, who lived at 33 Ellesmere Street and had known Emily for the past year, also told the court that she seen Emily coming out of a sweet shop in Church Lane at 8.25pm on May 12th. Emily walked up to a man and handed the sweets she had purchased over to him. That man had been Mark Shawcross and Annie stated that they appeared to be on good terms at the time. This evidence, of course, proved that Shawcross was indeed the man who had been with Emily on the night she died, and as a result, he was remanded for a week.

Shawcross made his second court appearance on May 27th before the stipendiary magistrate, Mr J.M. Yates. The case for the Director of Public Prosecutions was put by Mr J. Crofton while the prisoner was represented by Mr T.H. Hinchcliffe. The detailed charge Shawcross now faced was that he 'killed Emily Ramsbottom on a footpath leading from Mount Road, Gorton to Knutsford Vale between 8.25pm on May 12th and 5.30am on May 13th.' The proceedings lasted two days and at the end, all the evidence on the capital charge was completed. However, the proceedings were again adjourned, this time to June 4th, because there was a second charge, that of threatening to murder Thomas Horsfield, and this could not be completed as Horsfield was ill at the time. In due course, however, this, too, was completed and Shawcross was sent for trial.

The trial of Mark Shawcross took place at Manchester on July 6th, 1909, before Mister Justice Hamilton. Shawcross was defended by Mr Bigham while the case for the Crown was led by Mr John Mansfield who was assisted by Mr Philip Walton. On the same day, that Shawcross began the fight to avoid the hangman's noose, Manchester was filled with crowds who had come to witness the visit of King Edward VII and Queen Alexandra.

Eliza Stephens, the dead woman's sister, said that she had known Shawcross quite well for the last two years. At Christmas, 1908, she and her brothers and sisters had been present when Shawcross threatened Emily and said he would 'swing for her'. The cause of this particular row had been Emily not turning up at a meeting she and Shawcross had arranged. The following Saturday, Eliza had seen Emily meet Shawcross in Church Lane and for no apparent reason, he had struck her in the face and tried to choke her. Seeing that he was being watched, Shawcross told Eliza to 'clear off', but she pushed him away from her sister. Eliza also told the court that she believed that many of the problems stemmed from Shawcross being jealous of his own brother. Eliza knew that this brother was fond of Emily and she apparently returned the feelings.

In addition to the letters already referred to, Shawcross had written a third, while he was in custody. James Dyer was a warder at Strangeways and he had handed paper to Shawcross on May 20th when he said he wished to write to his sister. That letter read, 'Dear Sister, A few lines to hope you are all in good health as I am at present. I want you to send me a newspaper or two. Send Thursday and Friday night's *Evening News*. I want none of the family to take this hard, as I am all right and will remain so. Never mind what the people say against me or any member of the family. They have their brains and their own way the same as I have.

'There is no one that can tell another soul, mind, and so you don't know what people come to. Tell Jack I send him my best regards, and tell him to give the same to J, the brass moulder, he knows who I mean.' This letter, along with the one sent to the police and the one to Thomas Horsfield, had since been examined by Frederick Smart, a handwriting expert with 30 years' experience. He testified that all three were in the same hand.

There had been an interesting event after the police court hearing of May 27th. After Shawcross had been remanded to the following day, his sister Mary had asked permission to see him. At the time she had been with a friend, Sarah Ainfield and both women were escorted down to the cells by Inspector George Crossley. Mary had testified that she had asked Shawcross directly if he had killed Emily but he had failed to reply. However, both Sarah Ainfield and Inspector Crossley reported that Shawcross had replied, "Did I do it? Certainly I did it." After this, Sarah had asked him why he had not done away with himself after committing this terrible deed and Shawcross had told her to mind her own business.

Dr Thomas Morton had performed the post-mortem at the mortuary on May 14th. He explained that in his opinion, Emily had been dead for somewhere between 24 and 36 hours and death was due to suffocation caused by pressure on the windpipe. The handkerchief tied around Emily's throat had left a distinct line of discolouration but the throttling had been performed by someone's hands. The handkerchief accounted for the absence of finger marks on the neck but in Dr Morton's opinion, this was certainly a case of murder. He had never heard of anyone committing suicide in such a manner and, indeed, did not think it possible.

Shawcross gave evidence on his own behalf. He said that he had known Emily for seven years and lived with her for varying periods. They had always been on good terms and their relationship had broken up only because he had lost his work. He denied that he had ever assaulted Emily in any way, despite what her family had said.

Turning to the night of May 12th, Shawcross admitted that he had arranged to meet Emily and take her to the King's Theatre to watch a play entitled, *Was She to Blame?* They left the theatre together at 10.50pm and he walked her to Stanley Grove where he left her after saying that he was going to walk to Yorkshire to find work. She seemed to be a little depressed at this news and her last words to him had been, "Be sure you write."

That night, Shawcross walked to Todmorden and there bought a newspaper which carried a report of Emily's death. Her loss depressed him greatly so, from the reports in the paper, he concocted a fictional account of how he had killed her and wrote the letter to the police under, as he described it, 'the influence of destruction'. As he saw it, he had no money, no food, was out of work and had lost the woman he loved. He was tired of life and wanted to be found guilty so that the State would take his life. He had not killed Emily and he could only think that she had taken her own life while she was depressed over him leaving for Yorkshire and not knowing when she might see him again.

Not surprisingly, Shawcross was found guilty and sentenced to death. Almost immediately a petition was organised for a reprieve and one week after the trial it had already attracted over 1,000 signatures. Meanwhile, notice of appeal was entered and this was heard on July 16th before the Lord Chief Justice, Lord Alverstone, and Justices Darling and Jelf. Here, the defence claimed that the only real evidence against Shawcross had been his own 'confessions' in the letters. If those confessions were disposed of, then the entire case against him collapsed. In giving his judgement, Lord Alverstone said that it was true that circumstantial evidence alone was insufficient to find Shawcross guilty, but the evidence must be looked at as a whole and this, together with his own admissions, entitled the jury to reach the conclusion they had. After all, if Shawcross was not guilty, then why had he not rushed back to the scene to see what help he could be to the police?

By the appointed hour, 9.00am on Tuesday, August 3rd, 1909, a crowd of around 400 had gathered outside Strangeways jail. Many believed that Shawcross had been due to hang at 8.00am and held that this 'delay' was a sign that he was to be reprieved at the last minute. In the event they had all been mistaken and no such escape came for Mark Shawcross. He was hanged at the correct time by Henry and Thomas Pierrepoint who gave him a drop of 7ft, and as the prison bell began to toll, a cart, laden with lime, arrived at the prison gates.

CHAPTER SEVEN

THE POSTCARD

JAMES Ryder was a drunkard who mistreated his wife, Elizabeth Ann Ryder, to such an extent that she was really only happy when he was on one of his extended periods away from the family home during the course of his job as a ship's fireman. And by November, 1912, things between Ryder and his wife had become so bad that one night while he was out drinking, she and her two sons moved from their lodgings at 5 Ernest Street to a new address at 32 Briscoe Street, off Dark Lane, Ardwick. They did not bother to tell Ryder where they had gone.

It took James Ryder some time to trace his family and so it was not until May 8th, 1913, that he knocked on the door of the house in Briscoe Street. Ryder was sober, and although he appeared friendly enough towards his wife and sons, he was not asked to stay the night.

Ryder called again on May 9th, and again he was sober. Elizabeth opened the front door to him and Ryder walked in without being asked, saying, "I want my things." There was no venom in the request and after talking to Elizabeth for some hours, he was given permission to stay, not just for the one night, but on a permanent basis. It was a decision the family were soon to regret.

James Ryder remained sober until Wednesday, May 14th, when, at 6.00pm he came home drunk. Elizabeth, who was employed as a piecer in a mill in Jackson Street, returned from work some ten minutes later. At that time, all the family – James Ryder, his wife Elizabeth, and their two sons, James and Jack – were in the kitchen together. It was then that Ryder asked his wife about a 'letter' that had arrived the previous day.

That letter, which had in fact been a postcard, began, 'Dear L,' and continued, rather cryptically, 'I will see you if possible between five thirty and six o'clock on Wednesday evening by Ardwick Green.' It was signed, 'With love. P.' Ryder had asked Elizabeth about the message when it had first arrived and now she repeated the story she had told him. She claimed that the note had come from her aunt Polly, but Ryder had refused to accept this, choosing instead to believe that Elizabeth was seeing another man, someone with the initial P.

Ryder would simply not let the matter drop and continued pressing Elizabeth, demanding to know who had really sent the card. She continued to maintain that it was her aunt, and it was clear that a major argument was about to develop. James, Elizabeth's son, told Ryder, "If you don't give over talking about it, you will go outside." Ryder remarked that he still thought the card was from a man, but at this point he let the matter drop and fell quiet. The rest of the evening passed without incident. Jack retired to his bed first, his brother following him at 12.05am on the 15th. Five minutes before this, at midnight, Ryder had also gone up to the bed he shared with his two sons. Once all the men were upstairs, Elizabeth Ryder settled down on the sofa for the night.

Jack Ryder rose at 5.00am on Thursday, May 15th, his brother James coming downstairs five minutes later, leaving their father alone in bed. At 5.20am the two brothers left number 32 together. At the time their mother was busying herself in the kitchen. Ryder was still in bed.

When James Ryder arrived home for lunch at 11.45am, he found the front door shut and locked, something which was highly unusual. James used his key to let himself in and, going through to the kitchen, noticed that the back door was bolted on the inside. He called upstairs for his mother, but received no reply, and then saw that some of her clothing was on the sofa in the kitchen and her purse was still in her apron pocket. Puzzled, James Ryder went upstairs to see where she was and the sight which met his eyes froze his blood. Elizabeth Ryder was lying across the bed, a gaping wound in her throat and James' own razor was lying on the floor at the foot of the bed.

James fled downstairs and ran to fetch a neighbour, Mrs Charlotte Haslam, who lived at number 32a. She went to number 32 with James, saw that Elizabeth was beyond help and told James to fetch the police. Bravely, she stayed with her neighbour's body until James returned with two police constables.

Constable Thomas Maskery went upstairs to the front bedroom where he saw the body of Elizabeth Ryder, lying on her back but slightly turned on to her left side. The body was stiff and cold, suggesting that she had been dead for some time, and was covered in blood. Elizabeth was fully dressed but her skirt had been turned up to her waist and bed clothes had been thrown over her lower legs. The razor, still lying at the foot of the bed, was only partly open but Constable Maskery could see that it was heavily bloodstained and the blade had been broken. The corner of the bedsheet, some feet away from where Elizabeth lay, was also bloodstained and it appeared that someone had wiped their hands there. Soon afterwards, Dr Heslop arrived and Constable Maskery helped him to remove the body to the mortuary.

Attempts were made to locate the missing husband and a description was flashed to all the local police forces, especially those officers serving on Salford and Liverpool docks. Ryder was, after all, a seafaring man and it was reasonable to assume that he might try to make good his escape by joining a ship. The police message said, 'Wanted by the Manchester police on a charge of wife murder, James Ryder, aged 43. Height five feet seven inches, fairly high cheekbones, sandy moustache cut short, brown hair turning grey becoming bald at front, dressed in a blue serge suit, black silk muffler with a pattern of dull red flowers, plain flannel shirt, 'pot' hat, black boots without toecaps.'

In fact, such precautions were not to prove necessary. Amongst the police officers checking Ryder's usual haunts were Detective Inspector Richard Thomas and Detective Sergeant Evans. They were in Store Street at 2.30pm when they saw Ryder, who was very drunk. Four hours later, at Whitworth Street police station, the prisoner had sobered enough for him to be charged with murder, to which he replied, "What me? I know nothing about it." Inspector Thomas pointed to some blood on Ryder's shirt but he claimed that this had come from a fight. Further stains were noted on the inside of Ryder's right-hand trouser pocket but he claimed these were not blood.

Ryder made his first appearance at the police court on May 16th but the hearing was brief and he was remanded until May 19th. Asked then if he had anything to say when Inspector Thomas requested a further remand, Ryder replied, "There is no proof that I have had anything to do with it. I have no right to be remanded." The clerk of the court, Mr Heywood, asked Inspector Thomas if the police did have any evidence against Ryder to which he said, "We have very strong circumstantial evidence. It is only circumstantial. The inquest is fixed for today." This was enough for the chairman of the magistrates, Mr Halliday, who remanded Ryder for one day, pending the coroner's hearing.

Later that same day, the inquest opened before the Manchester City coroner, Mr Ernest Austin Gibson. Details of the arguments over the postcard were given by James Ryder. Other witnesses were also heard, including a number of neighbours, and members of Elizabeth's family who all testified to her exemplary character, and medical evidence was given by Dr Heslop who put the time of death at around 8.00am. Having heard all this, the jury took only a few minutes to return a verdict of murder against Ryder.

On May 20th, Ryder made another brief appearance at the police court when he was remanded for a week. It was on the third appearance, on May 27th, that the evidence of

George Smythe, who lived at 20 Love Lane, was heard. Smythe said that he had known both Ryder and the dead woman for 20 years, although he was not particularly close to either of them. According to Smythe, on May 15th, the day that Elizabeth met her death, he had been in the vault of the Cricketer's Inn between 9.00am and 10.00am when Ryder came in.

Ryder was already the worse for drink but asked Smythe to join him in a pint. Having been refused by the landlord, who felt he had already had enough, Ryder left the pub with Smythe who walked him to the corner of Berwick Street and Pollard Street where Ryder asked him to go to the Bridge Inn for a whisky. Smythe declined but Ryder was insistent, adding, "It will be the last drink you will ever have with me. I have cut my wife's throat." Smythe thought this was just the drink talking and placed no credence on these ramblings but Ryder fell to his knees, crossed himself and said, "Do you believe me now?" Still Smythe said he did not and after leaving Ryder there, returned to the Cricketer's and told the landlord about the conversation he had just had.

Two hours later, Ryder was back in the Cricketer's, and since the landlord was out at the time he managed to get himself served. Seeing that he was now extremely drunk, Smythe suggested that Ryder should go home sleep it off, but Ryder tried to lie down and said he would have a sleep where he was. Smythe walked him to the door and saw him off the premises.

Other witnesses were still to be called and so a further remand was ordered, this time until June 4th. On that date, all the other witnesses, except one, gave their testimony. Dr Heslop had been ill and had taken a voyage in order to improve his health and for this reason, one final remand was necessary, until June 11th. Only then was Ryder sent for trial.

James Ryder stood trial at Manchester on July 5th, 1913. The judge was Mr Justice Bailhache and Ryder was defended by Mr Merriman, while the case for the prosecution was led by Mr Henriques who was assisted by Mr Oliver.

It was important to show that Ryder had the opportunity to kill his wife, for he was claiming that he was simply not at home at the time she was attacked. To begin with, Ryder had been in the house at Briscoe Street at 5.20am when his two sons left for work. In addition to this evidence, James could confirm that the razor used to kill his mother belonged to him. He had last used it on the night of May 14th and at that time, the blade was not broken. Further, James confirmed that the only clothes his father had at the house was the blue serge suit he had been wearing when he was picked up in Store Street.

Jack Ryder told much the same story as his brother but added that when he came down for breakfast on the morning of May 15th, his mother had told him that she was going to the docks at Salford to see if his father could sign on the *SS Manchester Importer*. That day he had not arrived home until 2.30pm, by which time the police were already on the scene.

It could be shown that Elizabeth Ryder was alive ten minutes after her two sons had left the house. Sarah Hannah Whitlam was a knocker-up and had known Elizabeth for seven or eight months. At 5.30am on May 15th, she had knocked at 32 Briscoe Street, on both the bedroom and kitchen windows. Elizabeth appeared at the kitchen window and called out, "All right." Sarah passed back down the street several times that morning and saw no one leaving the house. The last time she was there was around 7.00am and she heard no noises coming from number 32.

Charlotte Haslam, who had been called to the scene of the tragedy by James Ryder, said that her bedroom was next to the front bedroom of number 32, the room in which Elizabeth was killed. Charlotte said that at 7.00am on May 15th, she heard a noise from next door which sounded like someone walking about in the bedroom. There were no other sounds, no screams and nothing that indicated that a struggle might be taking place. The inference was, though, that since these were the only sounds Charlotte heard, the attack upon Elizabeth might well have taken place at this time.

There was, however, a problem with this timing. Fred Birtwistle lived at the St Andrew's Hotel in Adam Street, Ancoats, and worked there as a barman. He had known Ryder as a regular customer for more than a year and testified that on May 15th, Ryder came into the hotel just before 7.00am. Ryder went into the vault where he had a bottle of beer, leaving after about three minutes. He was sober at the time but when he returned at 2.00pm, he was so drunk that Birtwistle refused to serve him. There was no blood on Ryder's hands or clothing when he came into the hotel that morning.

Frederick George Hodden was the landlord of the Cricketer's Inn which was situated in Berwick Street. He testified that Ryder came into his establishment between 8.30am and 9.00am on May 15th, had one glass of beer and left. By 9.50am, Ryder was back but appeared to be drunk and Hodden refused to serve him, even though he asked another customer, George Smythe, to have a drink with him. The two men left together, but Smythe returned a few minutes later.

All this testimony about Ryder's movements was, however, disputed by the evidence of two other witnesses. Elizabeth Smith lived at 35 Briscoe Street and knew Ryder, although only by sight. At 8.55am on May 15th, she had her front door open and was eating breakfast in the back room. She could see out into the street and saw Ryder pass by her house. Mrs Smith said that Ryder was wearing a blue serge suit.

Lily Pratt, who lived at number 31, a house opposite to the Ryders, ran a shop from that address and was dressing her window at 8.55am on the 15th. Lily determined this time by saying that a traveller had called about five minutes before and she had looked at the clock then, and it was 8.50am She saw Ryder leaving number 32. He closed the door behind him and thrust his hands into his pockets before walking off up the street. Lily, too, reported that Ryder was wearing a navy blue suit.

Although there was contradictory evidence about just where Ryder was on the morning of May 15th, there could be no dispute that he had been wrong about his wife being involved with another man. Mary Martha Thomasson, who lived in Greville Street, Rusholme, said that she was Elizabeth's sister-in-law and was known to the dead woman as Polly. Mary confirmed that she had sent a postcard to Elizabeth on May 13th, arranging to meet her on the 14th. They did, indeed, meet on the Wednesday and spoke about some wool which Mary needed for a vest.

Something of the history of Ryder's relationship with Elizabeth was detailed by Mary Jane Mitchell who lived at 10 Ernest Street. At one stage, the Ryders had lodged on the opposite side of the street, a few doors down, and Jane had got to know the family well. She described a number of arguments between Ryder and his wife, these usually taking place when Ryder got drunk. Once, Jane had heard Elizabeth shout, "Oh give over you damn thing, you will be killing me." Jane went across to see what the problem was and found Ryder with a hook in his hand. Elizabeth was lying on the sofa and claimed that her husband had hurt her head. Jane tried to calm the situation down but Ryder slammed the hook into the table and screamed for her to get out.

What looked like blood had been seen on Ryder's clothing and he said that this must have come from a fight. Hugh Welsh had known Ryder for four years and often went out drinking with him when he was home from sea. On May 15th, Welsh had seen Ryder at 2.10pm By that time, Welsh was already very drunk himself and he recalled some conversation between him and Ryder but had no memory of what had actually been said. Whatever it was must have offended Ryder in some way, for he suddenly lashed out at Welsh and struck him in the face. The next thing Welsh remembered was a doctor stitching his lip at Ancoats Hospital.

The fracas between Welsh and Ryder had been witnessed by Isaac Farrington. He was standing at the corner of Betley Street and Adair Street when he saw Ryder and Welsh together. Farrington saw Ryder lash out at Welsh who was struck on the right side of his jaw. The blow had come from behind and Welsh fell forward on to his face as Ryder shouted, "I will murder you." Ryder walked away as Farrington rushed over to help Welsh to his feet. The man was bleeding from the nose and mouth but in Farrington's opinion, the fall had been such that none of Welsh's blood could have got on to Ryder's clothing.

Dr William John Heslop was the senior divisional police surgeon and had examined Elizabeth's body at the scene, later performing the post-mortem. Dr Heslop reported an incised cut extending down to the spine which divided the internal jugular vein on the left side and the common carotid artery and the vagus nerve on the right. The windpipe had been divided and there was a notch on the spinal column and a piece of blade embedded in the spine. He estimated that Elizabeth had been dead for some six hours and since his initial examination took place at 2.00pm, this would put the time of death at around 8.00am Later still, Dr Heslop examined Ryder's clothing and was unable to confirm that the marks on the blue suit were blood. Indeed, Dr Heslop said he did not even think this was a recent stain and did not believe it was blood.

Ryder gave evidence on his own behalf, saying that he left the house at 6.15am, leaving his wife alone. He went first to the Milton Hotel, where he had a single beer, before moving on to the Crown and Anchor, which he reached just before 7.00am From there, Ryder went to the St Andrew's Hotel, then to the Rodney in Pollard Street before going to the Mitchell Arms, the Cricketer's and then back to the Mitchell. Much of this alibi had, of course, been corroborated by other witnesses, no blood had been found on his clothing, and only the evidence of two witnesses who said they had seen him leaving his house just before 9.00am contradicted his story. Despite this, the jury returned a guilty verdict and several women in the public gallery wept as Ryder was sentenced to death.

The appeal was heard on July 28th before Justices Bray, Avory and Lush. The main grounds were that Ryder had been seen in the Cricketer's Arms between 8.30am and 9.00am This pub was 1,400 yards from the murder scene and it was therefore impossible for Ryder to have been the man seen leaving 32 Briscoe Street at 8.55am There was also some doubt over the alleged confession made to George Smythe. He had claimed that at one stage, Ryder had fallen to his knees in the street. This must have been a very strange sight indeed but no one had been found who had witnessed it.

Despite these reservations, the judges still felt that the case against Ryder had been strong enough and the appeal was lost. Just over two weeks later, at 8.00am on Wednesday, August 13th, 1913, a crowd of more than 200 people gathered outside the prison at Manchester as James Ryder was hanged by John Ellis.

CHAPTER EIGHT

THE TRIANGLE

ALTHOUGH 38-year-old Sarah Woodall was a married woman, she had been separated from her husband, William, for four years and by 1915 there were two other men in her life. One, George Wake, was supposedly only a friend but the other, 44-year-old Frederick Holmes, enjoyed a closer, more intimate relationship with her.

In October of that year, Sarah Woodall's mother died and she returned briefly to Doncaster for the funeral. It was then that Sarah discovered that her mother had left her between £200 and £300, a considerable sum. At the same time, Frederick Holmes was working in Ripon but once Sarah had returned to Manchester, she wrote to him and asked him to come back and live with her at 64 Higher Ardwick. This he duly did.

No sooner had Holmes settled down to life with Sarah, than her old friend, George Wake, reappeared on the scene. He had known Sarah for about eight years and one day in early November he walked into a pub and there saw Sarah who was with a friend of hers, Maud Barker. The three fell into conversation and went on together to another pub. After a while, Maud Barker had gone home, leaving George alone with Sarah. They had carried on drinking, finally leaving the pub just before 5.00pm

Before they parted, Sarah said she had to get back but added that she would like to see George again. He suggested they meet up later that evening and eventually arrangements were made for them to meet at yet another pub, at the corner of Downing Street, Rusholme, at 8.00pm. Both turned up at that time and after having another drink together, Sarah asked George to come home with her to Higher Ardwick. George Wake was happy to agree.

It was 8.45pm by the time George and Sarah arrived at 64 Higher Ardwick, where she knocked at the door which was opened by Holmes. Sarah marched straight into the house and ordered Holmes to "Get out". Holmes demanded to know the identity of her man friend, turned to Wake and shouted, "Who are you?" George Wake smiled and replied, "My name is Wake."

Although Holmes knew that Sarah had been friendly with Wake, he had never met him and so asked, "Are you George Wake?" When Wake replied that indeed he was, Holmes flew into a rage and screamed, "I'll murder the pair of you." He lunged at Wake, lashing out with his fists. A fierce fight ensued in which it was plain that George Wake was coming off second best, so Sarah took up a shovel from the fireplace in the front room and struck Holmes on the back, causing Holmes to loosen his grip on Wake, who fell down in the lobby.

Holmes was dazed for only a few seconds and seeing Wake lying on the floor in front of him, stamped one foot on Wake's chest, then kicked out at him and finally bit him on the left hand. As Wake screamed out in agony, Sarah pushed past the two men, ran into the street and shouted, "Police! Murder!" That was enough for Holmes. He did not want to be involved with the police and so ran from the house, leaving Sarah to dress Wake's injuries. That night, Wake stayed with Sarah. Holmes did not return.

One might have thought that this incident would mark the end of the relationship between Sarah Woodall and Frederick Holmes, but this was not the case. Over the next few weeks, they saw each other on a number of occasions and eventually became friendly towards each other again. The upshot was that Sarah eventually suggested that they should 'try again' and Holmes agreed, providing they find new lodgings for themselves. So it was that on November 24th, 1915, Sarah Woodall knocked at the door of 9 Clifford Street, Chorlton-on-Medlock, Manchester.

The house was owned by Ellen Weller who also owned another house, number 13, and that particular property she let out as furnished rooms. There were already a number of families living at number 13, but the front room downstairs was still available and Sarah Woodall asked if she and her husband could rent it. The 'husband' who was, of course, Frederick Holmes, remained silent as Sarah handled all the negotiations. Terms were agreed and Sarah confirmed that she would pay the weekly rent, in advance, every Wednesday.

Ellen Weller saw Sarah a number of times over the next couple of weeks, the last occasion being Tuesday, December 7th. The next day, though, when the rent was due, Sarah failed to call at number 9 Clifford Street to pay it. Ellen, a businesswoman to the end, walked down to number 13 where she noticed that the blinds in Sarah's room were drawn. There was no answer to her knocking. Nevertheless, Ellen Weller stayed in the house until 11.30pm. Neither Sarah nor her husband returned and the landlady finally returned to her own house, determined to call again the following day.

On December 9th, Ellen did, indeed, return, at around noon. She knocked on Sarah Woodall's door a number of times but again there was no reply and the blinds were still drawn. Enough was enough, she decided and returned home to get her duplicate key.

When she finally gained admittance to the front room at 13 Clifford Street, Ellen Weller could not see very much as the room was in darkness. She walked carefully over to the window, raised the blind and then, turning around, saw why there had been no answer to her repeated knocking. Sarah Woodall lay in the bed, the sheets pulled up almost covering her head. Ellen touched her forehead and felt that it was icy cold, but there had been no need to check if her lodger was dead. The bloodstained sheets and the large pool of blood on the floor confirmed that something terrible had happened here. Of Frederick Holmes, there was no sign.

Locking the door of the room behind her, Ellen Weller hurried to the police station in Cavendish Street and reported to Inspector Lloyd what she had found at number 13. At 12.35pm, Superintendent Taylor and Sergeant Thomas Singleton arrived at Clifford Street and entered the room where the tragedy had taken place.

They saw the body of a woman, covered with sheets and an eiderdown, in bed. Carefully pulling back the sheets, Singleton saw that the woman was saturated with blood and there was a large wound on the right side of her neck. On her forehead, just above her right eye, there was a second wound, a clean cut. Making a note of what he found, Sergeant Singleton saw that the woman was wearing her chemise, some stays, a bodice, drawers, stockings and one suspender. Her clothing had been turned up all around so that it lay above her waist and every item she wore was heavily bloodstained. There was a large pool of blood on the floor at the foot of the bed and on a cupboard in the room lay a razor and a knife. Although it was plain that the woman was beyond all help, the formalities had to be observed and Dr Heslop, a police surgeon, was summoned.

Before the doctor arrived, another police officer, Detective Sergeant George Allan, arrived on the scene. He had heard of the murder and went to number 13 to see if he could assist his colleagues. While Superintendent Taylor and Sergeant Singleton took care of the searching of the room, Sergeant Allan spoke to other people who lived in the house and obtained a detailed description of the missing 'husband' Frederick Holmes, whom he then went off to find.

It was not until 5.20pm that Allan located Holmes, in Copeland Street. Having identified himself and ascertained that this was indeed Holmes, Sergeant Allan cautioned him and asked Holmes to accompany him to the police station. Holmes replied, "It's all right. I could see it coming. How long is it since you found her?" Allan told him that the body had been found at noon, whereupon Holmes continued, "I couldn't have kept away from her much longer. I was going to have a drink and I might have given myself up. It's no use running away."

Holmes was escorted to Cavendish Street and there charged with the murder of Sarah Woodall. Having had the charge read to him, Holmes asked that it be read over a second time. This was done by Sergeant Allan and after hearing it again, Holmes muttered, "No malice aforethought. You can cross them two words out." At the same time, Inspector Cavanagh was writing the charge down and made a mistake, putting the victim's name down as Alice Woodall. Holmes corrected him, saying, "It is Sarah Woodall, not Alice."

Holmes was searched and on him was found a key and a letter from Sarah. As the key was placed on a table, Holmes said, "That is the key of the door at 13 Clifford Street." Two men's detachable collars, both bloodstained, had been found underneath the bed at Clifford Street and these were shown to Holmes who denied that they were his. This, it seemed, was true for one of them bore the name 'Wake'. Holmes looked at them carefully and said, "They don't belong to me. They belong to the man whose name is there."

On the same day that he was arrested, Holmes appeared at the Manchester City police court before the stipendiary magistrate, Mr E. Brierley. The mistake made by Inspector Cavanagh was repeated here and Holmes found himself charged with the murder of Alice Woodall. Once again the matter was corrected and Holmes was remanded until December 13th. On that date he made another brief appearance and was remanded again, this time until December 20th.

It was also on December 13th that the inquest on Sarah Woodall was concluded and the jury returned a verdict of wilful murder against Holmes. A week later he was back at the police court when he was remanded until December 28th, the case for the Director of Public Prosecutions now having been taken over by Mr W.L. Hockin. At his final appearance on the 28th, Holmes was sent for trial.

The case of the Crown against Frederick Holmes took place at Manchester on February 18th, 1916, before Mr Justice Bailhache. The prosecution was led by Mr Lindon Riley, who was assisted by Mr Oliver, whilst Holmes' defence lay in the hands of Mr F. Brocklehurst.

George Wake told the court of his argument with Holmes when Sarah had invited him back to Higher Ardwick. After staying that night with Sarah, he had risen the following morning and while getting dressed had noticed that his collar was heavily bloodstained as a result of the struggle with Holmes. Wake had left the collar with Sarah. He went on to deny that he had ever been to see Sarah at Clifford Street. Indeed, the last time he had seen her was a couple of days after he had fought with Holmes, and that, too, had been at Higher Ardwick. George Wake, though, also admitted, under cross examination, that he had had his own problems with Sarah and on one occasion, she had called the police to have him ejected from 64 Higher Ardwick.

William Woodall, who was Sarah's legal husband, said that he lived at 86 Lloyd Street, Chorlton-on-Medlock. He had made the formal identification at the mortuary and confirmed that the cause of their break-up had been the fact that Sarah was living an immoral life. She had once been in custody on a charge of accosting and he knew that she was seeing a number of men, although he had been unaware that she was living with Holmes.

John William Skinner was Sarah's brother and the executor of his mother's estate. He said that Margaret Skinner, Sarah's mother, had died on October 29th, at 151 Bentley Road, Doncaster. Sarah had been at that address at the time and he had advanced her £10 out of the estate. He estimated that Sarah had been entitled to around £250. Finally, Skinner confirmed that the letter found on Holmes when he was arrested was in Sarah's handwriting. This had been dated November 12th and had been the one asking Holmes to come and live with her.

Maud Barker said that she had been the woman with Sarah in a public house when George Wake had come in and they had all had a drink together. This was the first time she had ever met Wake and Sarah introduced them to each other. She saw Wake the next morning, by which time he had a black eye and marks on his hands and thumb.

About a week after these events had taken place, Maud had been with Sarah in the Ludlow Hotel, when Holmes walked in. On seeing him, Sarah became frightened and ran from the pub. Holmes saw her dash out and went after her, as did Maud. By the time Maud caught up with Sarah, she had stopped a police sergeant and told him that Holmes was trying to hurt her. Holmes had laughed and told the policeman, "It's only fun." The situation had been calmed down somewhat and Maud, Sarah and Holmes then went back into the pub to have a drink together. At one stage, Maud had referred to the problems which Holmes and Sarah seemed to be experiencing and had said, "Don't hurt her, Fred." He had replied, "I'll only kill her. If you take her part, I have hit you before for taking her part, I'll hit you again." Maud had thought he was joking, but Sarah had run out of the pub again.

Elizabeth Thompson was the wife of Alfred and they had lived at 13 Clifford Street for nearly five years. They acted as caretakers for Ellen Weller and knew of Holmes and Sarah moving into the property on November 24th. During the next couple of weeks, they only ever heard Sarah and Holmes arguing once, and that was on the second night they were there, November 25th.

On December 8th, at around 11.30am, Elizabeth saw Holmes emerge from his room and lock the door behind him. Soon afterwards, she knocked at the door, seeking to speak to Sarah, but got no reply. The implication was, of course, that Sarah was already dead by that time. Elizabeth went on to say that she had not seen Sarah since 10.30pm on December 6th when she and Holmes went into their room together. Earlier that same evening, at around 7.00pm, Sarah had called on her and in the course of their conversation had shown Elizabeth her arm which was swollen. Sarah suggested that this had been caused by Holmes.

Sarah Metcalfe lived at 3 Wilton Street and had known Holmes for more than three years. They had once lived together, parting only a couple of years before. At 10.15pm on Wednesday, December 8th, she had seen Holmes in Bridge Street and he had approached her and asked if she thought her landlady might put him up for the night. He said he only wanted a bed for one night as he intended going to Ripon the next morning to find work. Sarah said she would have a word with her landlady who agreed to Holmes staying. That night, Holmes slept in her room.

The next morning, Sarah left her room at 7.50am, expecting Holmes to be gone when she returned. She got back a few minutes after noon and he was still there, although he did leave a few minutes later. Sarah reported that at no stage had she seen any blood on Holmes' clothing.

Detective Constable Frederick Augustus George had been in charge of Holmes at the police station. Constable George had been expressly told that he was not to question Holmes but after they had been left alone, on the evening of December 9th, Holmes had asked him what day it was. George replied that it was Thursday, to which Holmes had said, "Thursday, how's that? I have been drinking this last three weeks. It must have been on Monday I was with Alice at the Ludlow. We had been drinking together and went home friendly. She put her arm round me in the street."

At the time, Holmes appeared to be in something of a daze and he got Sarah's name wrong, calling her Alice. This, indeed, may have been why the inspector later made a mistake in transcribing the victim's name. Holmes now paused for a full five minutes before saying, "After we got in the house there was the usual haggling. She's a very jealous woman." He paused for a few moments more and then continued, "I think I did it with a razor that I saw on the cupboard at the end of the sofa. I have got the razor here in my pocket." At this point, Holmes felt around in the pockets of his coat, but there was no razor there. He then said, "I couldn't believe she was dead. I went out next morning about 11 o'clock. I didn't go back to the house. I stopped with Sally (*sic*) Metcalfe. You know her, she works in a laundry in Wilton Street. I was going to give myself up tonight. I'm a bit dazed." At no time had Constable George administered a caution to the prisoner.

Medical evidence was given by Dr William John Heslop who arrived at Clifford Street at 1.15pm on December 9th. He estimated that Sarah had been dead for something between 24 and 36 hours and later performed the post-mortem. He stated that the wound on the right of the neck was three and a half inches long and had penetrated down to the spinal column, severing all the large blood vessels. The wound over the eye was only three quarters of an inch long and did go down to the bone. The nose appeared to have been struck at some stage and there was a good deal of blood in the nose and the mouth and she had obviously swallowed some as blood was also found in the stomach. Neither the knife nor the razor found at the scene could have been used to inflict the wounds as neither bore traces of blood. Stains had been found on these implements, but these turned out to be rust.

Holmes gave evidence on his own behalf. He said that Sarah had been addicted to drink and was very violent at times. She often threw things around and had once struck him in the breast with a pair of scissors. On Monday, December 6th, Sarah had started an argument over some other woman he was supposed to have been seeing. At one stage he turned his back to her and she flew at him with something in her hand, striking him on the head and shoulders. He felt a terrible pain, turned around and seized the weapon, whatever it was, from her. He struck out with his fists and with the weapon and suddenly saw that she was bleeding. Only now did he realise that the weapon he had seized and used, was a razor.

As Sarah collapsed, Holmes, believing she was beyond all help, cried out, "You are going to Heaven. Pray!" He then began to pray as she called out the name 'Doris' three times. Doris was Sarah's daughter and even though she did not live with her mother, Holmes tried to put the dying woman's mind at rest by saying, "Yes darling, I will look after her." Blood was welling up into Sarah's throat and in a few minutes, she died. Holmes then placed her in the bed and spent that night sleeping with the body, her arm across his chest.

The next morning, Holmes took the razor out with him, broke it into pieces and threw the bits away. That night, he returned to Clifford Street and again slept with Sarah's body. The next day he left the house for the last time and spent that Wednesday night with Sarah Metcalfe. Finally, at the request of his barrister, Holmes took off his jacket, the same one he said he was wearing when he struck out at Sarah. There was a long cut down the back, one which might have been made with a razor.

In the event, the jury took just 30 minutes to decide that Holmes had deliberately killed Sarah Woodall and he was found guilty of murder. He did not appeal against the verdict and on Wednesday, March 8th, 1916, a miserable, snowy day, Frederick Holmes was hanged at Strangeways by John Ellis. Only a few people braved the weather to read the execution notices when they were posted on the prison gates.

CHAPTER NINE

BIG JIM

EARLY in 1914, Caroline McGhee separated from her husband, Michael, and went to live with her mother in Ashton-under-Lyne. Soon afterwards, Caroline was on the move again, choosing now to live with James Howarth Hargreaves, a short but powerfully built man, known to all as 'Big Jim'. At 54, he was some 16 years Caroline's senior.

By Christmas, 1915, there were problems with that relationship and Caroline McGhee changed addresses yet again, this time going to live with her brother, Oscar Robinson, at 55 Elizabeth Street. However, even this arrangement did not last for long because Caroline was very fond of drink and after three months, her brother asked her to leave. Caroline, not one to outstay her welcome, returned to Hargreaves at 9 Orange Street, Ashton-under-Lyne.

One of Caroline's closest friends was Lily Armitage, who lived at 39 Tatton Street, also in Ashton. The two women had known each other for about a year but had only been really close for perhaps the past eight months. They often went out drinking together and sometimes, when Caroline was the worse for drink, she would stay with Lily at Tatton Street. This happened on the night of Monday, August 7th, 1916 and it was not until 3.00pm the following day that the two friends were out and about again.

Walking down Wellington Road together, Lily and Caroline met up with Hargreaves and told him where Caroline had spent the previous night. Hargreaves seemed unconcerned. After all, it was something she had done before. He seemed content with Caroline's explanation and arranged to meet them both later for a drink at the Nelson Tavern, a pub also situated in Wellington Road.

It was just ten minutes later that Hargreaves joined Lily and Caroline in the tavern and the three stayed together until some time between 5.00pm and 5.30pm Hargreaves left then, after suggesting that Caroline might come home with him for a bite to eat. Caroline, though, did not return to Orange Street, preferring instead to stay with Lily and carry on drinking.

At 6.00pm, Hargreaves returned to the Nelson Tavern and again drank with the two women. At 6.45pm all three left together. Hargreaves announced that he was going home, while Caroline said that she wished to return to Tatton Street with Lily. On the way there, Lily and her friend stopped at a chip shop and purchased some peas which they took back to Tatton Street and ate.

Deciding that she could do with another drink, Caroline then took Lily to the Commercial Hotel where, after about 45 minutes, they were joined by two soldiers who they had never met before. The soldiers introduced themselves as Edward Uttley and William Sumner, and offered to buy the women drinks, an offer which was not refused. At 9.15pm this group of four left the Commercial Hotel, but only to continue drinking at the Nelson. After a couple of drinks there, they returned to the Commercial where they stayed until 10.50pm

At Caroline's suggestion they then went to Hargreaves' house in Orange Street. She had mentioned that Hargreaves had a bottle of whisky there and the soldiers were more than happy to go. By the time the four of them arrived at Orange Street, it was almost 11.00pm

Hargreaves did not seem too annoyed that Caroline had brought the soldiers home with her and was friendly to both them and Lily. The whisky was produced and at one stage, Caroline suggested that Hargreaves went out to buy some tripe for their supper. He happily obliged and the meal was shared out amongst all five people in the house. At around 11.30pm, Lily Armitage left the house with William Sumner. Edward Uttley stayed on but half an hour later, at midnight, he also left. As he saw Uttley to the door, Hargreaves bade him a warm goodnight and shook him by the hand. It had all been a most enjoyable evening.

In fact, there had been a sixth person in the house at Orange Street that evening. Savinah Caroline Hindley was Hargreaves' married sister, but she had separated from her husband, John, and for the past seven weeks had been living with her brother. Savinah had returned home from work at 6.30pm on August 8th and did not leave the house again, going to bed at 9.15pm. At that time, Hargreaves was not in the house and she did not hear him return. Savinah had a peaceful night, her slumbers not being disturbed by anything untoward.

On Wednesday, August 9th, Savinah rose at 6.20am after her brother had woken her, something he did each morning. She dressed, went into the kitchen and helped herself to a glass of water from the tap. At the time she noticed four empty glasses and detected, from their aroma, that they had contained whisky.

While Savinah had the use of the back bedroom, Hargreaves slept in the front room downstairs which was also used as a sitting room. As she walked into his room to collect her shawl, she saw her brother sitting on the sofa. He was already dressed and Savinah remarked that he was up early. To this Hargreaves had replied, "Can't I please myself when I get up? I feel miserable."

Savinah did not inquire further but suggested that her brother got ready himself and came out with her. At this, Hargreaves burst into tears and muttered, "I wish I was dead out of the road. I've a good mind to poison myself." It was clear that Hargreaves was in a strange mood but, nevertheless, Savinah Hindley left for work. It was not yet 7.00am.

At 2.25pm on August 9th, Constable Robert Wilson was on duty in Katherine Street when Hargreaves, a man he knew well, approached him and asked, "Oh Bob, what must I do? I've murdered a woman at our house last night. I hit her on the head with a poker." Wilson cautioned Hargreaves at once and told him, "You'd better say no more." On the way to the police station, though, Hargreaves reached into his pocket, took out a key and handed it over to Wilson with the comment, "You know where I live and you will find her on the bed."

When he arrived at the police station, Hargreaves was again cautioned, this time by Sergeant Henry Gregson. Hargreaves told Gregson, "She came drunk and brought a bottle of whisky. We had it between us… She threw the bottle at me. I caught it. She said she was the missus there. One thing brought on another. She threw the bottle at me and smashed me in the face. I hit her back. She hit me again. I hit her with the poker and her number was up."

After Hargreaves had been placed in the cells, Sergeant Gregson and Constable Wilson went to 9 Orange Street. The door was locked but the key Hargreaves had handed to Wilson fitted the lock and opened the door. Gregson and Wilson entered the house where they found some female clothing on the sofa in Hargreaves' room. Pulling down the blinds, Wilson noticed that the curtains were spotted with blood on the inside. The reason why was easy to determine. There in the bed lay the body of a woman, later identified as Caroline McGhee, lying on her back, her head, which had been brutally battered, positioned below the pillows, resting on the mattress. Blood had soaked through the mattress and made a sizeable pool on the floor below. The attack upon the woman must have been a furious one for Wilson found in the fireplace her bloodstained dentures and two pieces of bone from her shattered skull.

Having been charged with murder, Hargreaves appeared at the Ashton Borough police court on August 10th, when he was remanded to August 14th. The inquest on the dead woman opened on August 11th, before Mr G.S. Laresche. Matters proceeded quickly and at the end of the day, all the evidence having been heard, the jury returned a verdict of wilful murder against Hargreaves. Three days later, on the 14th, Hargreaves was back before the magistrates and was sent for trial on the capital charge.

His trial took place at Manchester on November 28th, before Mr Justice Avory. Hargreaves was defended by Mr J.B. Sandbach while the case for the Crown was led by Dr Atkinson, who was assisted by Mr Lindon Riley.

After Lily Armitage had outlined what had taken place on the night of August 8th, the two soldiers confirmed that there had been no animosity shown by Hargreaves. Edward Uttley, a sergeant in the 3rd Battalion, the Manchester Regiment, said he was now stationed at Cleethorpes but at the time of the incident, had been based at Ashton. Uttley detailed their movements, first meeting Lily and Caroline in the Commercial Hotel. It had been his colleague who paid for the tripe which was consumed, but Hargreaves had been happy enough to go for it.

William Sumner was also a sergeant, but he was in the 13th Battalion, the Manchester Regiment. He told much the same story as Uttley, adding only that he had paid sixpence for the tripe.

In addition to giving details of the arrest and the prisoner's statement, Constable Wilson also stated that the only blood seen on Hargreaves' clothing was a small stain on the right shoulder of his shirt and a couple of specks on his vest. There was no blood whatsoever on the female clothing found on the sofa, suggesting that Caroline had been undressed at the time she was attacked.

Savinah Hindley said that she had seen nothing out of place when she entered her brother's bedroom on the morning of August 9th. The blinds had been up at the time and consequently the room was well lit. As for the dead woman, Savinah had met her only once and that had been at the beginning of August when she was getting ready for work one morning and had seen her in bed with Hargreaves. No one pursued the point that Caroline and Savinah had been living at the same house for some weeks and yet Savinah was claiming that she had only ever seen Caroline on one occasion.

Medical evidence was given by Dr Donald Gordon Falconer who had examined Caroline's body at the scene and later performed a post-mortem. Dr Falconer stated that the bed in which Caroline was lying was under the window, behind the door in the front room on the ground floor. A quilt and a piece of white calico, both of which were bloodstained, had been thrown over the body, but did not quite cover it. It was possible to determine that Caroline had died while lying in the bed, face down, although she may have been attacked elsewhere.

Describing the injuries, Dr Falconer said that there was a large gaping wound, three inches long, running diagonally along the left side of Caroline's head, from the back to the front. This had exposed the skull and the right half had been smashed into minute pieces. There were many pieces of the skull bones lying amongst the hair and the clothes and the brain had been largely exposed and lacerated. Many blows must have been struck and the weapon used was a poker, found in the room, which had blood, hair and brain tissue adhering to it. Finally, Dr Falconer said that death must have occurred at least 12 hours before he examined Caroline, putting the latest time of death at 3.10am on August 9th.

Giving evidence on his own behalf, Hargreaves said that he had consumed about ten drinks that afternoon and Caroline had probably consumed far more. When she brought the soldiers back to his house, they had entered without his permission and he and Caroline had quarrelled later because he had told her that the soldiers could not stay the night. One thing led to another and after she struck him with the bottle, he hit her with the poker. Later, he put the body in the bed and slept with her that night.

There could really be only one verdict and Hargreaves was duly sentenced to death. There was no appeal and on the morning of Tuesday, December 19th, 1916, James Howarth Hargreaves – 'Big Jim' – was hanged at Manchester by John Ellis and William Willis, who gave him a drop of just 5ft 4ins due to his heavily build and short stature.

There remain two unanswered questions. If the whisky bottle hitting him in the face was the cause of Hargreaves losing his temper, then why had he been totally free of any injury when examined by the police surgeon? Second, and even more curious, if Caroline McGhee was already dead, as everyone agreed, by 3.10am on August 9th, why had Savinah Hindley not noticed anything out of the ordinary when she entered the room where the body lay, just after 6.20am?

CHAPTER TEN

INDUSTRIAL RELATIONS

THERE could be little doubt that 39-year-old Hyman Perdovitch and Soloman Franks, ten years his senior, were not on very good terms. Perdovitch, who lived in Albert Avenue, Sedgeley Park, worked as a machinist for Wilks Brothers, garment manufacturers at their Booth Street, Salford factory. Franks was his foreman.

For his part, Franks was convinced that Perdovitch wanted to take over the department while Perdovitch believed that Franks deliberately gave him the most difficult and most poorly paid jobs. This had led to a good deal of bad blood between the two men.

In fact, this was the second period of employment that Perdovitch had served for Wilks Brothers. Born at Vilna in Russia, he had moved to England in the latter years of the nineteenth century and started work for Wilks' soon afterwards. Although England was not his country, Perdovitch had joined the Army in 1916 and served in the Border Regiment. At the end of that year, he was sent to France where he transferred to the Royal Irish Regiment and almost a year later, in August 1917, Perdovitch was wounded at Ypres. His injury was so severe that he then spent a considerable time in hospital back in England, finally being discharged from the Army in August 1918, when he returned to Salford and was given his old job back. Even now, in 1919, Perdovitch still attended the Salford Royal Hospital as an outpatient.

On August 12th, 1919, Morris Sherr, a seamer in the same department as Franks and Perdovitch, heard the foreman ask Perdovitch, "Can I have that work out for today, Tuesday?" The reply, also heard by Sherr, was, "You can have it when it suits me." This was typical of the way the two men spoke to each other and things continued in this vein for the next few days.

It was 8.25am on Friday, August 15th, when Perdovitch asked Sherr, who worked on the machine opposite, to bring him a drink of water. As this was something he had done for Perdovitch many times before, Sherr did as he was asked but noticed that Perdovitch seemed to be quiet and depressed. As Perdovitch finished his water, Soloman Franks walked past and made towards a door which led to the yard. Without speaking, Perdovitch followed Franks and after a minute or so, Sherr heard a groan and looked to his left in time to see Franks falling forward towards him. Sherr rushed forward to see what was the matter and noticed that there was blood coming from the back of Franks' neck. Morris Sherr undid Franks' collar so that he could breathe more easily, as other men dashed forward to offer their help. As they did, Sherr saw that Perdovitch was backing away from his own machine.

Nathan Nelson also worked at Wilks Brothers but he had his back to Perdovitch at the time Franks was injured. Nelson heard a low groan and turned around to see Franks lying on the shop floor. Perdovitch was standing by his own machine and Nelson heard another of the workers ask him what he had done. Perdovitch replied, "It's alright, I've finished him. He deserved it, the bastard." Seeing that Franks was in need of proper medical attention, Nelson ran to fetch a doctor.

Nathan Lewis had had a good view of what had taken place between Perdovitch and Franks. He saw Perdovitch lean over Franks' shoulder as if to speak to him, but then suddenly he struck out twice with his left hand, aiming blows at Franks' head. Franks groaned and fell forward into the room. At first, Lewis did not know that, as he lashed out, Perdovitch had held a knife in his hand, so he asked what he had done. To this Perdovitch replied, "You can see. I'm an injured man and you know how he has treated me." Lewis said, "Yes, but you shouldn't have hit him," whereupon Perdovitch had made the comment overheard by Nathan Nelson about Franks having deserved it. Perdovitch then added, "I've done it now, and I'll wait like a man for the police."

Abraham Wand was another of Wilks' employees but he worked in the room next door. At 8.45am he heard some sort of commotion in the next room and went to see what had taken place. He saw Franks lying on the floor close to the door which led to the yard at the back. Wand knew something about first aid so he rendered what assistance he could, noticing that there were two wounds on the back of Franks' neck. Later still, Wand accompanied Franks in the ambulance which took him to the hospital.

Ebenezer Everard Newbold ran a tobacconist's shop from 79 Chapel Street, Salford, close to where Wilks Brothers had their factory. It was around 9.00am that he saw the police ambulance pull up at the factory and went across to see what was happening. As he went into the factory, Newbold saw Perdovitch, who he knew as a customer at his shop, and asked, "What's the matter kid?" Perdovitch replied, "Oh nothing worth talking about. The man was never any bloody good to anyone, so I've done him in."

Although Perdovitch had said he was going to wait for the police to pick him up, he did not in fact do so, choosing instead to walk down to the Chapel Street police station where Constable Samuel Marsh was on duty at the front desk. Perdovitch walked up to the counter and said, "Do you want me?" Marsh, at this stage knowing nothing of the events at the factory, replied, "What for?" Perdovitch said, "I've injured a man over at Wilks'. If you don't want me now, you will later." Constable Marsh detained Perdovitch and contacted his headquarters who were by now aware of the attack. Perdovitch was cautioned, searched and told he would be detained on a serious charge. During the search, Perdovitch took a knife out of his right-hand jacket pocket and told the police officer, "That's the thing I did it with." The knife was closed up at the time and when Marsh opened out the blade, he saw fresh blood on it.

Later still, when Marsh discovered that Franks was dead and Perdovitch was charged with murder, Perdovitch replied, "I didn't intend to kill, although I have done."

Perdovitch made his first appearance at Salford police court on August 16th when he was remanded until the 19th. It was also on the 16th that the inquest on the dead man opened, before the deputy coroner, Mr A. Howard Flint. Evidence of identification was given by Harry Franks, Solomon's brother, who said that the dead man had lived at Bellott Street, Cheetham Hill, and left behind a wife and five children. Solomon had worked for Wilks' Brothers for the past two years and had confided in his family that he was growing increasingly concerned about a Russian machinist who also worked at the factory and wanted to 'boss the room'. At this point, the inquest was also adjourned to August 19th.

On August 19th, the inquest came to a conclusion with a verdict of murder against Hyman Perdovitch being returned. The police court hearing, however, was adjourned for a further week since the Director of Public Prosecutions was not in a position to proceed. The final hearing took place on August 26th, Perdovitch remaining quiet throughout until Dr Ghosh was giving evidence of the condition of Franks' body. At one stage, Dr Ghosh referred to the state of Franks' heart, to which Perdovitch shouted, "He had no heart." The evidence concluded, Perdovitch was sent for trial.

The case of Hyman Perdovitch opened at Manchester on December 5th, before Mister Justice McCardie. Perdovitch's defence rested in the hands of Mr Lustgarten while the case for the Crown was led by Mr B.S. Wingate Saul, who was assisted by Mr Gilbert Jordan.

There could, of course, be no doubt that Perdovitch was responsible for the death of Solomon Franks, but if it could be showed that he had been provoked beyond endurance then he might possibly escape with a verdict of manslaughter. To counter this, the prosecution called 16-year-old Rebecca Reuben who lived at 10 Elsworth Street, Cheetham. She told the court that Perdovitch had lodged at her family's home for 17 years before he joined the Army and still used to visit from time to time. His last call had taken place at 9.00pm on August 14th, the day before the attack upon Franks. At the end of his visit, Perdovitch had handed her a half-crown piece, saying that she should get herself some chocolates. He also handed over some money for the other children in the family, saying that he was going on his holidays. When Rebecca asked him where he was going, Perdovitch had replied, "Strangeways", implying that he was considering a course of action that might result in incarceration. Cross examined by Mr Lustgarten, Rebecca confirmed that Perdovitch had often given the children money before, but he had never made any previous comment about Strangeways.

Medical evidence was given by Dr Jotindranath Ghosh, the resident surgical officer at Salford Royal Hospital. Solomon Franks had been admitted at 9.00am on August 15th and had been dead on arrival, although two wounds at the back of the neck were still bleeding. Dr Ghosh performed a post-mortem the following day and described in detail the two wounds he examined. The first was one and three-quarters of an inch long, one inch below and behind the lobe of the right ear. It was conical in shape, the apex being at the deepest point some three and a quarter inches down. It had penetrated between the first and second vertebrae, divided an artery and partially damaged the spinal cord.

The second wound was in the middle of the back of the neck and some one and a half inches long. This, too, was conical in shape and the apex was two and a half inches deep. Both wounds could have been produced by the knife he had been given by the police and considerable force must have been used. Indeed, the first wound was deeper than the length of the knife blade indicating that it had been driven in with some effort. The cause of death was shock and haemorrhage due to the two wounds.

Detective Sergeant James Blakeley had been present at the Chapel Street police station when Constable Marsh had cautioned Perdovitch and charged him with murder. Blakeley was also present at the police court the next day and after the hearing was over, Perdovitch had said that he wished to make a statement which Blakeley had then taken down. The statement was read over to the prisoner who agreed that it was accurate and made his mark upon it.

That statement, and Perdovitch's evidence at the trial, contained much the same information. Perdovitch said that he had had a good deal of trouble with Franks over the heavy workload he had been given. He had complained about this to his employers, but the situation had not improved and finally, after enduring as much as he could, he had decided to leave his employment. Franks knew about this decision and seemed more than pleased at the news.

On the day of the stabbing, Perdovitch saw that some buckles on his machine had become clogged and he decided to clean them with his knife, something he had done many times before. As he walked to his coat which was hanging on the door, Franks came up to open some windows due to the stifling heat and Perdovitch remarked, "I should like to know why I should leave this place for you, you are all the cause of it." Franks had smiled and replied, "You can bark as long as you like, I don't care." Franks then sprang towards him and tried to get hold of him, whereupon he swerved to one side and struck out, hitting Franks somewhere about the head. Unbeknown to him, Perdovitch had already taken out the knife and opened the blade. He was unaware that, as he hit Franks twice, the knife was in his hand and his death was therefore accidental.

The jury were out for 20 minutes and returned a guilty verdict, although they added a strong recommendation to mercy. An appeal was entered and this was heard on December 19th. At the trial, the judge in his summing up had stressed that Perdovitch struck the blow unconsciously when in reality the defence was that he had intended to strike Franks but was unconscious of holding the knife at the time. Mr Justice Lawrence pointed out that this was not consistent with his remark about having finished Franks off and him deserving it. In reply Mr Lustgarten stated that Perdovitch denied ever having made such a statement but another of the judges, Mr Justice Avory, said that this was hardly relevant and in his summing up the trial judge had gone out of his way to suggest every possible defence. The appeal was dismissed.

At 8.00am on Tuesday, January 6th, 1920, Hyman Perdovitch mounted the scaffold at Manchester prison, alongside David Caplan who had murdered in Liverpool and whose own appeal had been dismissed on the same day as Perdovitch's. Just before he was hanged, Perdovitch thanked the prison authorities for all the kindness they had showed him since his incarceration. Both men were then dispatched by John Ellis who had two assistants, Robert Baxter and Edward Taylor, who hailed from St Albans. A large crowd had gathered outside the prison to wait for the notices of execution to be pinned to the gates.

CHAPTER ELEVEN

UNREQUITED LOVE

WILLIAM Thomas Aldred tried his very best to get a relationship with Ida Prescott off the ground, but she was having none of it. Aldred had known Ida, a 44-year-old widow, for more than a year and although they were on friendly enough terms, he wanted it to develop into something more. Repeatedly he asked her to walk out with him, but Ida always said no.

Saturday, February 14th, 1920 was, of course, St Valentine's Day, a day for romance and love, and so Aldred once again asked Ida if she would go out with him. Once again she refused. The following day, the same scenario was repeated and again Ida was immovable. Aldred was not one to give up easily, however, and on Monday, February 16th, 54-year-old Aldred decided that he would make one last bid to capture Ida's heart.

Ida Prescott lived at 90 Manchester Road, Clifton, and was employed as a cleaner at the Bridgewater Mill at Pendlebury, the same mill at which Aldred worked. Because she was at work all day, Ida did not have time to come home to cook meals for herself and her children, 12-year-old Irene Mary Hardy Prescott, and her son, 10-year-old William, so the three were in the habit of taking their meals at 132 Manchester Road, a house occupied by Ida's sister, Maud Mary Jones, and Maud's husband, William.

It was 9.00pm on February 16th when Ida called at Maud Jones' house, taking with her some batter and eggs so that Maud would be able to make pancakes for lunch the following day. Ida explained that she had left the children on their own in the house at number 90, and so she stayed for only about 15 minutes before returning home.

In fact, Ida's would-be suitor, William Aldred, had already paid a visit to her home. At 6.30pm, Aldred had walked in through the back door and asked Ida if he might take young William to Farnworth. Ida had given her permission and soon afterwards, Irene had gone out to play with some friends. By the time she returned to her house, her brother William was back home and there was no sign of Aldred. William, though, did have some tripe and chips for the family supper which he said Aldred had paid for. Once Ida returned from her sister's house, she, Irene and William sat down to enjoy their meal. Once the food was eaten, William got ready for bed while Irene, enjoying the privileges that her extra two years allowed, stayed downstairs with her mother.

It was 9.45pm when Aldred again walked into the house through the back door and entered the front room where Ida sat with Irene. He had been there no more than ten minutes when Ida went into the kitchen, which was in darkness, only to be followed immediately by Aldred. The couple stayed talking in the darkened room for a few minutes when Irene heard sounds which sounded like a scuffle. Before the girl could investigate, Ida Prescott staggered into the front room, holding her throat, blood running through her fingers and down on to her dress. Terrified at what she had seen, Irene, wearing only her nightgown, ran screaming from the house and into the cold of the street.

Charles Lewis Penberthy, a collier who lived at 103 Manchester Road, was standing by his front door, waiting for a sight of the tramcar which would take him to work. As Penberthy shifted his weight from foot to foot, a blood curdling scream filled the night air. Looking across the road, he saw little Irene at her front door, obviously very distressed. Penberthy dashed over to her and the hysterical child blurted out, "He's murdering my mammy." Through the open front door, Penberthy could see into the kitchen where he saw a good deal of blood on the floor. Believing that there might be burglars in the house, he stepped slowly into the darkened back kitchen, picking up a poker as he did so. Almost as soon as he entered the room, however, he tripped over something lying on the floor and when his eyes became accustomed to the dark, he saw that it was the body of a woman.

As Penberthy climbed to his feet, he was aware of two other men, obviously also attracted by Irene's screams, coming through the front door. Penberthy shouted, "Come on chaps, let's go through the back. There's been a murder done here." As the three men went to the back door, William Aldred returned to the house, also through the back door, and Charles Penberthy asked, "Who the hell has done this mate?" Aldred, his voice calm and unemotional, answered, "It's me that's done it. There's no need to get excited."

By now, the rooms had all been lighted. A terrible gash could be seen in Ida Prescott's throat and she was obviously dead. Aldred looked down at her and said, "I've done it and I shall have to sit up for it." Then Penberthy took Aldred to the front room, ordered him to sit down and asked the other two men to guard him. Before the police arrived, Penberthy searched Aldred and although he found a bottle of port wine and an empty beer bottle, there was no sign of any razor or knife.

Another man who had heard Irene Prescott's screams was Moses Hully, who was in bed at 109 Manchester Road at the time. Going to investigate, he entered the house at number 90 and found Aldred being guarded by other men. Moses asked if anyone had been for the police and when told that no one had, he walked to Bolton Road where he found Constable Holden on duty, told him what had happened and took him back to Manchester Road.

It was 10.25pm by the time Constable Holden arrived at 90 Manchester Road. He found fresh bloodstains on Aldred's shirt, right shoe and on a handkerchief, and arrested him. Holden and Hully then walked Aldred to the police station where at 11.00pm he was questioned by Inspector George Holt and eventually charged with murder. Aldred made no reply to the charge.

William Aldred appeared before the Manchester county magistrates when only evidence of arrest was given. The next day, the inquest opened before Mr G.S. Laresche. The proceedings moved quickly and the same day, a verdict of murder against Aldred was returned. Further appearances before the magistrates took place on February 19th and again on February 26th. On the latter date, evidence was given that after the hearing of the 19th, before he could be cautioned, Aldred had said to Inspector Holt, "It was a fit of lunacy. They should have kept me in when they had me. I have been in the imbecile ward twice." Nevertheless, one further court hearing was necessary and this took place on March 5th when Aldred was sent for trial. Asked if he had anything to say, Aldred replied, "I have nothing to say. I don't know much about it."

Aldred's trial took place at Manchester before Mr Justice McCardie on May 13th, 1920. The prosecution was led by Mr Merriman, who was assisted by Mr Derbyshire while Aldred was defended by Mr Jessel Ryecroft. As Aldred walked into the courtroom he appeared dazed and looked around the room. Asked whether he was guilty or not guilty, Aldred unhesitatingly replied, "Yes I am. I done it sir." There followed a brief conversation between the prisoner and his counsel, after which a plea of not guilty was entered.

Irene Prescott repeated the story she had told at the inquest and at the magistrate's court and stated that she had known Aldred as a visitor to the house for the past 12 months. He usually let himself in by the back door and was always on friendly terms with everyone. But his visits had become more frequent of late and just a few days before the attack upon her mother, Irene had heard Ida tell Aldred that he should not keep coming around as she did not welcome his visits.

Referring to events before the attack, Irene told the court that on February 14th, Aldred had arrived at 6.30pm, asked Ida to go out with him and she had refused, saying that she had too much work to do. Aldred came again the next night and sat in the kitchen talking to her mother. Once again Ida had asked him not to come around any more and he had left at around 8.00pm.

Thomas Haslam lived next door to Ida Prescott at 92 Manchester Road. He was in bed on the night of February 16th, when a young girl's screams disturbed his sleep. Dressing quickly, he took a poker from his front room and went outside. He saw Irene at her open front door and a man who turned out to be Charles Penberthy, entering the house. Thomas later saw Aldred enter through the back door and heard him admit that he was responsible for the attack upon Ida. After viewing the body, Haslam had been forced to leave the house as the sight made him feel as if he was going to be sick.

Maud Mary Jones, Ida's sister, said that Ida was the widow of John Prescott, a bricklayer who had died in 1918. After Ida had left at 9.15pm on the night she had been attacked, Maud knew nothing more until there was a knock at her front door at about 10.30pm Someone who had heard what had happened told Maud that Ida's children were screaming and there was something wrong at the house. Maud dressed but before she could go to her sister's house, a neighbour brought Irene and William to her and she put them both to bed. Only then did Maud go to 90 Manchester Road. There she saw Ida lying near the wash tub in the back kitchen. There was a large pool of blood around her and a large wound in the front of her neck. The attack upon Ida must have been swift and unexpected for the dead woman still wore her spectacles.

Ethel Fogg worked at the same mill as Ida Prescott and at 12.15pm on February 16th, she walked with Ida to her sister's house. Ethel then went to her own home in Colton Street but called for Ida on her way back to work. As the two walked, Aldred came up behind them and called out, "Ida." At first, Ida took no notice of Aldred but eventually she stopped to talk to him while Ethel walked on and stopped some 30 yards away. Ethel could not hear what was said but did hear Ida raise her voice at one stage and shout, "I shan't, I shan't, I shan't." Ida then walked briskly to catch up with Ethel but after a few seconds, she turned back, returned to Aldred and more sharp words passed between them.

Kate O'Donnell ran a lodging house at 57 Eaton Place, Pendlebury. She had known Aldred for 30 years and he had lodged with her since the summer of 1917. Kate reported that Aldred had often spoken to her about Ida Prescott and was of the opinion that Aldred felt nothing was too good for her. She had spoken to her lodger on February 15th when Aldred had mentioned that he had asked Ida out and she had refused him. The next morning, at 7.00am, Kate called Aldred for work but he said he was not going to bother going in that day. He eventually rose at 11.00am and stayed in the house until about noon. He came back for his dinner but went out again just before 6.30pm, saying that he was going to see Ida.

Joseph Smith was a first-class stoker in the Royal Navy and he, too, lodged at Kate O'Donnell's house, sharing a bedroom with Aldred for the last two years. Smith, too, said that Aldred had often spoken of Ida and seemed to be very fond of her. On February 15th, at some time between 10.00am and 11.00am, Smith had shaved himself with his razor. When he had finished, he put the blade back into its case and put it on a shelf in the kitchen of 57 Eaton Place. He next went to use the razor at 10.30am on February 17th, but though the case was still there, the razor itself was missing. A razor had subsequently been found by the police and Smith identified this as the one he had lost. It was by now heavily bloodstained and it certainly had not been when he cleaned it and put it away on the morning of the 15th.

That razor had been found by Sergeant Edwin Gerrard. Once Aldred had been taken into custody, a number of officers returned to the scene of the crime to search for the weapon which had been used to kill Ida Prescott. Some hours after the attack, Sergeant Gerrard had found a bloodstained razor on the roof of the water closet of a house some 15 yards from the back door of 90 Manchester Road.

Dr John Jackson Berry had been called to 90 Manchester Road and arrived soon after 10.30pm. He examined Ida Prescott and found that her windpipe had been completely severed, as had the main blood vessels on each side of the neck. The next day, he had performed the post-mortem and apart from the one deep wound in the neck, found no other signs of violence. Dr Berry had come to the conclusion that since there were no defence wounds, and the direction of the cut was from left to right, it was probable that the wound had been inflicted from behind.

There could be no doubt that Aldred had taken Ida Prescott's life, but was he responsible for his actions? Thomas Alfred Jones was the relieving officer of the north district of the Barton-upon-Irwell Union. He had known Aldred since 1903 when he first became unfit to work due to suffering from locomotor ataxy. This situation persisted until December 13th, 1912, when Aldred found himself a job at the cinema on Bolton Road, Pendlebury, when his financial relief stopped.

On April 25th, 1916, Aldred had again visited Jones and reported that he felt sick. Aldred looked very strange and it was quite obvious that he was ill. He was admitted to the mental ward for observation and stayed there until May 19th. On August 16th, Aldred was back again and was again admitted to the lunacy ward, although this time only for three days, being released on August 19th.

Richard Henry Davie was the superintendent of the male mental ward at the Union and he confirmed that Aldred was admitted to his ward at 2.10pm on April 25th, 1916.

The register at the time stated, 'Has been drinking heavily. Appeared to be under the influence of drink when admitted. Talking garrulously, quiet since tea-time, seems fairly rational.' The next day, Aldred had been examined by the medical officer, Dr David William Davidson, who said that he should be kept under observation. Aldred began to improve slowly and was released on May 16th.

At 4.50pm on August 16th, Aldred was readmitted and the register read, 'He appeared to be under the influence of drink on admission. Has been quiet since, marks of cut on right hand.' Once again, Aldred was examined by Dr Davidson who ordered him to be detained. He was examined for the last time on August 19th, adjudged to be well again, and released.

Dr Davidson confirmed all the evidence of the previous witness but added that at no time had Aldred been detained under the Lunacy Act. He had merely been detained for observation. The final medical witness was Dr Howard Shannon, the medical officer of Manchester prison, who reported that he had found no evidence of insanity in the prisoner. That seemed to shut off the last avenue of hope for Aldred and the jury had little trouble in finding him guilty as charged. Asked if he had anything to say before sentence of death was passed, Aldred merely replied, "I am sorry. I must have lost myself completely. That's all."

An appeal was heard on June 7th when the defence again claimed that Aldred was insane at the time of the crime. The facts of the case coupled with his past history proved, held Mr Ryecroft, that this was undoubtedly the case. Giving his judgement, the Lord Chief Justice, Lord Isaacs, stated that although Aldred seemed to be a 'queer creature', and troublesome to people associated with him, it did not come to more than this and there was no evidence of insanity.

On Tuesday, June 22nd, 1920, just 15 days after the appeal had been lost, William Thomas Aldred was hanged at Manchester prison by John Ellis. Only a few people gathered outside the prison for what was the fourth execution at that establishment in this particular year.

CHAPTER TWELVE

A MAN PROVOKED

JOHN Oakes was the owner of a large house at 64 Higher Cambridge Street, Hulme, and let out rooms there in order to earn himself a few extra shillings. Some time around the summer of 1921, Peter Drinkwater, his 50-year-old wife, Winifred, and their daughter, Mary, took a front sitting room and a back bedroom on the first floor of the house. Mr Oakes liked his new tenants, but the same could not be said about the couple who came to stay in the spring of 1922, for George Frederick Edisbury and the woman he called his wife, Annie Grimshaw, were rather too fond of drink and seldom came home sober.

On July 27th, 1922, an argument took place between Edisbury and Winifred Drinkwater. Annie Grimshaw claimed that it was Winifred who had started it, but whatever the truth of that, Winifred was so upset that she complained to her husband about what Edisbury had said to her. Peter Drinkwater had thought the matter serious enough to warrant him speaking to Edisbury in an attempt to calm the situation down. Two days later, though, the problems were to flare up again.

It was some time between 3.00pm and 4.00pm on Saturday, July 29th, when Peter Drinkwater walked into the kitchen of the house at Higher Cambridge Street and saw Edisbury there with Annie Grimshaw. In Drinkwater's opinion, they had both been drinking heavily and were already well under the influence. It was nothing to do with him, however, so, leaving them there he returned to his wife in their bedroom.

A few hours later, at some time after 6.00pm, Winifred Drinkwater said she needed to do some shopping for the weekend and left the house to go into town. A few minutes later, Peter Drinkwater followed his wife and met her, by arrangement, in Stretford Road. Peter and Winifred did the shopping together, at one stage calling into a public house where they each enjoyed a glass of beer. It was around 8.50pm when Winifred left to take the shopping home. Peter said he would follow after he had had another drink.

In fact, it was close to 9.50pm by the time Peter Drinkwater turned into Higher Cambridge Street to see his landlord, John Oakes, at the front door of number 64. Oakes told him that he had missed his wife who had just left. Drinkwater went back out to retrace his steps in an attempt to find Winifred.

After a few minutes there was no still sign of her, so Drinkwater decided to return home since she would be bound to turn up there in due course. Indeed she already had, but in the most horrifying circumstances. It was 9.57pm by the time Peter Drinkwater arrived back at 64 Higher Cambridge Street to find a small crowd gathered around the body of his wife. Winifred Drinkwater lay on the pavement outside the front door of number 64, her throat cut. And as a distraught Peter Drinkwater looked up the street, he saw George Edisbury running off in the distance.

Edisbury was fleeing to his family for shelter. At 10.30pm he arrived at the house of his niece, Alice Edisbury, who lived at 2 Sadler Street, Moss Side. Alice admitted Edisbury, who was bareheaded at the time. His first request was for a cap of some kind, but Alice told him that there was none in the house. Gertrude Edisbury, Alice's mother, was visiting at the time and she saw that Edisbury appeared to be very drunk, almost unable to stand in fact.

Having been told that there was no cap for him, Edisbury then asked for a cup of tea but as he drank it down, he exclaimed, "I've cut a woman's throat. She said I have been getting a pension under false pretences. She's been nagging me for days. She came into the room and I ordered her out. She wouldn't go."

After 20 minutes, Edisbury left the house but was back within a minute insisting, "I must have a cap." Seeing that he was very excitable and fearing what he might do next, Alice finally handed over one of her husband's caps and Edisbury left the house, never to return.

It was close to midnight when George Edisbury knocked on another door, this time at 21 John Street, Rusholme. The door was opened by Janet Georgina Knott, Edisbury's married sister. She was very surprised to see her brother at this late hour and asked him what he wanted. He replied, "I've come to see you." This in itself was something Edisbury very rarely did and Janet said as much, telling him, "And it's taken you long enough. Three years and drunk into the bargain."

She took her brother into the kitchen and it was there that he said, "I've come to say goodbye to you. I've cut a woman's throat. She's asked for it. I stuck it for weeks that I'm living on prostitution and getting my pension under false pretences. I owe the debt and I'll pay it."

This last sentence was probably a reference to the debt Edisbury would be forced to pay when the law finally caught up with him, but as Janet listened to this speech, she did not believe Edisbury's words, thinking that he was just drunk and rambling. As far as she was concerned, the best thing for him was to sleep it off, so she offered him a bed for the night. Edisbury, though, was so drunk that he simply fell to the floor and so Janet left him there to sober up while she went back to bed.

It was 9.00am on July 30th by the time Inspector Thomas Singleton, Detective Constable James Hodson and Detective Constable Butler arrived at 21 John Street. Edisbury was still asleep on the hearthrug, his coat thrown across his chest to keep him warm. Constable Hodson took the coat and on searching the pockets, found a razor and two handkerchiefs, all of which were bloodstained. Inspector Singleton woke Edisbury, identified himself and the other officers present and told Edisbury that he would be taken to the police station on a charge of murder. Edisbury replied, "I shan't cause any trouble. I made a mistake last night." Later that morning, he was charged with the wilful murder of Winifred Drinkwater.

On July 31st, George Frederick Edisbury made his first appearance at the Manchester City police court. Here it was revealed that he was a painter by trade and Inspector Singleton then gave details of the arrest. Matters were then adjourned until August 2nd. On that date, in addition to the second hearing at the police court, the inquest was opened, before Mr C.W.W. Surridge. Peter Drinkwater revealed the details of the argument which had taken place between his wife and Edisbury on the Thursday before Winifred died. Edisbury had insulted Winifred who had retaliated by saying that she would still be living in the house long after Edisbury had gone. To this, Edisbury had said, "I will see you out of the house before the week is out."

Further evidence as to the atmosphere between Edisbury, Annie Grimshaw and the dead woman was then given, Mr Oakes stating that he thought Winifred and her husband were a most sober couple whereas Edisbury and his common-law wife were always drunk and argumentative and this led to altercations between them. The inquest jury duly returned a verdict of wilful murder against Edisbury. A few hours later, the prisoner was back at the police court where he was remanded for a further week.

A third remand followed on August 9th, and it was not until August 18th that all the witnesses were heard at the police court, where Edisbury was represented by Mr T.H. Hinchcliffe. The case for the prosecution was given by Mr A.F. Pickford and after listening to the testimony of all the witnesses, the magistrates sent Edisbury for trial.

George Frederick Edisbury faced his trial at Manchester on November 27th, 1922, before Mr Justice Acton. The Crown's case was led by Mr Crosthwaite while Edisbury was defended by Mr Milner Helme.

The only person who had actually witnessed the attack upon Winifred Drinkwater, was

John Oakes. He was quite an elderly man but said he recalled exactly what had taken place on July 29th.

At about 3.10pm Edisbury and Annie Grimshaw had come into the house and both were already drunk. They helped themselves to some food and then retired to their room, probably to sleep off the effects of the alcohol they had consumed. Mr Oakes saw Mr and Mrs Drinkwater leave the house separately, some time after 6.00pm, Winifred Drinkwater returning at about 8.50pm. About 20 minutes later, though, at 9.10pm Winifred had gone back out, saying she was going to meet her husband again.

Peter Drinkwater returned to the house at 9.45pm and John Oakes had told him that Winifred had gone back out to look for him. Peter said he would go to find her but no sooner had he left than Winifred returned from the opposite direction. John Oakes was sitting on his front doorstep at the time and for a minute or two he and Winifred chatted about nothing in particular. It was then that Edisbury appeared, passed the time of day with Mr Oakes, and then went back up to his bedroom. Within a minute or so, however, Edisbury was back at the front door and this time his words were directed at Winifred Drinkwater.

"My wife's not a bloody whore," spat Edisbury, "I'm telling you that. You've wanted me out of here for some time but I'll see you out first." As Edisbury spoke, Mr Oakes could see that he held something in his hand, although it was impossible to distinguish exactly what it was. There was a sudden glint on some kind of blade and John Oakes thought that Edisbury might be holding a table knife but before he could even move from the step, Edisbury had lashed out at Winifred Drinkwater and a wound appeared in her throat. As she fell to the pavement, Edisbury rushed out into the street and ran off, just as Peter Drinkwater arrived at the house. Asked what he thought was the cause of all the trouble in the house, John Oakes had no hesitation in placing the blame firmly at the door of Annie Grimshaw. Oakes claimed that Edisbury was usually friendly towards Mr and Mrs Drinkwater, especially when he was sober. All the trouble had been stirred up by Annie who was constantly complaining to Edisbury about things Winifred Drinkwater was supposed to have said to her.

Peter Drinkwater told the court of his discovery when he had returned to Higher Cambridge Street for the last time on July 29th. When he arrived, Edisbury was rapidly disappearing up the street. He had thought of giving chase but his first concern was for his wife. Peter Drinkwater knelt down by her side and cradled her head in his lap but even as he asked someone to fetch the police and an ambulance, she died in his arms. Drinkwater confirmed that at the time, John Oakes was on the front doorstep, while Annie Grimshaw was inside the house, in the lobby, but made no comment on what Edisbury had done.

Annie Grimshaw testified that she was the legal wife of Edward Grimshaw, but they had been living apart for some time and she had been with Edisbury since 1916. She admitted that there had been bad blood between her and Winifred Drinkwater but claimed that the arguments had always been at the instigation of the dead woman, who had accused Edisbury of claiming a pension he was not legally entitled to, and claimed that Annie earned her living from prostitution. Things had been very strained, especially for the ten days or so prior to Winifred's death.

On July 29th, she had gone into town at 1.40pm where she met Edisbury. They had several drinks together and arrived back at Higher Cambridge Street at around 3.15pm. She denied that either she or Edisbury were drunk. Annie agreed that they had first had something to eat but even as they had their food, Winifred Drinkwater was constantly walking through the kitchen, making accusations about Edisbury's pension and saying that he lived on immoral earnings. Edisbury made no reply to these hurtful words, but simply ignored what Winifred was saying.

After they had finished eating, Edisbury went upstairs for a lie down, while she went out to do some shopping. When she returned it was 4.30pm and she expected that Edisbury would still be asleep upstairs. To her surprise, he was in the kitchen and she remarked, "You've come down rather soon." To this, Edisbury had said, "Yes, it's because I can't stand that woman. She's been on all the afternoon." Annie thought a cup of tea would do them both good and put the kettle on. Shortly afterwards, she went back out, finally returning some time before 6.00pm.

When Annie got back to the house, Edisbury had washed and changed and was ready to go out for the evening. As they left, at 6.00pm, they passed Winifred and Annie claimed that at the time Mrs Drinkwater was well under the influence of alcohol.

Annie and Edisbury returned to the house at around 9.15pm and although Edisbury was rather tipsy, he was not drunk. They both went into the kitchen and within minutes, Winifred had appeared and greeted them with, "Oh, here's the Army pensioner and his tally whore again." The remark was ignored, both of them choosing to go upstairs, but Winifred shouted more abuse after them. Then, as Annie and Edisbury sat in their bedroom, they heard more abuse being shouted from downstairs. In a rage, Edisbury leapt to his feet and, shouting that he couldn't stand it any longer, he flew downstairs. A few minutes later, Annie heard someone calling her downstairs. By the time she got to the lobby, Winifred Drinkwater was already lying on the pavement and Edisbury was nowhere to be seen.

Sarah Jane Gale, who acted as housekeeper for Mr Oakes, had been in the kitchen at Higher Cambridge Street when Winifred was attacked. Sarah was able to confirm some of the movements detailed by other witnesses and although she did not see or hear the attack, Mr Oakes had called for her immediately after it had taken place. Sarah had gone to the front door and saw Winifred lying on the pavement, her husband cradling her head in his arms. Sarah was also able to state that she had heard Winifred and Annie Grimshaw arguing several times although she was unable to say who had started the rows.

Inspector Thomas Singleton told the court how he had arrested Edisbury but he also spoke of what he found when he first arrived at the scene of the crime. At the time, Annie Grimshaw was in the kitchen and in Inspector Singleton's opinion she was very drunk, which seemed to cast a good deal of doubt on the evidence she had given. Constable Hodson confirmed that Annie Grimshaw was very drunk.

It appeared then that everyone, except of course for Annie Grimshaw and Edisbury himself, had confirmed that Winifred Drinkwater was a virtuous and sober woman who had probably been attacked by a drunken man without provocation. This scenario was not, however, backed up by the evidence of Dr William John Heslop.

Dr Heslop had attended Winifred at the scene and later performed a post-mortem on her at the Cavendish Street mortuary. He described a wound in the front of Winifred's neck, which was some seven and a half inches long.

This ran from a point below the angle of the jaw on one side to the corresponding point on the other and had severed the windpipe, gullet and the large blood vessels in the front of the throat. But it was Dr Heslop's findings on Winifred's internal organs which negated the picture painted of her as a sober individual.

To begin with, there was a small amount of what appeared to be beer in the stomach. The liver, though, was very enlarged, there were many gallstones and the kidneys both showed signs of chronic disease. Dr Heslop believed that although Winifred had only taken a small amount of alcohol on the day she died, she was in the habit of taking much larger quantities and had been for some considerable time.

Edisbury, giving his own version of events, said that he had borne no animosity towards Winifred Drinkwater but her comments had sorely provoked him. This, together with the fact that he had been drinking heavily, meant that his attack upon her had in no way been premeditated and therefore he was guilty of manslaughter and not murder. The jury did not agree, however, and Edisbury was found guilty and sentenced to death.

An appeal followed, on December 18th, the main line of defence being that the only witness, John Oakes, was an old man and had only a hazy recollection of what had really taken place. It was clear that Edisbury had been provoked and manslaughter was the proper verdict in this case. Giving the court's ruling, the Lord Chief Justice, Lord Hewart, said that there was ample proof that Edisbury had been fully aware of his actions, admitting to his family afterwards what he had done.

At 8.00am on Wednesday, January 3rd, 1923, George Frederick Edisbury was hanged at Manchester by John Ellis. The event passed with little comment in the newspapers of the day, they being much more interested in attempts to save the lives of Edith Jessie Thompson and Frederick Edward Bywaters who were due to hang in London on January 9th.

CHAPTER THIRTEEN

THE UPHOLSTERER

JOHN White was a cashier at the York Street, Manchester branch of the London County Westminster & Parr's Bank, and something of a creature of habit. Each working day he would have breakfast at the same time, catch the same train into the city and return home each evening to a hot meal, cooked by his sister, 50-year-old Margaret Gilchrist White, at the large detached house they shared together, Invermay, 96 Acre Lane, Cheadle Hulme, near Bramhall. The morning of Monday, December 18th, 1922, was no different. John and his sister enjoyed breakfast together and he left for work at 7.20am. At that time, Margaret was in excellent health.

Under normal circumstances, and allowing for possible railway delays, John White would normally arrive home at around 5.30pm On this particular Monday, though, work at the bank delayed him somewhat, so he did not catch a train from London Road station until 6.17pm. This got him into Bramhall at 6.40pm and by the time he had walked from there to Acre Lane, it was approaching 7.00pm

From the moment John White walked through his front gate, he knew that there was something wrong. The house, normally well lit and welcoming, was dark and cold. White let himself in using his front door key and walked to the kitchen, hoping that Margaret might be there, cooking their evening meal. The door was closed and as he opened it, Margaret's small and vociferous Irish terrier, Bruin, dashed forward to greet him, but of Margaret there was still no sign.

John White now entered the drawing room which was to the immediate left of the front door, and as he stepped into the darkness, his foot caught something on the floor and he stumbled, almost falling forward on to his face. Scrabbling with his hands in order to discover what had almost caused him to injure himself, John White felt the unmistakable shape of a body. Dashing back into the hallway, he lit the gas lamp and then to his horror saw the body of his sister lying on her back, her head pointing towards the french windows at the far side of the room and her feet close to the door through which he had just entered.

John White could still not see clearly but rushed to his sister's aid. Something seemed to be causing an obstruction around her neck and thinking that this might be due to the apron she was wearing, he took a penknife from his pocket and cut away at some of the clothing around Margaret's throat, being careful not to cause her further injury. But after realising that he was having no success in reviving his sister, White then ran next door to fetch their neighbour, Mrs Whiteley. She, too, was unable to assist Margaret White and instead telephoned a doctor.

Dr Andrew Thomson was soon on the scene and after a brief examination of the prostrate form he told John White the news he was dreading and probably already knew. His sister was beyond help. Margaret White was dead. Mrs Whiteley, John White and another neighbour, Florence Hill, then carried Margaret upstairs to her bedroom. At this time, Dr Thomson had no reason to believe that anything untoward had taken place in Invermay, and so he was in the house for only ten minutes in total, although he did conclude that Margaret had been dead for seven or eight hours, putting the time of her death at some time between 11.00am and noon that day.

Once Dr Thomson had left, Mrs Whiteley began to undress Margaret White's body, prior to laying her out properly. Only then did she and John White notice some red marks around the dead woman's throat, and also on her wrists. In addition, John White had noticed some strange things around the house. There was a piece of webbing on the drawing room floor, and a chair which had been in his bedroom was now in the hallway having apparently been newly upholstered. There were small tin-tacks on the kitchen floor, and a bowl in the sink contained the residue of some burnt material. Puzzled, John White called the police.

Sergeant Walter Postons arrived at Invermay at 8.40pm. He toured the house with Mr White and although there were no signs of a break-in or a struggle, it was clear that something strange had taken place inside the house. The fact that the dog had been shut in the kitchen meant that someone must have called at the house. Although the animal was not vicious, it barked furiously at any stranger who called and Margaret White had a habit, at such times, of shutting the dog in the kitchen. Upstairs, drawers had been forced open, as had three cash boxes and yet valuable jewellery had been left on Margaret's dressing table. What at first looked like a simple death from natural causes, now showed indications that this might well be a case of robbery and murder.

By December 20th, the police had released basic details of the case to the press. These reports stated that a careful medical examination of Margaret's body was being made since there were no obvious signs of violence. The only reason the police were treating the death as suspicious was the fact that parts of the house had apparently been ransacked and this pointed to the presence of an intruder. The newspaper report ended with the comment that a man had been seen in the neighbourhood, offering to do odd jobs for people, including upholstery work, and this man was now asked to come forward.

In fact, the police knew a great deal more about this upholsterer than they had so far released to the reporters. Amongst the items found at Invermay when it was carefully searched was a small blue postcard on which someone had pencilled, 'Fred Wood, c/o Mrs Cooper, Church Street, Wilmslow.' On December 20th, two Scotland Yard officers, Chief Inspector William Brown and Detective Sergeant Baker, arrived at Bramhall at the request of the Cheshire police. As part of their investigation, they had called on a Mrs Cooper who lived at 28 Church Lane.

Mrs Annie Cooper ran a lodging house and she confirmed that she had, until very recently, had a guest named Frederick Wood, who had paid his rent up to the December 17th, but on the night of the 18th, his bed had not been slept in. Her evidence led to the detectives interviewing two more former residents, Peter Gateley and Ellen Middleton, who had both been friendly with Wood, and this in turn led to an interview with Mrs Wilhelmina Rosina Wood of Yew Tree Cottage, Ack Lane, Bramhall, for whom Fred Wood – who was no relation – and Peter Gateley had done some work. In this way, the two Scotland Yard officers, working with their Cheshire colleagues, determined that Fred Wood had been the upholsterer working in the district, and he had left his lodgings on the very day that Margaret Gilchrist White died.

On December 21st, the inquest opened at the Wesleyan Chapel Room at Bramhall, before the coroner for the Stockport district, Mr A.E. Ferns. Only the most basic details were given, the coroner stating that he wished to reveal as little as possible so that the ongoing police investigation would not be hampered in any way. Matters were adjourned until January 4th, 1923.

The police, meanwhile, were finding still more information about the man they wished to interview and on December 22nd, a new press release gave precise details which were printed the same day. Topped with banner headlines, the newspapers stated that Scotland Yard wished to locate a man named Frederick Wood, who had also used the name of Ronald Lee. He was described as being 29 years old, clean shaven, 5ft 7½ins tall, with brown hair and eyes. As if this was not enough, the reports went on to say that he had an injured left forearm from a gunshot wound sustained in the Great War, and tattoo marks on his arms and chest. Born in Bradford, Wood had been discharged from the

Northumberland Fusiliers on November 30th, 1917. There then followed a list of 15 previous addresses where Wood had been over the past few years, ranging from Bradford and Harrogate to Glasgow, Birmingham and Macclesfield. About the only thing the police had omitted was a photograph of the man they were desperate to find.

On December 23rd, more information flowed from the police. They announced that two days after Margaret White had died, Wood had returned to the family home in Bradford. His widowed mother, brother, sister and brother-in-law, lived at 6 Roslyn Place, Bradford, and on December 20th, Wood had turned up there seeking to borrow some money. His brother had given him £2 and Wood had left without even bothering to see his mother.

The publicity had to pay off eventually, and that same day, December 23rd, a man walked into Lincoln police station and approached the officer on the desk, Detective Constable James Barker. Handing over a newspaper, the man said, "Read that." The paper was folded over to show an article headed, 'Cheshire Mystery: Search for man with many addresses.' Without waiting to be asked to clarify exactly what he wanted, the man continued, "I've just been in a barber's shop and while waiting, looked at the daily paper, where I read a report of the Cheshire mystery and giving a description of the man the police wanted. I now report myself to the police here, but I know nothing of the mystery. I left Bramhall that Monday about 12 noon." Frederick Wood had been found.

On Christmas Eve, Chief Inspector Brown, together with Detective Inspector George Kingman of the Cheshire force, travelled to Lincoln to collect Frederick Wood. Identifying himself, Chief Inspector Brown said that he understood that Wood had given himself up, to which he replied, "What else could I do? You've got every address in the papers where I am known. It says Fred Wood, five feet seven, tattoo marks on arms, grey suit. I couldn't go anywhere." After being formally cautioned, Wood made a long statement, outlining his movements over the previous few weeks.

According to that statement, Wood had been staying at Mrs Cooper's lodging house for some three weeks prior to the death of Margaret White. He claimed to have left Church Street at about 10.15am on December 18th, intending to go to Bradford to see his brother in order to get some money to last him over the Christmas period. Leaving Church Street, Wood said, he had walked to the Victoria public house where he had caught a bus at about 11.30am, travelling in to Stockport, his only stop on that journey being at a tobacconist's shop where he bought two packets of cigarettes and a box of matches. From Stockport he caught the 1.37pm train to Leeds and stayed there that night, in a lodging house in Armley Road.

Leaving Armley Road on the Tuesday, Wood said he had then caught a train to Middlesbrough where he saw his married sister. They had an argument and he left

Middlesbrough and caught a train back to Leeds. The next day he went out begging and then walked to Bradford, where he saw his brother from whom he got £2. From Bradford he caught the 12.22pm train to Hull, arriving there at about 3.30pm and staying in a lodging house in Queen's Road where he used the name R. Lee.

On the Thursday, Wood took the ferry across the Humber and later still, caught the train to Grimsby. On Friday he walked to Brigg, where he slept in a shed, and the next day walked on to Lincoln, arriving at 5.00pm. Deciding that he needed a shave, Wood went to a barber's shop where he picked up the newspaper and read the report of the crime in Cheshire. He had his shave and then walked straight to the police station to give himself up.

In addition to detailing his movements, Wood also admitted that amongst the various jobs he had done while in Cheshire, he had covered an ottoman for a woman in Acre Lane, giving her a blue postcard afterwards with his name and address written upon it. He also spoke of the job for Mrs Wood at Yew Tree Cottage and said he had been helped there by Peter Gateley. That particular job had been unfinished and Wood said he had intended returning on Monday, the day Margaret White died, but after arguing with Gateley he had thrown his tools away and decided to get out of the district. Wood finished the statement by repeating that although he had walked past Miss White's house in Acre Lane, he had not gone in on December 18th.

Chief Inspector Brown saw Wood again, in the cells at Lincoln, at 9.00am on Christmas Day, and told him that he had checked one or two points in Wood's statement and was not satisfied. Wood was cautioned again and told he would be taken back to Cheadle Hulme. His reply was, "I'll say nowt," although on the journey back to Cheshire he volunteered to show the officers where he had dumped his tools. The car was stopped in Acre Lane but there had been a fresh fall of snow and Wood was unable to pinpoint the exact spot.

On December 26th, when Wood was charged with murder, he said, "Yes, I know nothing about it at all." Later that day he made his first appearance at the police court and on the way told Chief Inspector Brown of some witnesses who would need to be traced to prove his story. According to Wood, he had noticed a number of passengers on the bus he caught from the Victoria pub and if these could be found, they would show that he could not have been in Acre Lane at the time Miss White met her death.

Wood appeared before the stipendiary magistrate, Colonel Stott, and was remanded to January 3rd. On that date, a further remand followed, this time until January 9th, but it was to be at the next hearing of the inquest, on January 4th, that matters were to take a curious turn.

Before the inquest began, Sergeant Postons took the prisoner his breakfast in the cells and Wood, who seemed to be very angry, said that as far as he was concerned, some of the witnesses had perjured themselves and he wanted to see that they would get their punishment. He said that he wished to write everything down and asked for paper and an envelope. He then wrote a four-page statement which he sealed in the envelope and handed to Sergeant Postons, asking him to pass it on to Chief Inspector Brown with the express instruction that it was not to be opened and read until after the inquest. In the event, the inquest was not concluded on that day, but merely adjourned with little new evidence having been heard. It was then that Chief Inspector Brown opened the envelope and read what Wood had written.

The statement began, 'I got up at the lodge about 9 o'clock. I then had breakfast. About 9.30 I got ready to go to Mrs Woods, Yew Tree Cottage, Ack Lane, Bramhall. On account of it raining I decided to wait until it had abated. About this time Mister Gateley and his wife [Ellen Middleton who was in fact not married to Gateley] as I knew her had then gone. I, Fred Wood, did not go out with them but waited till about 10.15 when it had ceased raining.'

Wood went on to describe the route he had taken until he found himself on the road to Bramhall. He explained that as he was walking, he made his mind up to go home to Bradford to see if he could get any financial help from his family as it was nearly Christmas. At the time, he was still heading for Yew Tree Cottage, intending to finish the upholstery job there. He continued his route until, at around 11.10am, he arrived in Acre Lane. The statement went on, 'Going down Acre Lane I had got about half-way down when a lady said, "Good Morning Mr Wood." I did not know the lady's name then. I went across as it was a lady I had worked for a week before repairing an ottoman for which I received 9s 6d.' At this point in his statement, Wood had placed the figure 7s 6d in brackets, unsure which was the correct amount.

Wood explained that he had done this first job, the ottoman, outside the house as the lady had explained to him that her dog was fierce. Going over to her now, Wood said that the lady, Miss White, said that she wished to pleat a chair but was unsure how to carry out the task. She asked Wood to instruct her, and she would pay him 2s 6d for his time and trouble. Wood agreed.

The statement now detailed exactly what Wood claimed had happened next: 'Miss White told me to wait at the garden gate till she had fastened the dog up. I then went to the front door. I was standing on the top step, Miss White working just inside the hall on my instruction. I told Miss White how to do it and she done it according to her idea quite satisfactory.'

Eventually the work was finished and Miss White thanked Wood and asked him to wait while she brought his money, first handing back the tools she had borrowed from him. Wood continued, 'She went upstairs then, I still standing on the door step, she returned coming down the stairs with an enamel bowl in her hands turning to the right at the bottom of the stairs as if to me she was going into the room. I could not see the room then on account of the door being half-closed. I heard a noise of the bowl dropping. I waited a moment thinking she had just dropped it …After probably a few seconds I heard a groan …I got frightened.'

Wood explained how he had slowly entered the house now and pushed the door open. 'So I put my head in after pushing the door open and saw Miss White laying on the floor clutching at her throat her face, to my idea at the same time, changing colour. I thought she was in a fit. I, of course, being frightened went in to her and attempted or tried to get her hands from her throat. She was very strong and I not being strong, and ill, it took me all my time to get her hands from her throat.

'I having a broking (*sic*) arm could not hold them down, so kneeling on one and holding the other with my good hand, I tied them with something which I cannot remember. I being very frightened on account of being in the house then alone with Miss White, I tried to revive her by rubbing her hands and holding her head up. Miss White appeared to me then to be very bad, she groaning and rolling her head about.

'Being frightened at being in the house and in all probability at no one seeing me or hearing our conversation at the garden gate, I went queer and having only about 12s 6d of my own then I dashed upstairs, why I did not know at the time, saw some boxes, broke them open and got about 15s. I came downstairs. Miss White was then breathing very heavy as if in an anaesthetic. I, knowing the sounds on account of my being in hospital, was still frightened and in an excited state I came out, shut the door. The dog barked once after that.

'I came down Acre Lane, got some cigs at a shop in Acre Lane and got the bus for Stockport. As regards the time then, I could not swear too. I got the train to Leeds where I got lodgings for the night. Going out at night time, I saw someone that had been in hospital with me and told him that I was out of work and he got me some money from himself and a few of his friends. I should think about 17s.'

Wood's statement went on to recall his movements after arriving at Leeds, which were the same as those listed in his first statement, made at Lincoln. It ended, 'That is about all I remember clearly but I say quite clearly that I, Fred Wood, did not kill Miss White, the other things happening in my frightened and excited condition.'

All this, of course, was valuable evidence for it was the first time that Wood had admitted being in 96 Acre Lane on the morning Miss White died. At the next police court hearing, on January 9th, the statement was alluded to but Wood shouted from the box that he did not want it read at this time. Eventually the magistrate ruled that, although admissible as evidence, the statement would not be read until Wood faced his trial. The rest of the evidence then having been heard, Wood was committed to the next Chester assizes.

The trial of Frederick Wood opened at Chester before Mr Justice Swift, on February 28th, 1923. There were ten men and two women on the jury and Wood was defended by Mr Goodman Roberts, who had only very recently called to the bar, while the case for the prosecution was led by Sir Ellis J. Griffith, who was assisted by Mr Austin Jones. The proceedings lasted until March 2nd.

One of the principle lines of Wood's defence was that he was simply incapable of having killed Margaret White. During the war of 1914-18, Wood had been advancing from his position when a German bullet smashed into his left forearm. As a result of this injury, the bones in that arm were no longer connected and much of the muscle had wasted away. The prosecution would have to prove first of all that Miss White was indeed murdered and that the man who had throttled the life out of her was Frederick Wood.

One of the early witnesses was Peter Gateley. He and his lady friend, Ellen Middleton, had, by December 18th, been lodging at Mrs Cooper's establishment in Church Street for six weeks. At the beginning of December, Gateley had first met Wood who informed him that he was an upholsterer by trade but was also in receipt of an Army pension of 12s per week. Wood went on to say he had been doing some odd jobs in the neighbourhood, that he had just got a big upholstering job for a Mrs Woods and that Gateley could help him out if he wished.

On December 14th, Gateley had accompanied Wood to the house in Ack Lane. Wood went inside and negotiated with the householder, returning after a few minutes to announce that he had agreed to start the job the next day. On the 15th, they walked to Ack Lane from Wilmslow and worked for Mrs Wood until about 4.00pm. Gateley recalled using a screwdriver with a worn top and was able to identify one produced in court. That screwdriver was now bent but Gateley swore that it was perfectly straight when he had used it.

On December 16th, Gateley and Wood returned to Ack Lane and again worked until 4.00pm. During the time they were there, Wood used both his hands with equal dexterity and at one stage stretched some webbing with his right hand while he knocked in some nails, wielding the hammer in his supposedly useless left. The job, though, was still not quite finished and Wood said he was returning on Monday to complete it

Wood had promised to pay Gateley for his help and on Monday, December 18th, he saw Wood at breakfast. Wood repeated that he was going to finish the job in Ack Lane but said he would not need Gateley for this. He left, promising to return at about 3.00pm when he would 'see him right'. According to Gateley, it was 9.30am not 10.15am when Wood left the lodging house and walked off towards Bramhall.

Ellen Middleton backed up some of this evidence and confirmed that Wood appeared to be short of money, for on December 17th, she gave him sixpence to buy himself some cigarettes. He told her at the time that he would soon pay her back as he had £2 to come from the job at Mrs Woods. The next morning, she, Gateley and Wood all left the lodging house at the same time. Ellen confirmed that this was at 9.30am.

Wilhelmina Rosina Wood told the court that Wood had first called at her house on December 7th, explaining that he was looking for odd jobs, especially upholstery work. She showed him a suite which needed work and he told her that if she would also provide all the necessary materials, he would do the job for £2.

Exactly one week later, on December 14th, Wood called again to see if she had purchased the material he would need. He mentioned that he was working in Acre Lane and after looking at the cloth. Wood asked when he should start work. Mrs Wood suggested Monday, December 18th, but Wood said he could not come on that date, so she then suggested the 15th.

On the 15th, Wood arrived with a man who he introduced as his cousin. After they had finished work, Wood asked to speak to her privately and said, "I should be glad if you could let me have a little on account, not so much for myself, but for the man who is with me and who has a wife and two children." Mrs Wood handed over a £1 note.

The next day, Wood again asked for an advance after they had finished work. At first, Mrs Wood was reluctant but he handed over his Army pension book and asked her to keep it, adding, "Do you think I would jeopardise this for a few pounds. I will leave it with you." Mrs Wood gave the book back and handed over a further 10s. Significantly, of course, Peter Gateley had already testified that none of that 30s found its way into his pocket. Wood was obviously spinning his employer a line in order to obtain money for himself, proving yet again that he was in financial trouble.

The prosecution now tried to pin down an approximate time for Margaret White's death. James Collie was a postman and part of his round included Acre Lane. At 9.15am on December 18th, he had called at Miss White's house to deliver a letter on which there was insufficient postage. There was a penny to pay and as she handed over the money, Miss White held her dog by its collar. The postman passed the house several times during the day but saw no further sign of Miss White.

Mrs Fanny Jane Pye lived next door to Invermay, at 94 Acre Lane. She saw nothing at all of her neighbour on December 18th, but some time after 11.00am she did hear the sound of someone hammering in number 96. Later still, at a time between noon and 12.30pm, she heard the dog barking. The suggestion was, of course, that the hammering was the chair being upholstered and Wood was therefore at the house after 11.00am. This timing seemed to be confirmed by three other witnesses. Nancy Russell, who lived in

Ethel Road, not far from Acre Lane, said that Wood had called at her house at about 11.00am on December 18th, asking if she wanted any upholstering doing. Robert Norbury was a roadsweeper and he was in Stanley Road before 11.00am. He saw a woman he knew, Fanny Slater, in the street and some 30 yards behind her was a man he subsequently identified as Fred Wood. Mrs Slater recalled seeing Robert, and also a man walking some distance behind her. She put the time at around 10.45am.

The prosecution had shown that Margaret White was alive at 9.15am when the postman called. They had also shown that Wood was in the area of Acre Lane before 11.00am. They now called 13-year-old Nora Bratt, the next caller at Invermay, to show that Miss White was dead by 4.30pm. Nora's father, Joseph, was a farmer who supplied eggs to Miss White. Nora called at 4.30pm on December 18th to deliver half a dozen fresh eggs but got no reply to her knocking, although she did hear the dog barking from somewhere inside the house.

Florence Hill lived at 126 Acre Lane and she knew Margaret White very well indeed, working as a housekeeper for her, two and a half days each week. Florence was another neighbour who John White had called when he discovered his sister's body, and she was perhaps able to pin down the time of Margaret's death more precisely.

She testified that it was Miss White's habit to have lunch some time between 12.00pm and 12.30pm. After she was called into the house, Florence had helped John White to look around the premises and among the things she had noticed was that the breakfast pots were still unwashed in the sink, while there were no signs of any plates or cups from lunch. This indicated that Margaret White was already dead by noon.

Evelyn May Whittle ran a tobacconist's shop from 136 Acre Lane. On December 18th, she had closed for lunch at 1.00pm and some time in the hour before that she had served a man with two packets of Woodbines and a box of matches. On December 26th, she had attended an identification parade and picked out Fred Wood as the man she had seen in her shop. Although Evelyn could not be absolutely sure that Wood was the man, she strongly believed he was and if so, this showed that he had already left number 96 by around 12.30pm

Fred Wood had stated that he had caught a bus from the Victoria pub at 11.30am. If this were true, then he would simply not have had the time to kill Miss White. Talking to Chief Inspector Brown, Wood had detailed a number of witnesses who would have proved very valuable to him. To begin with, while waiting at the bus stop, he had seen a young woman who had two children in her charge. The children had very frizzy hair. In addition, not long after the bus had set off, two young women had flagged the vehicle down and joked with the driver about almost missing it. Finally, two men sitting behind Wood had been talking about some deal involving a motor car.

The police were certainly thorough in their work and they traced every one of these witnesses. Miss Emmie Baker told the court that she was a nurse to Mrs Locke who lived in Ack Lane. Part of her duties was to take care of Mrs Locke's two children, aged five and three, and both had a shock of frizzy hair. Miss Baker confirmed that she was near the Victoria with the children on December 18th, but she put the time at 12.30pm not 11.30am Freda Thorpe and Marjorie Chapman said they had signalled for the bus to stop, close to Bramhall Hall gates. Both ladies agreed that the bus they flagged down had been the 12.30pm service.

James Pearson Chapman, who was no relation to Marjorie, and his friend, Mr Whitehead, said they had been talking about a car while sitting towards the back of the bus. Again, though, both men said that the bus they had caught was the 12.30pm.

Medical evidence was to prove crucially important in this case, for according to Wood's second statement, the one penned on January 4th, Miss White had died from some sort of fit. John White, the dead woman's brother, gave evidence about what he had found when he returned home from work on the evening of December 18th, but he also spoke of his sister's general health. He said that as far as he knew, Margaret had never suffered from fainting fits of any kind, although he admitted that she had been badly affected by the death of their mother early in 1922, and had been advised to go away on holiday for two or three months in order to prevent a nervous breakdown. Some of this testimony was confirmed, by implication, by Jessie Theodore White, Margaret's sister-in-law and first cousin. She said that two years before, Margaret had consulted a lady doctor in Manchester, even though there was nothing wrong with her. Had Margaret White suffered from some nervous disorder after all?

Dr Thomson, the family physician, said that he had attended Miss White for the past three years and there were no indications of any nervous disorder. He had last treated her for an attack of influenza and did not think she would have been liable to seizures or fits of any kind. The same doctor had, of course, spent less than ten minutes with the dead woman on December 18th, and believed she had died from a heart attack. Indeed, he stated under oath that he could not recall even looking at Margaret's face as he examined her.

The post-mortem had been carried out by Dr Roland Nightingale and Dr Henry George Sideley Anderson, on December 20th. Both men reported finding abrasions on Margaret White's arms and a bruise on her upper arm. There was a circular mark on her throat, some two inches below the point of her chin, which was well-defined in front and ran from ear to ear. Margaret's teeth were clenched and there were small dilated blood points under the skin beneath both ear lobes. The larynx and the upper part of the trachea were congested and the trachea contained a small amount of some frothy exudate. Both

Dr Nightingale and Dr Anderson agreed that the cause of death was asphyxia, due to violence applied to the neck, but they could not agree on how that violence was applied. Dr Nightingale felt that Margaret had been seized by someone standing in front of her, but to her left side. The killer had grabbed her with his left hand and applied pressure with his fingers while holding her right arm with his right hand. Dr Anderson, though, stated that Margaret had been grabbed from behind and gripped with both hands around her throat.

Dr Nightingale, who was suggesting that Wood had strangled Miss White with his weak hand, had also examined the prisoner on January 9th. Nightingale agreed that the left arm was badly injured but this did not affect the muscles or power of the wrist and hands. He believed that Wood was strong enough to throttle Margaret White with his left hand.

There were quite a few police witnesses. Sergeant Postons told the court what he had found when he attended 96 Acre Lane on the night of December 18th. He also referred to the events of January 4th when Wood had asked him for paper so that he could write a detailed account of what had taken place. After cautioning Wood, the prisoner had said, "You'll get a shock. Miss White was at the gate when I was passing and she asked me to show her how to pleat a chair and she would give me half a crown. I did the job and half a crown of what I got out of that house was my own. I only got 15s. Miss White was alive when I left. The dog was in the kitchen. He would have worried me if he could have got at me."

Constable James Cunliffe had been escorting the prisoner from Stockport police court to Strangeways prison after his appearance on December 26th. At one stage Wood had said, "Mr Brown is a very nice man. He thinks he has got me but I can beat him on the time. I did not leave Hazel Grove until ten o'clock. I got the bus at Bramhall and caught the 1.37 train from Stockport to Leeds, and Gateley left at nine o'clock and I left at ten."

Finally, after Chief Inspector Brown and Inspector Kingman had been heard, there was the testimony of Constable Wilfred Bowyer. At 11.20am on December 26th, he had been searching a field adjoining Acre Lane and previously indicated by Wood. There he found a bag of tools which included a hammer and a screwdriver. The screwdriver had been badly bent as if used to prise something open.

Wood went into the witness box and repeated much of what was in his second statement. He said that as he left the house, Miss White was still alive, although she was breathing very heavily. After this, his own medical history was given. Wood had joined the Army at Bradford on September 10th, 1914 and had been badly wounded in the forearm, by rifle fire, on April 9th, 1917. Discharged from the forces on November 13th, he had been under medical treatment ever since. Mr Henry Poston, a surgeon from the

Grangethorpe Hospital in Manchester, testified that he had examined Wood in October 1922, and had taken an X-ray of the injured arm.

In Mr Poston's opinion, the gripping power in Wood's left hand was very feeble and he would have been incapable of killing Miss White in the manner described.

In his closing speech, Mr Goodman Roberts, for the defence, said that there were two points for the jury to consider. First, was Miss White actually murdered and if so, was Wood the man responsible? If robbery had been the motive, as the prosecution suggested, why had Wood not taken the jewellery from the dressing table and why had he not gagged Miss White as well as tying her wrists?

The jury retired at 5.20pm on March 2nd, and considered their verdict for an hour. Frederick Wood played nervously with his hands as the foreman was asked for that verdict and replied, "Guilty but with a strong recommendation to mercy." Asked if he had anything to say, Wood replied, "I still maintain I am innocent."

An appeal was heard on March 26th, before the Lord Chief Justice, Lord Hewart, and Justices Branson and Salter. The grounds were that the trial judge had misdirected the jury by suggesting that they had but two choices, murder or acquittal. It was suggested that a verdict of manslaughter should also have been possible. The three judges considered the various arguments but made much of the two contradictory statements which Wood had made. In one he claimed to know nothing of the crime but the second made it plain that he was in the house at the time. The jury had come to the only possible verdict and the appeal was consequently dismissed.

On April 7th, Wood's solicitor received notice from the Home Office that there would be no reprieve. During his stay in the condemned cell at Walton prison in Liverpool, Wood received no visitors apart from his legal representatives. His family never came near and only a crowd of 20 or so people gathered outside the jail as the appointed hour approached.

At precisely 8.00am on Tuesday, April 10th, 1923, Frederick Wood, also known as Ronald Lee and George Wood, in which name he had once been fined for being drunk and disorderly, was hanged by John Ellis and Thomas Phillips. The drop was reported to be 8ft 7ins.

CHAPTER FOURTEEN

COPPER

HAROLD Pinchin watched with pride as his youngest son played outside their home at 9 Crescent View, Salford. Five-year-old Norman Widdowson Pinchin was well-known in the area. His cherubic looks and mass of curly reddish-blond hair had earned him the nickname of 'Copper', but others called him 'Jackie Coogan', as he looked so much like the child film star who was all the rage in the early 1920s.

Norman was playing with his best friend, eight-year-old Eric Wilson, when at 2.30pm on Tuesday, June 10th, 1924, the two boys bounded into the Pinchin household where Norman threw himself upon his father's knee and shouted, "Daddy, give us a penny." Laughing, Harold Pinchin reached into his pocket, only to find that he only had a halfpenny in change but this he gladly handed over to the son he doted upon. Norman scrambled down and crying, "Come on Eric! We've got a halfpenny again," went into the kitchen to ask his mother's permission to go down to the shops with Eric to spend his new found wealth on sweets. Permission was given and the playmates headed off together.

Harold Pinchin was at home until 4.45pm when he went off to work. He did not see Norman again that afternoon but there was nothing unusual in that. Norman had most likely gone on to Eric's home, especially as the weather was rather inclement. Later that day, however, Harold Pinchin's world was shattered when the police came for him at his work, took him to the mortuary at Pendleton Town Hall, and there showed him the body of a child who he identified as Norman. The son he loved so dearly had been sexually assaulted, brutally murdered and the man believed to be responsible was now held in the cells.

Once Norman Pinchin and Eric Wilson had left Crescent View, they had gone to play in Peel Park but soon afterwards it had started to rain and they had taken shelter in the summer shed. It was while they were there that a man had approached the boys and offered to buy them ice cream. Since Eric was the oldest, and probably the one most likely to carry out the errand correctly, he was given four pennies to buy two twopenny wafers. They then left the park with the man. Eric was holding Norman's left hand, while the stranger held his right. Eric dashed off to purchase the wafers but returned to find that his friend had gone. The man had said something about going for a walk along the canal and under normal circumstances, Eric would have followed, but it was coming on to rain again. To a small innocent boy, the solution was obvious. Eric ate both ice creams and then went home.

Norman Thomas lived at 11 Hall Street, Salford, and knew Norman Pinchin well. It was around 3.45pm when he was standing by some iron railings in Park View and saw Norman walking from Peel Park holding a man's hand. Thomas, who was 14 years old, watched the couple as they strolled down Wallness Road and headed off in the direction of the canal owned by the London, Midland & Scottish Railway Company.

The next sighting of the man and boy was made by Harry Barnes who worked in the timber yard of John H. Ashton Ltd. The back yard of the premises ran alongside the canal, close to Windsor Bridge, and it was the custom of men taking a break to rest on the wall that blocked the factory off from the canal towing path. It was around 3.45pm when Barnes was enjoying a quiet smoke, leaning on the wall and looking over towards the canal.

As he watched, a young man, holding a little boy by the hand, came on to the canal towpath through a small gate which led to Wallness Road. The man was holding the boy's right hand and Barnes saw them walk under Windsor Bridge where, due to a bend in the canal, he lost sight of them. For the next nine minutes or so, Barnes continued to enjoy his break and then he saw the man return with the boy, who he was now carrying in his arms.

At first, Harry Barnes did not take much notice but suddenly the man took hold of the boy by the middle of his back and threw him into the dark, dank waters of the canal. For a few moments, Barnes was stunned at what he had just seen and was rooted to the spot. But as he watched, he saw the man kneel by the side of the canal and look down into the water before standing up again and heading off for the gate which led on to Wallness Road. Barnes leapt down from the wall, dashed through the factory where he worked and on to the towpath of the canal to see if he could locate the body of the poor child in the water. He was unable to find any sign but on the way there, he had passed the man who had thrown the boy in and Barnes felt that the best course of action now would be to follow him and find out where he lived so that the matter could be reported to the police.

Harry Barnes followed the man down Wallness Road and into The Crescent. The man then turned towards Manchester and it was then that Barnes saw two policemen walking towards him but on the opposite side of the road. Quickly he crossed over, blurted out his story and pointed out the man he had been following.

One of the officers, Constable Walter Smith, introduced himself to the man and explained that he had received information that the man had just thrown a child into the canal. All four men now returned to Windsor Bridge where Barnes confirmed his identification by shouting, "This is the man that I saw throw a little boy into the canal there." So saying, he pointed into the water, whereupon the man held by Constable Smith shouted, "Nothing of the kind," and made to strike Barnes. He was restrained by Constable Smith and then escorted to the police station. Once there, the man who Barnes had pointed out was identified as 23-year-old John Charles Horner.

After taking Horner to Cross Lane police station, Constable Smith returned to the canal with some grappling irons. At the spot indicated by Barnes, he began dredging the canal and within minutes had recovered the body of a small boy. The boy was not wearing trousers, implying that the crime might have some sexual nature. Although it was clear that the child was beyond help, Smith applied artificial respiration and later accompanied the child to hospital in the ambulance. There it was confirmed that the boy was indeed dead, so Constable Smith returned to the police station, cautioned Horner and then charged him with murder.

On June 11th, Horner made his first appearance at the police court when he was remanded to June 13th. In addition to the evidence of arrest, details were also given of an identification parade conducted at Salford Town Hall. Horner had positioned himself amongst eight other men but he had been positively identified by both Eric Wilson and Norman Thomas. Sadly, it was also revealed that poor Norman Pinchin had only celebrated his fifth birthday two weeks before he died, and it was only five weeks since had started his first school, Christ Church School in Hulme Street. Further, on the very day of this first hearing, Norman had been due to go to Flixton to spend a few days holiday with some family friends.

On June 13th, the inquest opened and the second hearing at the police court took place. There were large crowds outside both the Pendleton Town Hall and the Salford police court and cries of "Lynch Him!" filled the air. It was only with great difficulty that the police managed to force a way through the mass of people and get their prisoner into the buildings.

The last hearing of the inquest was on June 18th before Mr Arthur Holmes. The case for the prosecution was put by Mr C.O. Hockin while Horner was not legally represented. Here it was admitted that Eric Wilson had very bad eyesight and at first had great difficulty in picking Horner out as the man he had seen with his pal, Norman Pinchin, in Peel Park. The boy was allowed to walk about the court, everyone being asked to stand up so that Eric could get a better look at them. After some time, he touched Horner's coat and said that this was the man he had seen. A verdict of wilful murder against the prisoner was then returned. The very next day, the police court hearing was completed and Horner was sent for trial.

The trial of John Horner opened at Manchester before Mr Justice Talbot on July 17th, 1924. The case for the prosecution was led by Mr William Madden, who was assisted by Mr Hugh Beazley, while Horner's defence rested in the hands of Mr McKeever.

Eric Wilson was a most valuable witness for the prosecution. He told the court of his trip to Peel Park on June 10th, where they were approached by a man he had since identified as Horner. The man spoke to him and Norman and said, "Come with me and I will show you something and shove my dicky up your bottom." As they had left the park, Eric had asked Norman to come home with him, rather than go on to the canal but Norman had refused. Finally, Eric told the court of the identification parade which had taken place at Salford Town Hall that same evening. He had picked out Horner, a man he had also picked out at the police court.

The story of the boy being thrown into the canal and the subsequent following of Horner to the point in The Crescent where he was apprehended was told by Harry Barnes. He agreed that the man he saw throw Norman into the water was then out of his sight for a few minutes while he got down from the wall and ran to the canal, but he was adamant that he was not mistaken and that Horner, the man he followed, was the same man.

Evidence of the arrest was given by Constable Walter Smith and the officer who had been with him at the time, Constable James Lorinson. They stated that even before the body was discovered, Barnes had given them a description of the clothing the boy was wearing. As for the trousers, missing when the body had been recovered, these had been found by Constable Henry Barlow, some ten yards from Windsor Bridge.

Detective Inspector William Jowett, gave details of the organisation of the identification parade. It had taken place at 8.25pm on June 10th and Horner had been allowed to inspect the parade first. He had made an objection to one man, who had immediately been removed. Horner was then told to position himself wherever he wished and chose to place himself second in the line from the right. Eric Wilson had entered the room first and picked out Horner without hesitation. Horner had then been told that he might change his position if he so wished but he stayed where he was. Norman Thomas then entered and he, too, picked out Horner without hesitation.

Medical evidence was given by Dr Talbot who had examined the body at the Salford Royal Hospital and pronounced life extinct. The post-mortem had been carried out by

Dr Stanley Hodgson and he told the court that there was only one sign of violence upon Norman Pinchin's body. The anus had been forcibly stretched and the lining torn. This was consistent with forced anal intercourse and was the direct cause of the child's death. Although the body had been recovered from the canal, there was no water in the boy's lungs and his heart showed none of the signs characteristic of death by suffocation. This meant that Norman was already dead when he was put into the water. The cause of death was shock, caused by the forced stretching of the anus.

The time came for Horner to give his own version of the events of June 10th. He explained that he had been going out for some time with a young lady named Sarah Verity who was a ward maid at the Salford Royal Hospital. On the day in question, he had made arrangements to meet her at Old Trafford station but the weather was bad and they had also agreed that in such circumstances, she would not turn up at Old Trafford but he would instead go to the hospital.

After waiting a few minutes at Old Trafford, Horner realised that Sarah was not coming and so got on to a tram at Salford Docks. He subsequently changed to another and finally alighted at the corner of Oldfield Road, opposite to the hospital. There was still no sign of Sarah but Horner thought she might come out during the evening meal time and so decided to while away the time by going for a walk. He strolled down Oldfield Road and did, indeed, walk along the canal to the gate at Wallness Road. Near that gate he saw a man who he did not know, rush past him on to the canal towpath. That man was the witness, Harry Barnes. Horner claimed that he had never set foot in Peel Park that day and had never seen either of the young boys who subsequently picked him out at the identification parades. This was simply a case of mistaken identity.

Some of this evidence was backed up by Sarah Verity. She had arranged to meet Horner at Old Trafford but did not do so as it was 'pelting down' at the time. She had known Horner for seven years and had no doubt that he was simply not capable of committing this terrible crime.

The jury, though, chose to believe the three witnesses who claimed to have seen Horner with the murdered boy, and a guilty verdict was returned. On July 28th, Horner's appeal was dismissed by the Lord Chief Justice, Lord Hewart, and Justices Shearman and Sankey. On the same day, the same men dismissed the appeal of Jean Pierre Vacquier, the Byfleet poisoner.

On Wednesday, August 13th, 1924, hundreds of people gathered outside Manchester prison, waiting for the notices of execution to be posted. The crowd included relatives of Norman Widdowson Pinchin, there to see justice done. At 8.00am, John Charles Horner, a man who had a police record but not for any sexual offences, was hanged by William Willis. To the very end, he maintained that he was innocent of any involvement in the crime which claimed his life and that of an innocent young boy.

CHAPTER FIFTEEN

—⟨∘⊙∘⟩—

THE SPIRITUALIST

—⟨∘⊙∘⟩—

JAMES and Sarah Ann Sykes had been married for some 20 years and James was now working as an ice-cream salesman, his wife making the product he sold. The couple lived happily enough at 8 Whit Lane, Pendleton, a house they shared with their lodger the past few months, 41-year-old Patrick Power. Sarah, though, had other interests besides maintaining the family home and making ice-cream, for she was also deeply involved in the spiritualist world, thought of herself as a medium, and often gave readings for friends and neighbours.

Patrick Power, a well-built Irishman, had lodged with the Sykes family since December 1924. Having spent 23 years in the Army, serving with both the Connaught Rangers and the Manchester Regiment, and having seen action in the Far East, Power had now fallen on hard times. His only income was an Army pension of just over £1 a week, and 18s unemployment benefit. Out of this he had agreed to pay the Sykes 14s a week for his board and lodgings, but eventually he fell into arrears.

By April 11th, 1925, Power was three weeks behind with his rent and consequently owed James Sykes £2 2s. That, though, was not the full extent of his indebtedness to the Sykes family, for he had also borrowed money from James, saying that he was waiting for some cash to come through from the bank. Power now owed around £5, but he had not been pressed for repayment and as far as James Sykes knew, there was no animosity between him, Sarah and Power.

It was 11.30am on Saturday, April 11th, when James Sykes left to do his round. At the time, Sarah and Power were in the house, and Sarah said that she would make some more ice-cream while her husband was at work. Four hours later, though, at 3.30pm, things at Whit Lane were never to be the same again.

It was just before that time that Power had walked into Pendleton police station, strolled purposefully up to the desk and told the officer on duty, Constable Frederick Gibson, "I wish to give myself up. I have killed my landlady." Power was cautioned and taken into the office at the back so he could be interviewed. There he continued, "I hit my landlady on the head with a hammer. If she is not dead now, she is near it, and she deserves it." So saying, Power placed a door key on the desk, telling Gibson that this was a key for his lodgings.

After arranging for Power to be taken down to the cells, Constable Gibson picked up the key and dashed around to 8 Whit Lane. There, in the front sitting-room, he found Sarah Ann Sykes lying on her side, bleeding profusely from a wound to her head. On the floor nearby lay a heavy, bloodstained hammer. Sarah, although deeply unconscious, was still alive and Gibson called for the police ambulance. She was rushed to Salford Royal Hospital where, a few minutes after she had been admitted, she died from her injuries without ever regaining consciousness. After escorting the body to the mortuary, Constable Gibson returned to the police station and charged Power with murder. Power made no reply.

Patrick Power made his first appearance at the Salford police court on April 13th, when the details of the arrest were heard by the stipendiary magistrate, Mr P.W. Atkin. In addition to police evidence of Power walking into the station to give himself up, Mr Robert Lightbody Galloway, the surgeon who had treated Sarah at the hospital, also gave information on the injuries she had sustained. Three of her ribs on the right side had been broken and her skull was fractured in seven places, four times around her right ear and three around her left. Her upper and lower jaw were fractured and the tip of her right thumb had been sliced off, for in addition to being battered with the hammer, she had also been attacked with a sharp knife, suffering 12 stab wounds. Power listened impassionately as the list of injuries was read out and he was then formally remanded in custody until April 15th.

On April 14th, the inquest opened at the Pendleton Town Hall. The coroner was Mr Arthur Holmes, but Power was not present in court as a verdict of murder against him was returned.

The next day, the police court hearing was resumed. By now, Power had obtained legal representation in the form of Mr Kenneth Burke. The prosecution asked for a further remand to which Mr Burke strongly objected. He stated that although he had received instructions only the day before, he was ready to proceed. How then could it be that the prosecution was not ready when they had held all the evidence for five days? Nevertheless, a further remand was granted, this time until April 23rd.

On April 23rd, all the evidence was heard and Power was duly sent for trial on the capital charge. That trial took place at Manchester on May 8th. Mr Burke continued to represent Power while the case for the Crown was led by Mr Neville J. Laski. The judge was Mr Justice Finlay.

James Sykes testified that on the day his wife had died, she had risen at 7.30am but Power did not get up until 11.00am and was washing himself when James left to sell his ice-cream. Power had done no work since moving into Whit Lane and relied on his pension, dole money and what money he had saved, an amount of some £40 which he had on deposit at the bank. Despite this, Power had borrowed money from Sykes, apparently reluctant to dip into his savings. During the time Power had been living with them, there had been no arguments between him and Sarah and while Power had once been a heavy drinker, he seemed to have curtailed this habit over the three weeks prior to Sarah's death, possibly due to his lack of money.

James Sykes went on to say that the hammer used to kill Sarah, and now produced in court, was one that belonged to him. He used it to break up large blocks of ice and had last used it on the morning of the attack. When he had last seen it, it had been left in the back yard. As for the knife which Power had apparently also used, that had been on the kitchen table when he left for work. James first heard of the attack when he arrived home at 5.00pm to find the police waiting for him. He was taken straight to the mortuary where he identified his wife's body. Finally, James Sykes confirmed that his wife had claimed to be a medium but he denied that she had ever done a reading for Power, or told him that she had seen people standing behind him.

Power had walked into the police station a few minutes before 3.30pm on April 11th and this must have been very soon after the attack had taken place. Edith Margaret Rollins ran a grocer's shop which was opposite the back door of Sarah's house. She testified that Sarah had called at her shop five times on April 11th, the last time being at 2.45pm. Edith had known Sarah for two years and reported that on April 11th, she appeared to be her usual cheery self.

Constable Gibson reported the conversation that had taken place at the police station when Power gave himself up. Going to the house in Whit Lane, Gibson said that the back door was not locked, only latched, but the door that led to the scullery inside was locked and he used the key Power had given him to open it. Sarah was in the sitting room, her head lying underneath the piano keyboard. Although there were blood splashes all over the room, there were no ornaments broken and no signs of a struggle, indicating that the attack upon her must have been sudden.

Detective Sergeant David Thompson told the court that he had seen Power at the police station at 4.10pm on April 11th and at the time, he appeared to be calm and sober. Ten minutes later, Sergeant Thompson went to Whit Lane and assisted in the investigation. He found splashes of blood on the wall near the fireplace and also on the piano. Nothing was broken inside the room, and nothing was out of place. The breakfast things were still on the table, as was a bloodstained kitchen knife.

Medical evidence was given by Mr Robert Galloway, the resident surgical officer at Salford Royal Hospital. Mr Galloway said that Sarah Sykes was admitted at 3.30pm and he examined her at 3.34pm. There were multiple injuries to the head and her body was covered in blood. Despite his attentions, Sarah died within five minutes. Finally, Dr Galloway stated that in his opinion the man who committed the attack upon Sarah would not have had full control of his mind at the time.

On April 13th, Dr Stanley Hodgson had performed the post-mortem on Sarah's body. In addition to the wounds that had already been detailed, Dr Hodgson described further injuries including a deep gash in the web of Sarah's right thumb and four cuts on her forehead, all of which penetrated down to the bone. The cartilage of Sarah's left ear was severed completely and a two-inch lacerated wound in front of this ear went down to the bone. Another deep wound extended one inch into the neck muscles and all these could have been caused by the knife produced in court.

Dr Hodgson detailed the skull injuries, describing a star-shaped wound the size of a shilling and another the size of a half-crown. Many pieces of bone had been driven down into the brain. Although there were many injuries, the cause of death had been shock following the injuries to the brain. The attack, in Dr Hodgson's opinion, was a furious one and had been carried out by either a man who was completely mad, or a sane man in a terrible rage.

Both Dr Galloway and Dr Hodgson had expressed their belief that the man who killed Sarah might well have been insane at the time. The prosecution now called Dr Shannon, the medical officer of Strangeways prison where Power had been held. He testified that he had examined Power a number of times and kept him under constant observation and his opinion was that there were no signs of madness.

Power stepped into the witness box to give his own version of the events of April 11th. He said that after Mr Sykes had gone to work, Sarah had mentioned to him the subject of him being three weeks in arrears with his rent. He recalled her saying that if he did not pay up by the coming Tuesday, he would have to find himself new lodgings. He remembered very little after that, except for picking up a hammer. The next thing he knew, Sarah was lying on the floor and he was standing over her. Realising what he must have done, he then went straight round to the police station. Power also stated that on more than one occasion, Mrs Sykes had told him that she was a spiritualist and had seen a figure standing behind him.

There could be no denying that Power had killed Sarah Sykes but the defence asked that a verdict of 'guilty but insane at the time' be returned. In the event, the jury took only ten minutes to decide that Power was guilty of wilful murder and he was sentenced to death.

There was no appeal and no reprieve. A crowd of around 100 gathered outside the prison in Manchester on the morning of Tuesday, May 26th, 1925, as Patrick Power was hanged by William Willis. The man whose sanity two doctors had expressed doubts about, was finally at rest.

CHAPTER SIXTEEN

--- ❧ ---

THE WOMAN IN THE GREEN HAT

--- ❧ ---

I N JANUARY 1925, James Makin, a 25-year-old bleacher, married and with his new bride moved, on the 10th of that month, into the house owned by Makin's uncle, Joseph Howsley, at 3 Cross Street, Newton Heath, Manchester. For a time, the newly-weds appeared to be a devoted couple, but then, on May 4th, an event occurred which was to change everything.

May 4th, 1925, was a Monday and Makin had a day off work. The same could not be said for Joseph Howsley and Mrs Makin, who both left for their respective jobs, at the usual time. It was Mr Howsley who returned home first that evening, arriving at Cross Street at around 5.50pm to be followed, just minutes later, by Mrs Makin. Her first action was to go up to the bedroom she shared with her husband but as she tried to gain entrance, something blocked her way. Pushing the door a little harder, she managed to see what was preventing her entry and the sight caused her to scream at the top of her voice. Joseph Howsley dashed up the stairs and he found to his horror that the battered and bloodstained body of a strange woman lay on the floor. Of his nephew there was no sign and Howsley wasted no time in contacting the police.

Constable Edward Smith was soon on the scene, to be followed within minutes by Dr Howard Buck who confirmed that the woman was indeed dead. Constable Smith noted that the woman's body lay across the floor with her head underneath the bed. A bloodstained knife, presumably the murder weapon, lay nearby and there were obvious signs of a struggle having taken place. Smith contacted his superior, Superintendent Joseph Lansberry, and later went with the body to the mortuary where the post-mortem was carried out.

The dead woman was soon identified as 24-year-old Sarah Elizabeth Clutton of 13 Manor Street, Ardwick. Sarah had a number of other names including Sarah Barker and May Smith, and earned her living as a prostitute.

An official identification was made on May 5th, by Amelia Hughes, a waitress who knew Sarah and said she had last seen the dead woman at around 5.15pm on May 3rd. Amelia knew Sarah as 'a woman about town' and went on to say that when she had seen her last, Sarah appeared to be upset and looked as if she had been crying.

The initial police investigation turned up two useful witnesses. Gertrude Jackson lived at 42 Cross Street but at some time between 3.30pm and 3.45pm on May 4th, she had been in the shop at 10 Cross Street, which was almost directly opposite number 3. As Gertrude chatted to the shop owner, Hilda Collinge, she saw James Makin walk down the street and enter the house owned by his uncle. At the time he was wearing a jacket but moments later he reappeared at the front door in his shirt sleeves. He seemed to be rather furtive and looked up and down the street before vanishing back inside. Some minutes later, as Makin came back to the door, a woman wearing a green hat, went to the door of number 3. She paused for just a few seconds before walking into the house. Makin remained standing on the steps for a short time and then went back inside.

Hilda Collinge confirmed all this evidence and both women agreed that the woman they had seen enter Makin's home, was not his wife. Among the clothing found inside the bedroom at 3 Cross Street, the police had discovered a bright green hat which Mrs Makin confirmed did not belong to her. It was clear then that Makin had admitted the woman who had been found dead in his bedroom and since he had now disappeared, it became a matter of urgency to find him.

It was 9.45pm on May 4th when Superintendent Lansberry was standing outside Newton Heath police station. A tramcar pulled up outside the station and among the passengers who alighted was a young man who seemed to be very drunk. The man staggered up to Superintendent Lansberry and slurred, "I am Jimmy Makin."

He was so drunk, in fact, that he had to be assisted into the station where he was examined by a police surgeon who noted that Makin had what appeared to be congealed blood on the finger nails of his right hand, recent abrasions on the same hand and bloodstains on his clothing.

Makin was not charged with murder until 10.00am on May 5th. In reply to that charge he replied, "I was under the influence of drink. I believe the woman had a bad disorder or was in a bad way." Later that day, Makin appeared at the Manchester City police court before Mr E. Brierley, when only evidence of arrest was given, Makin then being remanded to May 7th.

By May 7th, the case for the prosecution had been taken by Mr Fred Webster while Makin was represented by Mr T.H. Hinchcliffe. Once again only the briefest details were given and Makin was again remanded, this time until May 21st. Earlier, on May 7th, the inquest had opened before the coroner, Mr C.W.W. Surridge, and having heard the details of the case, the jury returned a verdict of murder against Makin.

The final police court appearance took place on May 21st when Makin was sent for trial. Those proceedings took place on July 25th, at Manchester, before Mr Justice Wright. The case for the Crown was led by Mr Cyril Atkinson MP, assisted by Mr Goldie, while Makin was defended by Mr W. Gorman and Mr Percy Butlin.

Joseph Howsley testified that he was the owner of 3 Cross Street and that prior to his marriage, Makin had lived with his step-sister. On the day in question, Howsley had been unable to open the bedroom door properly and had looked around it to see the body of a woman, who he did not know, lying in a pool of blood. Nothing had been touched inside the room before the police arrived and later, Howsley had identified the bloodstained knife found on the bedroom floor as one which belonged to him and was normally kept in a kitchen drawer downstairs. A broken dandelion and burdock bottle had also been found on the floor, by the police.

At the police court, Makin had claimed that he had served in the war and since his return to civilian life, he had tried to kill himself on three separate occasions. Further, Makin had testified that his brother had been an inmate of the Prestwich Lunatic Asylum for the eight years prior to his death. In the final part of his testimony, Joseph Howsley was able to say that although he knew that his nephew had been in the forces, he had not seen much of him during the past few years and so knew nothing of his suicide attempts, or of his brother being in an asylum. Howsley was also questioned about reports that Makin had been forced to leave his step-sister's home after issuing threats to kill both her and her husband. He claimed to know nothing of this incident.

Attempts were made to trace Makin's movements after the attack upon Sarah Clutton. It had already been shown that he and the dead woman had arrived at Cross Street some time after 3.30pm. The next sighting took place at about 4.30pm. Sarah Alice Wilcock had known Makin for more than four years and it was 4.30pm on May 4th when she alighted from a tram at the corner of Thorpe Road and Oldham Road. Sarah lived at 8 Cross Street and as she walked from the tram-stop to her home, she passed Makin who was walking in the opposite direction. Makin appeared normal in his behaviour, but he also looked somewhat preoccupied as he brushed past her without speaking. The last time she saw him, Makin was getting on to a Hollingwood tram in Oldham Road.

It was not until 8.00pm that Makin was seen again by anyone who knew him. Arthur Green, a carriage cleaner of 67 Whitley Street, Collyhurst, had known Makin as a friend for a number of years and he saw him standing outside the Falstaff Hotel in Market Place, Manchester. They fell into conversation and went inside the pub where they each enjoyed a half-pint of Bass. Makin had obviously taken a few drinks already as he was somewhat under the influence by the time he met Green. Then, as Arthur Green took a sip of his beer, Makin suddenly announced that he was under arrest.

Thinking that it was the drink talking, Green told his friend not to be silly but asked him what he might have done that warranted such a comment. Makin replied, "I have done a woman in." Green, still not convinced that Makin knew what he was saying, had suggested that his friend had better go home but Makin said, "I'm not going up there. It's up there I've done it, in the wife's bedroom."

The two men continued drinking and Makin eventually announced that he was going to give himself up to the police. Arthur Green asked Makin if it was his wife he was claiming to have killed and Makin replied, "No, one from down the town." He paused for a few minutes and then continued, "It was in the wife's bedroom and the woman asked for a bowl of water to clean herself." He went on to say that he had asked her if she was unwell or diseased and she had started crying. Makin continued, "I hit her on the head with a bottle. I went downstairs, got a knife and drew it across her."

Having finished his story, Makin then told Green that he was the only friend he had met that night, and shook him by the hand. He then took some money out of his pocket and handed it to Green, asking him to pass it on to Mrs Makin. Green counted £9 in banknotes and tried to give it back to Makin who would have none of it. The friends parted outside the pub after being in there for perhaps 20 minutes, during which time they each consumed three or four drinks.

Constable Smith gave evidence that he had been on duty in Oldham Road, some 25 or 30 yards from Cross Street, at 6.05pm when he had been approached by Mr Howsley who informed him that a woman was lying in one of his bedrooms, having apparently been murdered. When he arrived at the scene, Constable Smith noticed that the woman was lying on her back with her legs wide apart and a knife lying near her left thigh.

Superintendent Lansberry was at the scene soon after, arriving there at 6.10pm. He noted that the bed appeared to have been moved after the attack upon the woman, as a mark from the castor had been made through a pool of blood. The woman's combinations had been pulled up and open and her skirt and petticoat had been turned up to her waist. All these items were covered in blood, as was the clothing around the neck, and there were spots of blood on the bed linen and the pillows. The bed itself was disordered and a stained shirt and collar lay nearby. Superintendent Lansberry had also found a green woollen hat, a pair of gloves, a pair of shoes, a handbag and a pair of bloodstained women's knickers, on a chair in the bedroom, along with two tram tickets.

Dr Buck detailed the wounds inflicted upon Sarah Clutton. She had a bruise on the right side of her head and two long narrow bruises on her right cheek. There were three skin-deep cuts on the left side of her cheek and two cuts on the left side of her neck. The first of these was three inches long and had penetrated into the muscle of her neck while the second was five inches long and ran downwards and across the front of the neck dividing the jugular vein and the carotid artery.

There was evidence that Sarah had tried to defend herself as three of the fingers on her right hand had been cut down to the bone. Dr Buck further testified that the bruises on her head could have been caused by a blow from the bottle found at the scene and that considerable force would have been needed to inflict the throat wounds. Finally, Dr Buck stated that Sarah was just finishing her monthly period at the time she had been killed, and was suffering from no form of disease.

When giving evidence on his own behalf, Makin had claimed that he had travelled into Manchester city centre on May 4th, and there he had met Sarah for the first time, in a public house in Market Street. She had asked him to buy her a drink and at that time, he had been unaware that she was a prostitute. They had a few drinks together and in the course of their conversation, Sarah revealed what she did for a living and insisted on accompanying Makin back to his house. He tried to lose her but she followed him home and after he had entered his house, she had hammered on the door, demanding to be let in. At first he had gone to open the door intending to give her a piece of his mind, but seeing that he was being watched from the shop opposite, he reluctantly allowed her in. Eventually he consented to sex but afterwards he noticed that she was bleeding and believed that she might have some disease which she would now have passed on to him.

Three times he had asked her what was wrong with her, and three times she had failed to answer. Then she started to cry and he was convinced now that she had given him some disease. Before he could face her with this, Sarah leapt to her feet and pushed him backwards, into the fireplace, shouting that she wanted to 'do him in'. Makin had then run downstairs to get a knife, intending only to frighten Sarah and get her to leave the house but she rushed at him again and they both fell over. The next thing he realised, Sarah's throat was bleeding and he knew he was in trouble.

While Makin's story might have been acceptable if Sarah had suffered one wound in her throat, it went little towards explaining away the two cuts Dr Buck had described. Further, another witness, Howard Yates, gave evidence which appeared to refute Makin's claim that he was a reluctant party to Sarah's advances. Mr Yates was a tram guard for Manchester Corporation and he was on a tram which left Stevenson Square for Newton Heath at 3.00pm on May 4th. He identified the two tram tickets found at 3 Cross Street as ones issued on his route and was also able to say that Makin and a woman in a green hat had boarded together. Mr Yates remembered the two particularly because they had to run to catch the tram and jumped on just as it started moving. He also recalled them getting off together and noticed them as the woman smiled at him as they did so.

One of the final witnesses was Makin's step-sister who testified that he suffered from 'severe head attacks' and that at such times he was 'very queer', but this did nothing to help Makin's case. The jury took only 20 minutes to arrive at their guilty verdict and Makin was duly sentenced to death. He did not appeal against that sentence and there was to be no reprieve. By 8.00am on Tuesday, August 11th, 1925, a crowd of around 250 people gathered outside Manchester prison as Makin was hanged by William Willis and Robert Baxter. Originally, Makin had been due to hang alongside Francis Hyland, but he had entered an appeal and was subsequently to escape the gallows, leaving Makin to die alone.

CHAPTER SEVENTEEN

A VERY HONEST MAN

SAMUEL Johnson, a 29-year-old slinger who lived at 9 Wellington Street, Stretford, had been walking out with Beatrice Philomena Martin for something like two years and in that time he had been quite open with her about his circumstances. Johnson had freely admitted that he was a married man and had three children, but there had been talk of a divorce so that he would be able to marry Beatrice. These plans proceeded well until May, 1925, when Beatrice's attitude appeared to change and she finally told him that she did not wish to get married after all.

In due course, Samuel Johnson discovered that there might well be an excellent reason for Beatrice having changed towards him. Beatrice, it seemed, was not the most faithful of ladies and had been seeing other men, including a seaman named John Hunter. Johnson was not one to give up easily though, and he still paid attention to Beatrice, even though she often made it plain to him that she thought there was no future for them.

On the evening of Saturday, July 25th, 1925, Beatrice met her sailor at the Palace Cafe in Manchester. Unfortunately for Hunter, though, Johnson was also there and at one stage tried to offer a gift to Beatrice which she refused. This annoyed Johnson and when Hunter later escorted Beatrice to her home at 13 Wingfield Street, Stretford, they found Johnson waiting for them. Beatrice let herself in and Johnson announced menacingly that he was also coming in to talk to her. Eventually she managed to calm him and he left the house.

The next evening, Sunday, July 26th, Hunter again took Beatrice out but this time they went to the Fox Inn. Once again Johnson was there and again he tried to persuade

Beatrice to go with him. She turned him down flat and added insult to injury by telling him that he was 'not big enough for her'. At this Johnson said that he intended proving who was the better man and challenged Hunter to fight him. Hunter was not to be provoked and left the pub, leaving Johnson with Beatrice. They were not together for long, though, as a few minutes later, Hunter saw Beatrice in the street outside, talking to some women she knew. By now there was no sign of Johnson, so Hunter and Beatrice went elsewhere for a drink and it was not until around 2.00am on the morning of Monday, July 27th, that Beatrice and her sailor friend once more turned into Wingfield Street.

To Beatrice's dismay, Johnson was once again standing on the doorstep of her house, waiting for her to come home. John Hunter watched from a discreet distance as Beatrice approached her front door with some apprehension. Words passed between Beatrice and Johnson but Hunter could not make out what was said. As he turned to walk away, Hunter saw Beatrice knock on her front door, half-push Johnson away and shout, "You're not coming in here."

Mary Alice Martin, Beatrice Martin's mother, had seen Johnson hanging about outside for some time before her daughter arrived home. Now, at her daughter's knock, Mrs Martin dashed downstairs to open the door, heard Beatrice shout something about Johnson not coming in and then heard what sounded like a scuffle. Suddenly a shrill scream shattered the night air and Beatrice cried, "Murder! Police!"

By the time Mary Martin had opened the door, Beatrice was standing on the doorstep and Johnson was aiming blows at her. Mary saw something glinting in Johnson's hand and tried to pull her daughter into the house. It was too late. Beatrice was already lying on the doorstep, bleeding from a number of stab wounds. John Hunter had by now dashed back to the front door and seeing that Johnson had attacked Beatrice, shouted that he would go for the police. At this Johnson replied calmly, "I've done it." He then walked off to give himself up to the first policeman he came across.

Constable Benjamin Whalley was on duty in Chester Road, Stretford, when Johnson walked up and told him, "I want to give myself in charge." He went on to explain that he had just stabbed a woman in Wingfield Street and was escorted back to the scene of the crime. As they arrived, Johnson pointed out a dagger sticking up in the soil of the front garden of number 13 and commented, "This is the knife I did it with." Constable Whalley then took Johnson in charge until Superintendent Yates and Inspector Nixon arrived to take him to the police station.

Soon afterwards, Dr William Isbister arrived and pronounced Beatrice Martin dead. The body was lying face upwards in the passageway of the house, with her head just over the doorstep into the street. Her upper clothing was saturated with blood and a large fresh pool of the crimson liquid lay on the pathway and over the front door step. Although Dr

Isbister later conducted a full post-mortem, his initial examination showed that there were a number of stab wounds centred about the neck and chest.

Samuel Johnson made his first appearance at the Manchester County police court on July 27th. Here some brief details were given of Beatrice's movements on the night she died. Evidence was given that she had met John Hunter on Trafford Bridge and they had gone to the Fox Inn in Salford. Here an argument had broken out between Johnson and Hunter and just when a fight had seemed imminent, Hunter had walked out of the pub. Soon after 10.00pm, Hunter had met up with Beatrice again and they had gone to a cafe and from there for a walk. They arrived back at Wingfield Street at around 2.00am. After this evidence was head, Johnson was remanded until July 29th.

The following day, July 28th, the inquest opened before the county coroner, Mr R. Stuart Rodgers, at the Stretford District council offices. Here all the evidence was heard and Johnson was committed for trial on the coroner's warrant. On the 29th, the police court hearing resumed. For the police, Superintendent Yates said that he had not yet heard from the Director of Public Prosecutions and asked for a remand until August 5th. Asked if he had any objections to a further remand, Johnson replied, "I should like the case to be dealt with as quickly as possible." Superintendent Yates said that the next assizes were not due to start until November and he did not see any way that Johnson could be dealt with before that time. The remand was granted and when Johnson did appear next, on August 5th, all the evidence was heard.

Mrs Mary Martin told the court that Johnson had last visited her home on the afternoon of July 26th when he had brought with him some presents for Beatrice. Her daughter had told Johnson that she did not want his gifts and further, that she did not wish to see his face again. That evening, Beatrice had gone out to meet Hunter but at some time between midnight and 1.00am, Mary had noticed Johnson hanging about near the front gate.

She told him to go away and had then gone upstairs to wait for Beatrice to return home. From time to time she had looked out of the bedroom window but there had been no sign of Johnson. She went on to tell of the events that took place when Beatrice finally did arrive home at 2.00am. When Mary Martin was cross examined however, she was forced to admit that her daughter was 'completely out of hand' and that Mary had tried to reason with her in an attempt to get her to improve her behaviour. These pleas had fallen on deaf ears.

William Thomas Martin was the dead girl's father and he stated that Beatrice had celebrated her 23rd birthday on May 29th, 1925. He went on to admit that his daughter had not led a straight life and that she had been keeping bad company for the last couple of months of her life. It was about that same time that he noticed an appreciable deterioration in her relationship with Samuel Johnson. Eventually the quarrels between them became so fraught that William had told his daughter to ask Johnson to stay away from the house.

The dead woman's father further stated that at one stage, Beatrice had been engaged to an American. A special licence had been obtained but at the very last moment the wedding had been cancelled and the American had sailed from Salford docks. William knew that Beatrice had started seeing another sailor, John Hunter, and since that relationship began he had heard Johnson threaten Beatrice, saying that no other man should stand between them.

Turning to the night of his daughter's death, William testified that he was asleep in bed when he was woken by his wife's screams for help. By the time he got downstairs, Beatrice was lying across the doorstep. It was then about 2.05am. Finally, William Martin agreed that when he had made his first statement to the police, he had commented that 'it's a blessing she has gone.'

John Hunter said that he was a native of the Shetland Isles and an able seaman, serving on the *SS Iceland*, at present tied up in Salford docks. He had first met Beatrice some two months before, in a public house, the Fox Inn on Regent Road, Salford, and since then they had been out together about eight times. Speaking of the night of the attack, Hunter testified that he had said his goodnights to Beatrice and was already across the other side of the street when he heard the sound of a struggle. He heard Beatrice scream and ran back to help her, but by the time he got to her front gate she was already lying in a pool of blood with her mother standing over her. Johnson then turned to him and said, "Jock, take me to the police," but before he could do anything, the attacker had walked off down the street.

Winifred Parker was a married woman who was now separated from her husband and lodged at 31 West Bank Street, Salford. She was a close friend of Beatrice's and had known her for about four years, having once lodged with Beatrice at her parent's house. On July 18th, Winifred was at Beatrice's house when Johnson appeared. In his presence, Beatrice had announced, "Oh Winnie, one of my boys is coming home tonight. I shall have to put Sammy on one side." This was an obvious reference to Hunter's ship being about to dock at Salford and Beatrice was taunting Johnson with the other man.

Soon after this comment had been made, Beatrice had gone into the kitchen and Winifred had turned to Johnson and asked, "What will you do Sam?" He had replied, "I'll show you what I'll do," and had then brought out a dagger from inside his coat pocket, adding that he intended to use it to kill Hunter. Winifred had told him not to be foolish as he would do himself more harm than good, but Johnson had shrugged his shoulders and replied, "I don't care. If I can't have her, I'll see nobody else does have her." At this point Beatrice had returned and rubbed salt in the wounds by saying, "I'm going to see one of my boys tonight. I'll have to put you on one side." Johnson then leapt to his feet, clutched Beatrice around the throat and shouted, "I'll kill you before I've finished."

On July 26th, Winifred had seen Beatrice at the Palace Cafe on Regent Road. Beatrice was with Johnson and another man who turned out to be John Hunter. They appeared to be quarrelling and Beatrice had called Winifred over and pointed to Johnson saying, "I can't get rid of him. He won't leave me alone." Hunter had then walked away, at which Johnson had partly pulled a dagger out of his pocket. He quickly put this away again and Winifred left soon afterwards.

Dr Isbister gave details of his findings at the post-mortem. He described seven wounds in the chest, neck and back, five of which were superficial. The wound which had caused Beatrice's death had severed two-thirds of the aorta and this had caused her to rapidly bleed to death. Dr Isbister was also able to say that Beatrice was suffering from a sexual disease at the time of her death.

At this final police court hearing, Johnson stepped into the witness box to give his own version of the events of the early hours of July 27th. He stated that the trouble had started two months before, soon after Beatrice had met John Hunter. He had tried a number of times to get Beatrice to resume their relationship, but she had persistently refused. On July 27th, he had put his hand upon Beatrice's shoulder as she tried to enter her house and struck a blow at her with his other hand, in which he held a knife. He continued striking at her until she fell to the floor when he dropped the weapon and walked off to find a policeman.

The final witnesses were the police officers involved in the case. They testified that in addition to the knife, they had also discovered a knuckle duster in the garden next door. It seemed likely that Johnson had come to the scene equipped for a fight with Hunter but had turned his attentions instead to Beatrice who had paid with her life for rejecting him. Not surprisingly, Johnson was sent for trial.

The trial took place at Manchester on November 23rd, 1925 before Mr Justice Wright, and was nothing if not sensational. When asked how he pleaded to the charge, Johnson replied that he was guilty and wanted no defence of any kind. The judge, reluctant to accept such a plea, asked, "Have you seriously considered the course you are taking?" Johnson said he had, whereupon Mr Justice Wright continued, "Do you realise that what you are pleading guilty to is killing this woman intentionally and of set purpose?" Once again Johnson said that he did, and the judge added, "And you know that by pleading guilty the sentence which the law must pass on you is in no way affected?"

Johnson replied in a firm voice, "I realise that," to which Mr Justice Wright asked, "You have been offered counsel and you have refused it?" Johnson nodded and replied, "Yes, I have refused it." The plea of guilty was then accepted and Johnson was sentenced to death. The entire proceedings had taken just four minutes and was the shortest murder trial ever heard at Manchester. Having heard the sentence of death, Johnson turned on his heel and caught sight of a friend in the courtroom, to whom he waved as he was escorted to the cells below.

On Tuesday, December 15th, 1925, Samuel Johnson was hanged at Strangeways by William Willis, who was assisted by Thomas Phillips. At the inquest afterwards, it was stated that whilst he was in prison the prisoner had been received into the Church of England by the Bishop of Manchester. The coroner, Mr Rodgers, said that this was a very sad case. Johnson had served in the Army and had received an honourable discharge. Prison officials said that Johnson was the best-behaved prisoner they had ever had and they greatly admired his conduct since his arrest.

CHAPTER EIGHTEEN

MURDER WITHOUT MOTIVE

LATE on the night of Friday, October 2nd, 1931, a man and a woman booked in at the Station Temperance Hotel in New   Bridge Street, Manchester, using the names of Mr and Mrs Harry Stanley. Walter Stead, the manager of the hotel, watched Mr Stanley sign the register and then, after accepting 10s as payment, handed over the key to room number six. As the couple retired for the night, Mr Stanley asked Walter Stead to call him at 8.00am the following day as he had to get off to work.

In fact, Mr Stanley did not need his early morning call, for it was just a few minutes before eight when Mary Casey, a domestic servant at the hotel, entered the lobby from the yard at the back and saw him in the hallway, looking at himself in a mirror, apparently checking that he was neat and tidy. Although Mary said nothing beyond, "Good morning," to Mr Stanley, she got the impression that he was in a hurry and held the door open for him as he left the hotel. She then returned to her duties.

By about noon, there was still no sign of Mrs Stanley and Mary Casey needed to get into the couple's room to clean it. She knocked on the door and called out, but there was no reply and so eventually she used her pass key to gain entrance to room six. Once inside, she saw that Mrs Stanley was still in bed, apparently asleep, but on closer inspection she saw blood upon the pillow and something tied tightly around Mrs Stanley's throat. Pausing only to tell Mr Stead what she had found, Mary Casey ran outside to find a policeman.

Constable Gilbert Westwell was on duty in Great Ducie Street at 11.50am when Mary Casey dashed up to him and told him what she had found. He accompanied her back to the hotel and there saw the body of Mrs Stanley, almost completely covered by bedclothes.

Pulling back the top sheets, Constable Westwell saw that she was lying on her back in the centre of the bed and that there was a piece of a man's dark brown knitted tie, fastened loosely around her neck. Feeling the body, Constable Westwell found her still warm and, believing that she might still be revived, undid the piece of brown material which had been fastened by means of a double granny knot below the right ear. Underneath, however, was a second, longer piece of brown tie but this was knotted much tighter and had bitten deeply into Mrs Stanley's throat. Westwell also unfastened this and applied artificial respiration but it was soon apparent that he was too late. Mrs Stanley was already dead, a fact confirmed by Dr Arnold Renshaw who had also been called to the scene.

In due course, Detective Inspector Huntingdon arrived at the hotel and began to search the room, finding a woman's purse between the bed and the mattress. There was still money inside the purse, suggesting that the motive for killing the woman had not been robbery, but then other items revealed that the woman lying in the bed was not after all Mrs Stanley, but 28-year-old Annie Riley who lodged at 25 Camp Street, off Deansgate. The important thing now, of course, was to trace her companion, the mysterious 'Mr Stanley'.

Hilda Ambler lived at the same lodging house as Annie Riley and had known the dead woman for more than three years. When Hilda was interviewed by the police, she could tell them only that she had seen Annie leave Camp Street at 7.30pm on October 3rd. Later that same evening, Hilda had gone into town and happened to see Annie outside the Victoria Hotel, by which time it was around 10.45pm. Just ten minutes later, Hilda walked past the same spot, but by then Annie had gone.

Many of Annie's other friends were traced and interviewed. One man, who had known her very well, was actually held by the police and interrogated for some hours before being released. Meanwhile, the investigation spread to Liverpool, where Annie had spent some time, and some of her friends were taken by car to Bolton when a man who had spent some time with the dead woman was reportedly seen there.

Through Mr Stead, the hotel manager, and Mary Casey, the servant, police had been able to piece together a very basic description of the man who had shared the room with Annie Riley. This description was published on October 4th and read, 'Five feet four inches tall, dark complexion, clean shaven, fairly well built, and dressed in a dark suit with a bowler hat and black patent shoes.' It was not much to go on and it appeared that this would be a difficult case, but in the event, the man for whom the police were looking was soon in custody.

At around 5.20pm on October 5th, Detective Inspector Valentine and Detective Sergeant William Malcolm were talking together in the detectives' office at the Town Hall when a man walked in and announced, "I want to give myself up for the murder of the woman at the Station Hotel." The man identified himself as 21-year-old Solomon Stein of 110 Charlotte Street, Hightown. Stein was cautioned but he seemed to be totally indifferent to the consequences of what he was saying and went on to make a lengthy written statement outlining exactly what had happened between himself and Annie Riley.

Stein's statement began, 'On Friday night, I went to the Theatre Royal picture house in Manchester and saw *City Lights*. I came out of the pictures about 10.30pm. I walked steadily to the corner of Market Street and Cross Street and there saw a young woman.'

The statement went on to give a full description of the woman Stein had met and there could be no doubt that she was Annie Riley. Stein's statement continued, 'She spoke to me as if she knew me. She said, "Hello, where are you going?" I said, "I'm just having a walk round". She asked me which way I was going and I said, "Down Corporation Street," and she asked if it would be all right if she walked with me and I said, "Quite all right."

'She started to tell me she had come from Liverpool that day and had been looking for an hotel to stay the night, and then she noticed an hotel on the other side of Corporation Street, just past Hanover Street.

'I said, "You will probably be all right there." We both went across but the place was in darkness. We knocked at the door and were there about two or three minutes.' Stein's statement went on to say that there had been no reply at the hotel and Annie had then asked him if he knew of any others nearby. He told her that there were one or two he knew and they walked off together to find one. The statement went on, 'On our way there she suggested to me that I stay the night with her at the hotel, providing I paid for the room. I agreed and we went down New Bridge Street and I knocked at the door of the Station Hotel.

'A gentleman opened the door and I asked him if he could let me have a room for the night and he said, "Yes, I think I have a spare room." He asked me to sign the register, which I signed as man and wife in the name of Mr and Mrs Harry Stanley, of Liverpool. The man asked for 10s and I gave him a 10s note. He took us upstairs to the third or fourth floor, and showed us into the bedroom. There was one large bed in it and I told him to call me at eight o'clock in the morning. I and she undressed and went to bed after turning out the electric light.'

Stein did not go into any detail over what took place in that bed during the night, but he was not so reticent when describing in detail how he had killed Annie Riley. Stein wrote, 'I woke up at six o'clock in the morning and reminded myself that I had to be at work. I decided to dress.

'When I had partly dressed, I picked up my jacket for a cigarette and discovered a tie. It was not the one I was wearing. It was a brownish knitted tie. While I held the tie in my hands I noticed the girl was in bed. She appeared to be fast asleep and before I could realise what I was doing I had tied it firmly round her neck.

'To make sure to do the job properly I wound it round her neck again, this time pulling tightly with both hands. I pulled so hard that the tie broke so I tied one half round her neck and knotted it and then tied the other half round her neck and knotted it. I stood by and watched her struggles, which lasted about five minutes. She suddenly lay still and I realised it was over. I then fully dressed and discovered 15s was missing from my trousers pocket – a 10s note, a half crown, a florin, a sixpence, or two separate shillings and sixpence. I searched high and low. I looked into her handbag and could not find the money. It was eight o'clock and I then gave up looking and decided to go out.'

Stein went on to say how he had turned the door handle and been unable to open the door. He had thought of escaping through the bedroom window but trying the door again, he found he had been turning the handle the wrong way and this time, the door opened easily. He had gone downstairs and heard the maid carrying out her duties so turned to straighten his collar and tie in the mirror. After leaving the hotel, Stein said he had run up New Bridge Street and then along Cheetham Hill Road and finally arrived home. Here his mother asked him where he had been and he told her that he had met a friend outside the pictures and stayed overnight at his house.

The statement ended, 'I had breakfast and got washed and told mother I was going to work, where I arrived at 9.15 in the morning. I was late. I worked ten minutes but could not keep my mind on my work so put on my coat and walked out. At ten minutes to five I found myself near Victoria Station and I decided to have another look at the hotel. I stood at the gateway of Victoria Station and watched a small crowd which had gathered around. There was a policeman standing by the door of the hotel.

'I realised that the crime had been discovered and walked away and bought a paper to read about the hotel tragedy. I thought it best to get out of the way. I took the bus to Belle Vue district and walked around there until eight o'clock. I went to the Osborne Theatre and later slept in the name of Leonard Harris at Walton House, and told them that I had come from Leeds. I slept there on Saturday night and Sunday and, through having to keep out of the way of the police, got fed up and decided to give myself up and so came to the Town Hall and made this statement.' Having completed this lengthy document, Stein was charged with the wilful murder of Annie Riley.

Stein appeared at the Manchester City police court on October 6th. The hearing, before the stipendiary magistrate, Mr J. Wellesley Orr, lasted for just three minutes and Stein was remanded until October 14th. On that second date, the hearing was even shorter, Mr Lawrence Marks for the defence saying that he was not ready to proceed. The final police court hearing took place on October 21st, the case for the Director of Public Prosecutions being given by Mr John Heyes while Stein was represented by Mr B.S. Wingate-Saul who was instructed by Mr Marks.

In addition to the witnesses already referred to, Jacob Stein, the prisoner's father, told the court that his son, who was a machinist at a waterproof garments factory, lived at the family home in Charlotte Street and had left there on the night of Friday, October 2nd, and had not returned until some time between 8.45am and 9.00am on the Saturday. He had told his mother that he had stayed with a friend who he met after leaving the picture house. Mr Stein added that his son had celebrated his 21st on October 3rd, the very day he had killed Annie Riley.

Important evidence was given by Dr Renshaw, the police pathologist who had examined Annie's body in the hotel and later performed a post-mortem. As he examined Annie at the hotel, Dr Renshaw noticed that there was blood on the left shoulder strap of her chemise and further stains on the top left-hand portion of the pillow which lay nearby. The necktie had been removed by Constable Westwell but there remained a livid mark around the neck where it had been. After carrying out a post-mortem, Dr Renshaw was able to confirm that death had been due to asphyxia. The doctor added that he believed Annie had been asleep when the attack upon her had started but bruises showed that she had revived and tried to remove the ligature.

The evidence being concluded and Stein's statement having been read out, the prisoner was sent for trial at the next Manchester assizes. These opened in mid-November and on the 25th of that month, Stein was brought before Mr Justice Finlay. The prosecution lay in the hands of Mr T. Eastham and Mr Redmond Barry while Stein was defended by Mr Neville J. Laski and Mr Wingate-Saul.

Asked how he wished to plead, Stein replied, "Guilty." Mr Laski immediately stood up and said, "Not guilty," but Stein replied, "I say guilty." Seeing that there was some difference between the prisoner and his barrister, Mr Justice Finlay allowed Mr Laski to consult with his client for a few minutes in the cells below the court. However, when they returned to the court, Stein stated that he would not change his guilty plea. He was spoken to by Mr Marks, the solicitor who had represented him in the early hearings, but Stein was adamant that he would not change his mind.

The judge called Dr Howard Shannon, the medical officer of Strangeways prison, who said that he had observed Stein since he had been admitted to jail on October 6th. There was no sign of any mental disorder and in Dr Shannon's opinion, the prisoner was fit to plead and fully aware of the consequences of his actions. To this, Mr Justice Finlay stated that since there was no evidence of insanity, he had no alternative but to accept the guilty plea but asked Stein if he understood what he was pleading guilty to and if he fully grasped the consequences. Stein replied, "Yes," to both questions, the guilty plea was recorded and the death sentence passed.

Not surprisingly perhaps, Stein did not appeal against his sentence. His last visitor on the morning of his execution was the Jewish chaplain, Jacob Phillips, after whose ministrations Stein enjoyed a breakfast of two eggs. Later he knelt and said some prayers with Reverend Phillips and at 9.00am, as the executioner entered his cell to pinion Stein's arms behind his back, he grasped Jacob Phillips' hands as a gesture of farewell.

A crowd estimated at 1,500 had gathered in the streets outside Strangeways prison, even though there was a heavy drizzle. Most of that crowd were people of the Jewish faith and many were the same age as Stein. At 9.00am on Tuesday, December 15th, 1931, Solomon Stein, who had celebrated his 21st birthday on the day that he murdered Annie Riley, was hanged by Thomas Pierrepoint. Stein was only the third Jew ever to die on the gallows at Manchester.

A few minutes later, a prison officer tried to place the notice of execution on the prison gates but the hook which held it snapped and it had to be tied on with string. Meanwhile, a man and a woman, taking advantage of the large crowd, circulated amongst them with a petition for the reprieve of Peter McVay, who was due to hang in the same prison on December 22nd. Luckily for McVay, those efforts would prove successful and Stein was the last person to die on any gallows in 1931.

CHAPTER NINETEEN

A CASE OF MURDER

I T WAS around 6.30pm on Tuesday, September 22nd, 1931, and 11-year-old Olga Roberts was playing in the street outside her house at 73 Victoria Road, when she saw her friend, Constance Inman, who was just eight, running from the area behind her own house at number 56.

The two girls often played together, so Olga called out to Constance, hoping that she might join her in some game or other. Constance, however, either did not hear or chose to ignore Olga, for she made no reply. Olga called out again, noticing that her friend seemed to have been crying. This time, Constance did reply, shouting that she couldn't stop, she was going to join some other children. Under normal circumstances, Olga might well have joined Constance and gone off with her, but she was under express orders from her mother not to move from outside her house. The reason for that precaution was not simply normal maternal concern, though, for recently, there had been reports of a man in the area who had accosted children.

This man, whoever he was, rode an old and battered bicycle around the streets of the Victoria Park area and he had already attacked one girl in Raincliffe Avenue. The poor child had arrived at school in a distressed condition and told her teacher, Miss Clark, that the man had promised to show her some cigarette cards, but had then assaulted her. Some days later, a man had stopped a boy in Victoria Road itself, asked him where he was going and tried to entice the boy away. Luckily, the boy's mother, Mrs Brandon, had seen this conversation taking place and had come out of her house in time to chase the man away. The best description she could give was that he was middle-aged and well dressed.

Soon after seeing Constance run off down the street, Olga Roberts went inside her house to have her evening meal. It was not until about half an hour later, at 7.00pm, that Christopher Inman, Constance's father, knocked on Olga's door and asked her if she had seen anything of his daughter. Olga told him that she had seen Constance at 6.30pm but had no idea where she was going. By now, Mr Inman was growing concerned. Constance was usually home by this time and he had asked at a number of houses, but it seemed that no one had seen her.

Christopher Inman continued the search, helped by his wife, Lilian, and a number of friends and neighbours. By 8.55pm there was still no sign of the missing girl and when Mr Inman discovered that Constance had told her sisters that she was off to meet a man who was going to give her some cigarette cards, the now-distraught father hurried to Claremont Road police station and reported her missing. The police said they would take over the search, but Inman continued looking for her himself until late that night.

Jane Birkett worked as a domestic servant for Mrs Warne, who lived at 42 Park Range, Victoria Park. At 8.20am on September 23rd, Miss Birkett opened the study window to let in some fresh air. The window overlooked the back gardens of some houses in Dickenson Road and it was in one of those gardens, a particularly overgrown and unkempt one, that she saw what she at first took to be a very large doll. Looking more carefully, Jane Birkett saw that the 'doll' was in fact a little girl who was lying perfectly still in the long grass. Thinking that the child might be in need of assistance, Miss Birkett shouted down, "Little girl, are you hurt?" When she received no reply, she dashed downstairs and told her employer, Mrs Warne, what she had seen.

At first, Mrs Warne told her maid to calm down and not to be silly, but then seeing how distressed she was, the owner of 42 Park Range decided that Jane Birkett should investigate further. The maid went into the back garden with a set of ladders, climbed gingerly over the fence and crouched down beside the little girl. Touching the child's hand, she felt it ice-cold and realised that the girl was dead.

Within minutes, Superintendent Townsend, Superintendent Fisher and other police officers were at the scene. The body was that of a young girl, no more than ten years old. She lay on her back, her knees half raised and her head inclined slightly towards the right. The girl's dress had been pushed up but there were no obvious indications of sexual assault. Some of the girl's clothing, including her red jersey, bore stains which might have been blood and there was a large ball of froth near her mouth. A string of blue and white beads around the girl's neck had been broken.

At 9.45am Dr Arnold Renshaw, a pathologist, arrived to examine the body in situ. He noticed some irregular marks on the girl's flesh, 19 brown marks on her right arm, and six on the left. There were similar marks on both legs and Dr Renshaw concluded that these were almost certainly insect bites, caused after death. There was an abrasion on the left knee and one of the left side of her head, but these might have been caused by the child falling. The doctor did not believe that these marks had played any part in the girl's death.

Of greater importance were three small, indistinct red marks between the girl's chin and neck and a further mark on her larynx. These might have come from finger nails or possibly from the beads being pulled tight against the girl's throat if she had been grabbed from behind. A full post-mortem would reveal more but for now, Dr Renshaw could tell the police that it appeared that the child had died through some external violence.

There was only one child in the area who had been reported missing and the clothing worn by the dead girl matched that detailed by Christopher Inman. Later that morning, police officers called at 56 Victoria Road, told Mr Inman what they had found and asked him to come with them to the mortuary. There, the body was formally identified as that of Constance Inman.

During the time since Constance had been reported missing, there had been some curious happenings at 97 Dickenson Road. That address was a large house, split into separate lodgings. On the ground floor lived Annie Francis Broadhurst and her husband, John Joseph Broadhurst. The Broadhursts acted as caretakers at number 97. With them lived their servant, Rose Powell, and the only other tenant on that floor was Eva Radford, who lived alone in two of the rooms. There was, however, one other person living at 97 and he occupied a room up in the attic. Although known to all the others as Mr Price, his real name was George Alfred Rice, a one-eyed, unemployed labourer aged 32.

On the night of September 22nd, at around 11.15pm, Annie Broadhurst and Rose Powell had been alone in Mrs Broadhurst's kitchen when they heard a strange noise which seemed to come from the foot of the stairs. To the two ladies, it sounded as if someone had stumbled downstairs. This was followed by a light thud and the noise of someone dragging something across the floor towards the back door.

Thinking that they might be the victims of burglars, Mrs Broadhurst and Miss Powell moved to the front bedroom. If there was a stranger in the house, then he would have to leave either by the back door, or the front. If he left through the front door, they would see him, but if he escaped out the back, then the only way for him to go was down a passageway at the side of the house and around to Dickenson Road. Either way, he would eventually have to cross their field of vision and they would see who he was.

To the surprise of the two ladies, no one appeared and after ten minutes or so, they heard the unmistakable sound of the back door being bolted. Footsteps then crossed the hallway and climbed the stairs. It was Rice coming in and at first, Annie Broadhurst assumed that the noise of him returning had scared off the intruder, but then she realised that the man would still have been forced to come around to the front. There was only one explanation, the sounds they had heard must have been made by Rice himself.

Rice was still behaving strangely the following morning. Eva Radford heard him up and about at 6.30am. Even at the time she thought this to be totally out of character. Rice was, after all, unemployed and seldom rose before noon, often staying in his room until the late afternoon. An hour or so later, when Eva went to the front door to collect some letters, she saw Rice sweeping the stairs, a job he habitually carried out on a Saturday: today was Wednesday.

Later that day, at 12.45pm, Annie Broadhurst, her husband John, Rose Powell and others were at 73 Dickenson Road, the house where John Broadhurst's mother lived. By now, the discovery of Constance Inman's body was common knowledge and formed the main topic of conversation in the house. After a few minutes, Rice came in and Rose Powell asked him if he had heard the news. Rice said he had, adding that he had bought a newspaper which gave all the details. This in itself was highly curious for Rice could neither read nor write.

Referring to the noises of the previous night, Annie Broadhurst asked Rice if he had heard anything. Rice paled visibly and asked, "Was that before I came in?" Annie replied that she and Rose had heard the sounds about ten minutes before they heard him bolting the back door and then remarked, "I heard something being dragged along the hall to the back door last night." Rice appeared to ignore this and remarked cryptically, "You will see, they will take me because I am out of work."

Officers investigating the death of Constance Inman were calling on a number of people in Dickenson Road and at 4.00pm that day they visited George Alfred Rice in his attic flat. Rice was asked to account for his movements of the previous night and told Detective Sergeant John Blinkhorn that he had left 97 Dickenson Road at 6.25pm on September 22nd. He had walked to the corner of Wilmslow Road where he stayed until about 7.00pm when he called at a shop for some cigarettes. Returning to his home, he went to see Eva Radford and told her he would be out late that night as he was going to see a film at the Ardwick Empire. He asked her to mention this to Mr and Mrs Broadhurst and ask them to leave the back door unlocked for him.

Leaving the house again soon afterwards, Rice said he caught a tram to Brunswick Street and went to the Empire, speaking to an attendant there when he asked if the programme was continuous. Rice claimed that after the film had ended he walked along Brunswick Street, passing a jeweller's shop in which there was a large clock, before getting to Upper Brook Street where he caught the tram home.

Sergeant Blinkhorn had already spoken to the other occupants of the house, and heard details of Rice's strange behaviour. Eva Radford had confirmed that Rice had knocked on her door and asked her to tell the Broadhursts to leave the door open but even this was curious. There had been an arrangement, for some months past, that the back door was always left unlocked for Rice and it was he and he alone who locked it each night when he came home. Sergeant Blinkhorn told Rice that he was not completely satisfied with the details Rice had given and he would be taken to the police station pending further inquiries. At this Rice handed over two tram tickets and the torn portion of a picture house ticket.

Rice did not seem to be unduly worried and that night he slept soundly in the cells at the station. Waking at 4.30am, Rice greeted Sergeant Blinkhorn and said, "Give me another cup of tea and I'll tell you all that happened." He then made a detailed statement which was taken down, read back to him and upon which he then made his mark in the presence of a number of officers. At 1.00pm he was charged 'that he did feloniously, wilfully and with malice aforethought, kill Constance Inman'. After hearing the charge, Rice asked, "That means I did it on purpose?" Sergeant Blinkhorn answered that it did, to which Rice remarked, "I could not do it."

On September 24th, Rice appeared at the Manchester City police court where, after a brief hearing, he was remanded to October 1st. Five days later, on September 29th, the inquest on Constance Inman opened before the city coroner, Mr C.W.W. Surridge who, after hearing evidence of identification, and confirmation that Constance had been the third child of four, adjourned the matter until after the conclusion of the criminal case against Rice.

The second police court hearing took place on October 1st, before the stipendiary magistrate, Mr J. Wellesley Orr. The prosecution case was put by Mr John Heyes, while Rice was represented by Mr T.H. Hinchcliffe.

Mrs Radford, who had already given the police much information, also mentioned an incident which had taken place at 5.30pm on September 22nd. A hawker had called at 97 Dickenson Road and as she was talking to him, Rice ran downstairs and asked if it was someone for him. Mrs Radford said that it wasn't, to which Rice had added that he was expecting a man to call and see him about a job. This, too, was unusual. Rice had not received a single visitor since he had arrived at the house in December 1930.

Confirmation was heard that Rice had indeed called at a shop in Walmsley Road to buy cigarettes, but this had taken place at 6.00pm, not an hour later as Rice had claimed. Some of the most telling evience, though, was Rice's statement to the police, made early on the morning of September 24th. After saying that he had purchased those cigarettes in Walmsley Road, Rice went on to say, "I met a little girl in Dickenson Road, Rusholme, about 7.15 on Tuesday night. I done it. I met her near home. I had never seen her before. I took her down by the side of the house where I lived and took her behind the garage. I was cuddling her, but I did nothing wrong to her.

"I must have hit her on the head or something. I do not know what happened. She collapsed at my feet. I spoke to her and could get no answer and so left her." Continuing to talk of his movements, Rice went on to say that when he went back inside his house, it was just getting dark and it was then that he called on Mrs Radford, told her he was going to the Empire and asked that she tell the Broadhursts to leave the door open for him. He continued, "I then left and went to the second house at the pictures, next to the Ardwick Empire, and remained there to the finish of the pictures. I then returned on a tramcar to Dickenson Road. I went behind the garage, where I had left the girl. When I touched her I found she was going cold and appeared to be dead.

"I picked her up in my arms and carried her to the bottom of the garden and laid her gently on the grass at the bottom of the garden. I then went into the house and went to bed. This is the truth. I can't tell you anything more. When I first took the girl behind the garage my nerve seemed to go and I went dull."

With all this evidence against him, Rice was then sent for trial at the next Manchester assizes. That trial opened on December 14th, before Mr Justice Finlay and a jury which included three women. The Crown's case was led by Mr J.C. Jackson MP, who was assisted by Mr Redmond Barry. Rice was defended by Mr E.G. Hemmerde and Mr T.H. Hinch-cliffe. The case lasted for two days.

There could be little doubt that when Constance Inman died, George Alfred Rice had been with her. For the prosecution, the suggestion was that Rice had killed her while either raping her, or attempting to rape her. In such a situation, medical evidence was to prove crucial.

The post-mortem had been performed by Dr Arnold Renshaw, the same physician who had first examined Constance Inman at the spot where her body was found. He had discovered that both of Constance's lungs were congested and appeared to be collapsed. She had bitten her tongue in three places and at the police court, Dr Renshaw had stated that these were evidence of death from asphyxia which could be explained either by pressure on the neck, or by holding the child's clothing tightly from behind, thus causing the beads to choke her.

Dr Renshaw had come to three conclusions, which he had stated under oath, in the police court on October 1st. These were that there was no definite evidence of rape, that the abrasions seen had probably been caused when the child fell forward on to her face, and that the marks on the neck were too small and closely set to be caused by fingernail pressure and had almost certainly come from the glass beads of her necklace.

Now, at the assizes, Dr Renshaw elaborated on those findings. He had now come to believe that Constance had been raped and that her assailant had, at some stage, grasped her so tightly that all the air had been squeezed out of her body. In effect, she had been crushed to death. This was a very rare form of asphyxia where death had come on very quickly once that pressure was applied.

In the witness box, Rice denied that he had ever held Constance so tight as to crush her. He had cuddled her and she had simply collapsed at his feet. He also claimed that his so-called confession to the police was nothing of the kind. He had been woken, in the early hours, by Sergeant Blinkhorn who handed him a piece of paper and told him to sign it, which he did. When Blinkhorn was questioned, he, of course, denied that the confession had been manufactured and swore that it was a verbatim report of what Rice had said, even when it was pointed out to him that Rice was of low intellect and yet had apparently made a statement grammatically correct apart from the one phrase, "I done it."

The problem for Rice was that his version of events did not fit the known facts. He had claimed that he had gone to the cinema on the night of September 22nd and had even handed over a ticket stub to the police. Although the cinema staff could not pinpoint the exact date it had been issued, they were able to show that it had been issued some time before February 19th, a full seven months previously. There was also the evidence of the noises, heard by his fellow tenants, on the night Constance died. The prosecution suggested that this was Rice disposing of the body. His statement simply did not fit what was known.

In his summing up, Mr Hemmerde told the jury that they had three options. They could acquit Rice or they could believe that he was guilty of either raping or attempting to rape Constance, during which she died. If that was the case, then they must find Rice guilty of murder. If, however, they felt that Constance had somehow died accidentally while with Rice, then they could return a verdict of manslaughter against him.

Mr Justice Finlay clarified this point for the jury. If they came to think that the child had died as the result of violence while being raped by Rice, then he was a murderer, but if they felt he had only indecently assaulted her, then he was guilty of manslaughter.

The jury retired and returned after 35 minutes to ask the judge for further clarification. They sought to know if it was still murder if Rice had attempted rape but not completed the act. Mr Justice Finlay stated that it would be murder and added that they must be certain that the child died from violence and that this violence had been caused by Rice. They retired for ten more minutes before filing back into court to announce that Rice was guilty. As he heard the word 'guilty', Rice almost collapsed in the dock and began to groan. By the time the sentence of death had been completed, he was crying bitterly and had to be helped down to the cells.

An appeal was heard on January 18th, 1932, before Justices Avory, Talbot and Macnaghten. Here the defence again referred to the entire matter of whether Constance had been raped or not. There was no evidence of any struggle having taken place, no sign of bruising and none of Constance's clothing had been torn or removed. There was no evidence to support the view that Rice had sexually interfered with the child and the worst that could be accepted was that Rice had indecently assaulted her, in which case the correct verdict was one of manslaughter.

It was plain that Rice was not an intelligent man and some of his answers in court had plainly shown this. Asked at one stage why he had not taken the child back to the house if he thought she was still alive, he answered that he was afraid he would be charged with an assault upon her.

Mr Justice Talbot remarked that there was ample evidence that extreme violence had been used against Constance. The doctor had said that all the breath had been squeezed out of her lungs. Mr Justice Avory, announcing that the appeal was lost, said he was satisfied that the trial judge had freely invited the jury to return a verdict of manslaughter and there were clear indications that Rice had attempted something far worse than indecent assault.

On Monday, February 1st, Rice learned that there was to be no reprieve. Just two days later, at 9.00am on Wednesday, February 3rd, 1932, he was hanged at Strangeways by Thomas Pierrepoint. It was reported that Rice had broken down and had to be half-carried to the scaffold.

At the inquest afterwards, the county coroner, Mr R. Stuart Rodgers was asked if there had been any petition for a reprieve for Rice. Saying that he thought there had not, he added, "I was just wondering if those who sign petitions for reprieves ever send a letter of sympathy to the relatives of the murdered person."

What really happened to Constance Inman? While it was possible that Rice might have attempted to rape her and killed her during the process, it was also possible that she may have died from vagal inhibition, a phenomenon where sudden pressure on the neck, even light pressure, can cause death. He might well have been simply cuddling her, during which process the beads tightened slightly around her throat and killed her. If so, that was manslaughter, not murder.

It is likely, too, that this took place inside Rice's room and not at the back of the garage. Later, once it had gone dark, Rice took the body out of the back door and dumped it at the bottom of his garden. That was what Mrs Broadhurst and Miss Powell heard. There remains, though, one unanswered question. Who was the man who had offered children, including Constance Inman, free cigarette cards? It could not have been Rice for he did not own a bicycle and did not fit the description of the man seen in the area.

CHAPTER TWENTY

THE THIRD DEGREE

THE summer of 1933 was gloriously hot and the month of July was particularly stifling. For day after day, the sun beat down on the baking streets of Manchester and even the most conservative of people cast off the odd layer of clothing. So it was on Wednesday, July 19th.

There were, in total, six people living in the large imposing house named Claremont, situated at 453 Cheetham Hill Road. The matriarch of the house was 61-year-old Frances Levin, a woman who was not in the best of health. She shared the house with her two brothers and two of her daughters. The other person living at Claremont was a 17-year-old maid, Freda Phillips, who had been a resident there since February.

The family being a closely knit one, it was the custom whenever possible for all the members to return home for lunch. On July 19th, however, at 1.15pm it was only Louis Henry Davis, Frances' brother, and her two daughters who shared a light meal in the front room of number 453. After the meal, Frances, for some reason which she was never to explain, asked for her purse and in front of one of her daughters, Clara Levin, counted her money. Clara noticed that Frances had just 9s which she placed in a purse which was in turn, put inside Frances' handbag.

At 1.45pm the two daughters left the house to return to work, leaving their uncle, Louis, with their mother who was resting on a couch before the bay window in the sitting room at the front of the house. They chatted for perhaps half an hour, after which Louis went to his room upstairs. A few minutes later, he came downstairs again and saw that the maid, Freda Phillips, was attending to Frances. He then left the house by the front door, making sure that it was securely locked after him. It was now almost 2.30pm. Louis Davis, an antiques dealer, would normally have returned to his shop but for some reason, that afternoon he decided to take advantage of the fine weather and walked to nearby Cheetham Park instead. By the time he returned home at 4.40pm he found that something terrible had occurred in his absence.

Freda Phillips had taken Mrs Levin some books and magazines and, after seeing that her mistress was comfortable on the settee, had retired to the kitchen at the back of the house where she busied herself with her electric sewing machine. She sat close to the back door which, because of the oppressive heat, had been left open all that day.

At 3.30pm Freda decided to finish her sewing by hand and thought that it would be a good idea to do so in her own room which was on the second, or top floor of the house. The back door was still left open, though, to allow at least some air to circulate through the rooms.

As Freda sat near her window, she looked over to the house next door, a surgery, occupied by Dr Lees and his family. There in the driveway, which ran alongside that of Claremont, she saw Samuel Norman Woodcock, the man who worked as the doctor's chauffeur. He had started working on Dr Lees' car at 3.15pm and now he saw Freda, sitting at her window, and the two exchanged polite waves.

At 4.00pm, Mr Woodcock found that he would need a part to fix the car, so climbed on his bicycle and pedalled off to Brocklehurst's garage which was further up Cheetham Hill Road. He was away for no more than 15 minutes but in that intervening period, Freda Phillips looked down from her lofty window to see a man walking down the driveway of Claremont.

The man was walking from the back of the house, through the large wicker gate at the side and out into Cheetham Hill Road. Freda, though, was not unduly concerned. Only a couple of days earlier, a man had called to see the family about some chickens they kept at the back of the house and he had intimated that he might call again some time. This caller looked something like that man and Freda assumed that he had merely kept his word, and visited Claremont again. She did not see more than a brief glimpse of the man's chin but put his height at around 5ft 9ins and noted that he was dressed in working clothes, a brown coat, dark brown trousers, a pinky-brown shirt and he wore a light trilby hat. He was of medium build and perhaps around 45 years of age.

By 4.15pm, Samuel Woodcock had returned from the garage and started work again on Dr Lees' car. He looked up from time to time and saw that Freda was still working at her window on the second floor. Then, at around 4.30pm, Freda motioned that she was going downstairs and Samuel nodded his understanding.

It was perhaps two minutes later that Samuel Woodcock heard Freda call him from the kitchen steps. There was an element of panic in her voice and Samuel quickly dashed around to number 453. As he passed through the lattice gate, he noticed that it was closed but not latched, which was just as well as the gate was very difficult to open. Freda beckoned him into the kitchen and pointed to what looked like a poker, lying on the floor. He bent down to pick up the poker but at the last moment saw that the square end was covered with blood. Even as he gazed at this, Freda pointed out a shirt which was also heavily bloodstained and which had been taken down from a clothes rack and thrown on to the kitchen table.

Samuel asked Freda who else was in the house and she told him that she was alone apart from Mrs Levin, who was resting in the front room. Samuel and Freda walked together towards the front room and saw that the door was closed. Samuel knocked and receiving no reply, knocked again, turning the door handle as he did so. The door opened and he stepped into the front room of the house, leaving Freda waiting outside in the hallway.

Frances Levin was still lying on the settee in the bay window and Samuel Woodcock saw instantly that there was something very wrong. Frances' head was a mass of blood, there were splashes of blood on the walls, curtains, pictures and floor, and the pillows on which Mrs Levin rested were also saturated with the crimson liquid. Moving forward, Samuel spoke to Mrs Levin who opened her eyes and moved her head to one side. She did not speak, though, and instantly slipped into unconsciousness. Closing the door behind him again, Samuel Woodcock dragged Freda out of the house and ran to the nearest telephone box from where he called the police ambulance.

As he finished the call, Samuel saw a police officer, Constable James Turner, on duty in Cheetham Hill Road. Samuel quickly told Turner what he had found and the officer went with him to the house, where Freda was waiting for them at the front gate. Telling Samuel to wait outside the room, Constable Turner went in to make his own inspection of the scene.

Turner noted that Frances Levin was lying on her back on the settee with her head slightly inclined towards her right and away from the bay window. Her knees were drawn up slightly, her left arm resting on the settee, her right arm hanging off the side of the settee and almost touching the floor. Her face and head were covered in blood and there were signs that a number of blows had been struck. As Constable Turner tried to render first-aid, Mrs Levin again briefly opened her eyes but she seemed not to hear as the officer spoke to her, for she made no attempt to reply.

Looking around the room, Constable Turner saw there were no signs of disorder. No ornaments or other items had been scattered about or smashed and there were no indications that a struggle had taken place. On the settee lay two magazines, a newspaper and a book, and there were other magazines on the floor immediately in front of the settee. Finally, Turner noticed that the centre portion of the bay window had been opened, to a distance of about six inches, apparently to allow air into the room.

The police ambulance arrived and the officer who travelled with it, Constable Cecil Hartman, was shown into the house by Freda Phillips. As he entered the front room, Turner was still attempting to revive the badly injured woman and he now assisted Constable Hartman to lift Mrs Levin into the ambulance so that she could be taken to the Jewish Memorial Hospital. As the ambulance sped off, Detective Inspector William Malcolm Page arrived at Claremont to take charge of the investigation.

It was 4.45pm when Frances Levin was admitted to the hospital, situated on Elizabeth Street. Dr Isaac Goldberg, the resident surgical officer, saw that his patient was deeply unconscious and required treatment for extensive scalp wounds and a fractured skull.

Dr Goldberg saw, too, that both of Frances' hands were bruised and the bones in her left hand were broken, almost certainly sustained as she attempted to ward off the blows her assailant had inflicted upon her. However, despite all the attention which Frances Levin received, she never regained consciousness again and at 8.53pm died from her terrible injuries.

The police concentrated their efforts on finding the man who Freda Phillips had seen walking down the driveway of 453 Cheetham Hill Road. Although the description was fairly basic, it was known that there a number of unemployed and homeless people on the streets of Manchester and it seemed likely that the killer would be found amongst this particular class. The description was circulated to all police forces, railway and bus stations were checked, taxi drivers were spoken too and many lodging houses visited.

On July 21st, detectives working on the case announced that no fingerprints had been found on the murder weapon which was, in fact, not a poker but a heavy iron tool used to lift the grate in the kitchen. It was normally kept on the fireplace and the killer had taken from there, used it to batter Frances Levin to death and then returned it to the kitchen. The police said that they were not surprised that no fingerprints had been found on the weapon since the murderer had wiped it on the shirt before throwing it on to the floor. One foreign print had been found, though, on Mrs Levin's handbag and it was held that the motive for the crime had been robbery for the money which had been inside the purse was now missing. On the same day, July 21st, the inquest opened before Mr C.W.W. Surridge, and Frances Levin was buried at the Jewish cemetery in Crumpsall.

There were some leads flowing into police headquarters, for on July 25th, the newspapers carried reports that a definite line of inquiry was being followed. The police had stated that they were particularly interested in finding one man who was now believed to be in Darlington. This man, whom the reports did not name, had apparently almost been captured the previous weekend. He had been seen in Ormskirk a couple of days before the crime, in Manchester on the day of the murder and had since been spotted in Redcar and Darlington, which was where the last sighting had been made.

Other press reports asked the public to look out for a man whose clothing would be bloodstained and who may well have currency notes in his possession which might also be stained. At this stage, the police were still of the opinion that Mrs Levin might have had banknotes in her purse at the time she was attacked.

In the event, all such suggestions as to the identity of the culprit were soon conveniently forgotten, for at 10.30pm on July 26th, police in Hyde, Cheshire, picked up a vagrant. They saw that he fitted the general description issued by the Manchester police and when the man stated that he had been in Manchester on the day of the crime, the Manchester force was immediately contacted. At 1.30am on July 27th, two police inspectors, Page and Willis, travelled to Hyde where they interviewed the man, 47-year-old William Burtoft, before taking him back to Manchester with them for further questioning.

What happened over the next few hours proved to be highly contentious, with Burtoft insisting that his version of events was true. Ranged against him, though, were the words of a number of high-ranking and very experienced police officers who all agreed that Burtoft made a voluntary statement admitting that he was responsible for the death of Frances Levin. Consequently, Burtoft was charged with her murder.

Later that same day, July 27th, Burtoft made a brief appearance before the magistrates in the police court. He was described as a short, stocky man, who had only one eye and whose face was rather red and weather beaten owing to the amount of time he had spent out of doors. Only evidence of arrest was given before Burtoft was remanded until the 29th. On the second appearance, the hearing again lasted for only a few minutes and the prisoner was remanded this time until August 3rd.

By August 3rd, the case for the Director of Public Prosecutions had been taken over by Mr John Heyes, and Burtoft had obtained the services of Mr Boyd Hotchen to defend him. Reference was made to the confession which Burtoft had allegedly made and Mr Heyes suggested that this was made under duress. At one stage, Inspector Page denied that during his interview at Manchester, Burtoft had written on a piece of paper, 'This is to certify that I have been subjected to the third degree, which I cannot stand any longer.' Inspector Page also denied that any inducement had been held out to Burtoft to make any statement whatsoever. Nevertheless, after hearing the confession which the police said that Burtoft had made, the magistrates had no difficulty in sending him for trial.

William Burtoft's trial opened at Manchester on November 13th, before Mr Justice Atkinson who had been appointed to the bench as recently as May 15th. Burtoft was defended by Mr B.S. Wingate Saul and the case for the prosecution was led by Sir Walter Greaves-Lord MP, who was assisted by Mr E. Shackleton-Bailey. The trial lasted for two days.

In addition to relating what she had seen on July 19th, Freda Phillips also confirmed that on July 28th she had attended an identification parade at the Albert Street police station.

Because of the way she had observed the man leaving down the driveway, she watched from a window set at approximately the same height while a number of men walked passed her. She had picked out a man but this had not been the prisoner. Freda also stated that she had heard no noise or disturbance on the afternoon Mrs Levin was killed.

Samuel Woodcock detailed what he had observed and told the court how he had dashed to the nearest telephone box to contact the authorities and summon medical help. No reference was made, as had been at the police court on August 3rd, to a curious piece of behaviour on Mr Woodcock's part. His employer was a doctor and, of course, lived next door to Claremont, yet Woodcock had not run to him for help when he found Mrs Levin. Asked by the magistrate to explain this, Woodcock had replied that Dr Lees' door was closed and he thought he might be asleep!

The testimony of both Freda Phillips and Samuel Woodcock narrowed down the time of the attack upon Mrs Levin considerably. Woodcock had been working in the driveway of the house next door and swore that he saw no one walk down the side of Claremont. He left to go to the garage just before 4.00pm and was back by 4.15pm. Soon after he had gone, Freda saw the man walk from the back of the house, so, since no one else was seen, the attacker must have entered the house immediately after Samuel Woodcock had ridden off on his bicycle. Frances Levin was attacked at around 4.00pm.

There was another witness who described a man in Cheetham Hill Road on the afternoon of July 19th. Henry Rourke Willcock left his home at Bank Street, Higher Broughton, to attend Dr Lees' surgery at 2.50pm. Arriving at 451 Cheetham Hill Road at 3.20pm, Willcock sat down in the waiting room and a few minutes later, heard someone knock at the front door. Looking through the window he saw a man walk down the garden path. The man was of medium height, stockily built and was wearing a trilby hat. This testimony, though, provided the prosecution with two difficulties. In the first place, Burtoft was a most distinctive figure, since he had only one eye, and Henry Willcock made no mention of such a facial deformity, and second, if this man had been Burtoft, why had it apparently taken him more than half an hour to get to the house next door?

If Burtoft was the killer, then it was important to show that he was in the area of Cheetham Hill Road at 4.00pm on July 19th. Amy Wale lived at 72 Stockton Street, Moss Side, but at 2.45pm she was at 13a Elizabeth Street, a lodging house run by one of her friends, Bertha Edwards, when Burtoft called and asked to see another woman, Maggie Creamer. After being told that Creamer was not there, Burtoft asked for a cigarette and Amy Wale bought a packet for him while Bertha Edwards gave him some tea and sandwiches.

During his snack, Burtoft remarked that he had no money, but added that he might have some 'by tonight'. Both Amy and Bertha noticed that Burtoft, who had a severe drink problem, was carrying a bottle half-full of a purple liquid which they both recognised as methylated spirits. Burtoft left the lodging house at 3.15pm, saying that he was going off to get some money selling cards door to door. Amy testified that she saw Burtoft walk off towards Cheetham Hill Road and this was backed up by Bertha Edwards who said that her house was about 15 minutes walk from Claremont. This would mean that if Burtoft walked directly to the murder scene, the earliest he could have arrived was 3.30pm. This, in turn, meant that it was unlikely that Burtoft was the man who had been observed by Henry Willcock, since he put his sighting at just after 3.20pm.

The next positive sighting of William Burtoft was made by James Hughes, a newsagent whose premises were situated at 9 Angel Street. It was 4.20pm and Hughes was in Kane's lodging house in Angel Meadow when Burtoft came in with his hands thrust deep into his pockets. Hughes, who had known Burtoft for many years, greeted his old friend but Burtoft did not acknowledge him. Hughes was about to leave the lodging house but before he went, he saw Burtoft go into the kitchen and start to wash his hands.

Three days later, James Hughes saw Burtoft again, this time in the George and Dragon public house. Hughes asked Burtoft why he had not spoken to him the previous Wednesday but Burtoft, still apparently did not recognise Hughes and it was not until Hughes identified himself that Burtoft realised who he was talking to. He and Hughes then had a drink but as they were leaving the pub together, Burtoft asked Hughes if the police were visiting lodging houses in the area in connection with the Cheetham murder. Hughes said that the lodging houses had had 'no peace' and the police were coming 'in droves'. Rather cryptically, Burtoft had said, "I'll beat it," and had then walked off alone.

Dorothy Roberts ran a small cafe from 33 Swan Street and at some time between 4.45pm and 5.00pm on July 19th, Burtoft had come into the shop and purchased a cup of tea and a meat pie, for five pence. She was absolutely positive that Burtoft was the man because he had only one eye and she had plenty of time to observe him as he was the only customer there at the time. Dorothy Roberts also confirmed that Burtoft had been wearing a light, dirty trilby hat, a brown coat and dark trousers.

As soon as Inspector Page stepped into the box to give evidence, the defence objected again to the admissibility of the statement Burtoft had signed. The jury was asked to leave the court while the matter was discussed and Burtoft briefly stepped into the witness box to give his version of his interrogation. This contrasted totally with the version of events given by Inspector Page and his colleagues and the judge eventually ruled that the document should be read out in court.

The jury having been readmitted, Inspector Page began to give his testimony. He first described what he had found when he attended the scene of the crime at 4.30pm on July 19th. Frances Levin's handbag was lying open, on a small chair behind the door of the front room. Her purse had been removed from the bag and was lying, also opened, on the piano lid. Its only contents were a single bent penny and a miniature horseshoe-shaped good luck charm.

On July 27th, after he had arrived back at Manchester with Burtoft, Inspector Page had cautioned his prisoner in front of Detective Inspector Arthur Willis and Detective Sergeant John Blinkhorn. Asked to give an account of his movements over the past few days, Burtoft detailed what he had done and where he had been on July 18th, 20th, 21st and 22nd. He spoke for perhaps half an hour, during which none of the police officers present made any remarks whatsoever. At the end, Inspector Page remarked that Burtoft had said nothing about July 19th. Burtoft hesitated for a few seconds and then said, "Go on, I want to tell you everything, write it down." Burtoft then made a statement in which he admitted killing Frances Levin. That statement was taken down and read over to Burtoft who then signed it.

According to Inspector Page, it was around 3.00am on July 27th when Burtoft signed his statement, having arrived at the police station at 2.00am. He was not, however, charged immediately for Page thought it important to show the statement to his superiors first. Consequently, Burtoft was placed in the cells and not charged until 5.00am. Inspector Page went on to deny that any other officer had spoken at any stage, that any pressure had been brought to bear on Burtoft, or that he had been offered a tumblerful of whisky if he confessed.

Inspector Page also gave evidence of the identification parade at which Freda Phillips had picked out the wrong man. There were eight men besides Burtoft and he had been invited to take any position he wished in the line-up. Burtoft placed himself in position number one as the men walked past a window where Freda sat. There was then a few minutes pause before the men were asked to parade a second time during which Burtoft changed his position to number four.

After giving this evidence, Inspector Page read out the statement which Burtoft had made on July 27th. This read, 'Go on, I want to tell you everything, write it down. I admit being the murderer of Mrs Levin owing to drinking methylated spirits and also to the maid being where she was, the old lady lost her life. I was cool, calm and collected, of course. When I got in the front room there, the old lady got up and asked who was this and I went back and got the poker off the fire range and struck her repeatedly.

'When I left the house she was not dead but owing to the state of my nerves, I thought everyone was looking at me. I went down Angel Meadow into Kane's lodging house, washed my hands and threw the handkerchief down the lavatory and pulled the chain. Then I walked calmly into Swan Street and had a bit of tea and jumped on a tram for Oldham. I wasn't three minutes or so in the house. I was selling discharged soldiers' cards, Big Bertha will tell you I left her to sell some.

'I had no intention to do it but, well, I did it. I was sorry when I thought about it after. After I did it I took the poker back into the kitchen and wiped it on a shirt to remove my finger prints.'

Inspector Willis confirmed the details of the interview with Burtoft in the early hours of July 27th and also said that no inducements had been made to Burtoft. More important perhaps, Willis had also taken charge of the identification parade on July 28th. There had been a gap between the two parades, during which Burtoft had asked for a cigarette. Sergeant Yarwood had handed one over and Burtoft, in taking, it had said, "Why all this messing? You know I sold some of the cards in the side streets and called at that doctor's next door." Sergeant Yarwood immediately cautioned the prisoner, pointing out that he need not say anything, but Burtoft had continued, "I know that, but there was a man working at the doctor's place. I don't think he saw me." The details of this conversation were confirmed, by Detective Sergeant Samuel Yarwood.

Detective Sergeant John Blinkhorn agreed with his colleagues about what had taken place in the interview room on July 27th, but added that on the following day, he had handed all of Burtoft's clothing to the city analyst. It was that analysis which caused further problems for the prosecution for Mr Harri (sic) Head who had carried out the examination had found no trace of blood whatsoever on any of Burtoft's clothing despite the fact that all those who had examined the murder scene had described splashes of blood on the furniture, walls, curtains and paintings.

The post-mortem had been carried out by Dr Reginald Ellis who described three distinct wounds at the front of the head, one over the left eye, one over the right and one on the forehead. The central wound was by far the deepest, extending well down into the bone. There was a four-inch long wound on the back of the head, towards the right side and one of similar size on the left. Under this latter wound, the skull was shattered over an area the size of a human hand. Dr Ellis also stated that Frances Levin's left wrist had been fractured and that the cause of death had been shock and haemorrhage due to the head wounds.

In his summing up for the defence, Mr Wingate Saul made an excellent speech. In his so-called confession, Burtoft had said the woman rose as he entered the room, but she had been found lying in the same position as when she had last been seen by the maid. Were the jury seriously to believe that a stranger entered the room, Mrs Levin rose and then sat down again as he went out to fetch the weapon which he would use to batter her? Why had Mrs Levin not called out for help when she saw a stranger? If Burtoft was the man seen calling at the doctor's house next door, what did he do in the half hour or so before he entered Mrs Levin's house and why had the police analyst found no blood on Burtoft's clothing if he had been responsible for the bloody battering which killed Mrs Levin?

The jury retired and after an hour, returned to court to ask for clarification of one part of the evidence. The judge said he was unable to recall the doctor who had given evidence but, reading from his statement, said that there had apparently been no blood found on the front of the settee.

The jury retired for a second time and after a further hour, filed back into court to announce that Burtoft was guilty as charged. Mr Justice Atkinson donned the black cap and pronounced his first death sentence, and Burtoft was taken to the cells below.

On November 21st, Burtoft's solicitor announced that an application to appeal against the death sentence had been lodged. That appeal was heard on December 4th, before the Lord Chief Justice, Lord Hewart, and Justices Avory and Lawrence. The grounds were that the confession was wrongly admitted in evidence as the onus was on the prosecution to prove that this was a voluntary and free confession and not obtained under duress. Lord Hewart answered this by saying that it was for the judge at the trial to decide whether the document was admissible and he had ruled that it was. The appeal was dismissed.

Still determined to save his client, Mr Hotchen wrote to the Home Secretary, Sir John Gilmour, but on December 16th he received a reply stating that no grounds had been found for advising His Majesty to interfere with the due course of the law.

At 9.00am on Tuesday, December 19th, 1933, five months after the death of Frances Levin, William Burtoft was hanged at Manchester as a crowd of 100 people waited outside in the heavy fog which lay over the city. At the inquest afterwards, the coroner, Mr R. Stuart Rodgers, made a rambling speech about the morbid curiosity of people who wanted to know all the details of the condemned man's last hours. He launched into a strange diatribe about murder not being the 'sin of sins' adding, "Adultery is a sin against the soul, hypocrisy is our national sin and apostasy, which is treason against heaven, is the unforgivable sin."

There was no hard evidence to link William Burtoft to the murder for which he paid with his life, apart from his own confession. It has to be for those who study the case to decide whether that confession was true or whether four police officers worked together to exhort a signature from an innocent man.

In addition, a number of unsettling questions need to be answered. If Freda Phillips saw a man leaving the house, why did she not see him arrive? Why did Freda not check for herself what had taken place inside that front room before calling for help? Why were no screams heard from Frances Levin? The bones in one of her hands were broken showing that she had tried to defend herself, so why did she apparently not scream also? Why did Samuel Woodcock not run to his own employer, a doctor, for medical assistance instead of going to a telephone box down the road; and why did Louis Davis, the dead woman's brother, choose that day of all days to spend a couple of hours sitting in a park?

CHAPTER TWENTY-ONE

———— ❧◉❧ ————

A SALFORD TRIANGLE

———— ❧◉❧ ————

AMELIA Nuttall had known John Harris Bridge for most of her young life, the two having grown up together. By 1935 they had been walking out with each her for seven years and had been officially engaged since 1932, when Bridge had given her a ring. The wedding date had now been set – the ceremony was due to take place on June 8th, 1935 – but then, in February of that year, Bridge's attitude towards his fiancée changed and his behaviour cooled appreciably.

Amelia lived with her father, John Andrew Nuttall, at 52 Symons Street, Broughton, Salford. Mr Nuttall, too, had noticed a marked change in Bridge's attitude towards Amelia and, more distressing for him, he had seen the affect that this had upon his daughter. Amelia was distressed and that distress became all the more acute when she and her father discovered that the cause of Bridge's sudden disinterest was perhaps the oldest reason in history: John Bridge had found himself attracted towards another girl, Eileen Earl, who worked with Bridge at a jeweller's company, Greene & Calvert Ltd.

On April 12th, 1935, Bridge took Amelia to the pictures but the evening was not a pleasant one. When she returned home to Symons Street, a somewhat tearful and saddened Amelia reported to her father that throughout the entire time they had spent together, Bridge had never even so much as smiled at her. On hearing this, John Nuttall decided to tackle Bridge and went around to his house. He confronted the man he thought was to be his son-in-law and told him, "After you have been courting the girl for seven or eight years, you should know whether you want the girl or not." Bridge made no reply to this admonishment.

Two days after this, on Sunday, April 14th, John Nuttall announced to Amelia that he was going to visit his son's house. It was 6.00pm when he left Symons Street and at that time, Amelia was left alone in the house. She was wearing her overall and went upstairs to her room as her father closed the door behind him.

John Nuttall spent more than four hours away from home and it was not until 10.15pm that he returned to number 52. To his great surprise, the house was entirely in darkness and when he called out for Amelia, there was no reply. Going into the kitchen, John Nuttall struck a match so that he could light the gas, but as he did, he saw to his horror that his daughter was lying on her stomach in a large pool of blood. He ran for help.

Police Constable Henry James Evans was on duty at Great Cheetham Street police station when he received information that there had been an incident at a house in Symons Street. By the time he arrived, it was 11.00pm and Dr Kathleen O'Donnell was already there. She told Constable Evans that Amelia Nuttall was dead and Evans, turning the body over, saw that there was a large wound in the neck. Looking around the kitchen, Constable Evans noticed that the bottom sash of the scullery window had been pushed open as far as it would go. The door between the kitchen and the scullery was wide open, as was the door which led out into the yard, although the yard gate itself was securely bolted. All the kitchen drawers had been thrown open but there was no sign of a forced entry, indicating that whoever was responsible for killing Amelia had most probably been known to her and been admitted to the house by her. After speaking to Mr Nuttall, Constable Evans knew that he had to trace John Bridge as soon as possible.

Constable Evans was told that Bridge had been seen in Buile Street but when he visited that address, there was no sign of him. However, on his way back to Symons Street, Evans, who was with Mr Nuttall, came across Bridge who was in the company of a young woman. Seeing John Nuttall, Bridge walked over to him as if to engage him in conversation, whereupon Constable Evans demanded to know who he was. "I am Millie's fiancé," replied Bridge, and Evans then asked him when he had last seen her. Bridge thought for a second or two before replying, "About a quarter to eight." This was, of course, during the time that Amelia had been alone in the house, and quite probably around the time she was killed, and Bridge was told that he must accompany the officer back to 52 Symons Street.

By the time Constable Evans escorted Bridge back into the house at Symons Street, Detective Constable Harold Derbyshire had arrived and was standing at the parlour door. Soon afterwards, Superintendent Frederick Stear arrived and took charge of the investigation.

By coincidence, the officer in charge of the case knew the chief suspect very well. Superintendent Stear had known Bridge's family ever since John Bridge was a small boy and knew them as a very respectable family. Stear, though, had not seen Bridge for several years and at first was not aware of who he was speaking to when he arrived at the house. He asked Bridge to identify himself and Bridge replied, "I'm her fiancé. We should have been married in June." Bridge then asked to see Amelia and was told that he would be able to do so later. Soon afterwards, Inspector Barnfield arrived at Symons Street and on Superintendent Stear's suggestion escorted Bridge, John Nuttall and Amelia's brother-in-law, who had turned up at the murder house, to the police station where they could all make statements.

John Bridge made his first statement to the police in the early hours of April 15th. He said that he was 25 years old, single and lived at 11 Beaumont Street, Broughton. He went on to say that he was employed as a warehouseman and driver by Greene & Calvert of 55 Marshall Street, off Rochdale Road. Bridge admitted that he and Amelia had been keeping company for some time and had been engaged for more than two years. On the night in question he had arranged to see her at 6.30pm at her home, but did not arrive until 7.05pm.

Amelia opened the door and at the time was wearing a green overall and slippers. She greeted him with, "You're late again," to which he had replied, "It's not my fault this time." Amelia was not to be mollified, however, and continued, "You were late last week," Trying to avoid an argument, Bridge had responded with, "Now don't start rowing or I am going," but Amelia had simply retorted, "All right, go."

Thinking that things might be better if he asked her to come out with him, Bridge asked her to get ready and go with him. She said she was not interested and walked to the kitchen door. Seeing that he was not getting anywhere, Bridge shrugged his shoulders and said, "Okay then, I'm off. Are you coming or not?" When Amelia had again refused to budge, he had given her a cheery goodbye and left the house. As he pulled the front door closed behind him, Amelia was sitting in a chair and the time then was around 7.30pm.

Continuing his story, Bridge said that after leaving Amelia he walked home but as there was no one else in, he left after 20 minutes and went to the Griffin Hotel. From there he caught a bus to Pendleton and after getting off at the church, walked to Swinton Park Road where he met the other woman in his life, Eileen Earl. The two strolled to Eileen's house at Radcliffe Park Crescent. After seeing her safely home, Bridge caught a bus back to Pendleton Church and from there got a second bus, this time to Bury New Road from where he walked home. By then it was 10.45pm and his father and sister were both at home. By now, of course, the police had been to Bridge's house and told the family that something had happened to Amelia. Bridge's sister, Olive, told him that he had better come with her to Millie's house and they were walking there when they had seen Constable Evans with John Nuttall.

As a matter of routine, Bridge was asked to remove his clothing so that it could be scientifically examined. Those clothes were handed over to Sergeant John Howarth who had custody of Bridge, along with Detective Sergeant Smith. By now it was 7.30am on April 15th and Bridge was taken from the superintendent's office to the refreshment room. It was there, at around 8.00am that Bridge turned to Sergeant Howarth and said, "I've told the inspector lies. I did it with the bread knife. You'll find it in the knife box." Inspector Barnfield was immediately summoned and in due course, Bridge was returned to the office where he made a second statement.

This second version of events began, "Millie and me had trouble a few weeks ago when I told her of the other girl, Eileen. I could not make my mind up what to do." He continued, "I have been out with Eileen three times this week and I intended to finish it last night with Millie. I had mentioned it to her one night through the week.

"I went round last night to finish it. When I went in she started with, 'You're late again.' I said, 'Don't start rowing, we may as well finish it now without any bother.'

"She got hysterical and her nerves went. I got hold of her to quieten her. I slapped her. I pushed her down in the chair and turned to get my coat. She came flying at me with the poker. We struggled. I grabbed it off her and before I knew what I had done, I'd hit her with it. She fell down in the hearth. I lost my head. I hit her again with the poker.

"The first time I didn't know what I was doing. It came all of a sudden. The second time I was frightened. She was still speaking and I didn't know what to do. Then I went and got the knife and cut her throat when she was on the little chair. I went and washed the knife and wiped it on some newspaper. I was frightened and I went upstairs.

"I opened the drawers in her bedroom and scattered the things. I did the same downstairs. I opened the scullery window and then went out through the front door. I then did exactly as I said in that first statement. I must have been daft. I had no idea of finishing it like that. It was when she got hysterical that I lost my head."

At 8.56am, John Bridge was charged with murder. He had no comment to make in answer to the charge but Inspector Barnfield noticed that Bridge had become emotional towards the end of making that second statement, and the right side of his face had begun to twitch uncontrollably.

Later that same day, April 15th, Bridge appeared before the stipendiary magistrate, Mr Percy Macbeth, at the Salford police court. Superintendent Stear gave details of the arrest and Bridge was then remanded in custody until April 17th. By that date, the case for the prosecution had been taken over by Mr E.G. Robey and Bridge had obtained legal representation in the form of Mr T.H. Hinchcliffe. Matters were again adjourned, this time until April 23rd. On that date, all the evidence was heard and Bridge was sent for trial.

That trial took place at Manchester, before Mr Justice Hilbery on May 3rd, 1935. Bridge was defended by Mr E.G. Hemmerde and Mr Hinchcliffe while the case for the Crown was led by Mr Maxwell Fyfe, who was assisted by Mr Hartley Shawcross.

Eileen Earl, of 2 Radcliffe Park Crescent, Pendleton, testified that she had worked for Greene & Calvert for the past three years and that was where she had first met and become friendly with Bridge. They had started going out but she knew about Bridge's involvement with Amelia and thought the situation hopeless, so, in 1934, had started walking out with another man. This relationship had ended in February 1935 and almost immediately the friendship with Bridge had been rekindled. By the beginning of April, Bridge was already talking about breaking off his engagement to Amelia and on April 6th, had told Eileen that he had spoken to Amelia and that she had been very upset.

On the day that Amelia died, Bridge had spent some time with Eileen but left her at 5.00pm after arranging to meet her again at 8.30pm, saying that he would probably call at her house for her. Bridge did not turn up at the appointed time, so Eileen went outside and they met in the street soon afterwards. Bridge appeared to be cheerful and happy and they went for a walk, during which Bridge told her he had been to see Millie and she was fine and had been reading a book when he left her. He and Eileen stayed together until some time between 10.30pm and 10.45pm, when Bridge left her outside her house.

Sergeant Howarth told the court about Bridge informing him that he had lied in his first statement and wished to speak to Inspector Barnfield. After Bridge had made his second statement, Sergeant Howarth returned to Symons Street and searched through the knife drawer in the kitchen. There he found a large bread knife which appeared to be clean, but since Bridge had claimed that this was the weapon he had used to cut Amelia's throat, it was taken back to the police station and later, along with Bridges clothing, had been taken down to London where, on April 16th, they were handed over to Dr Lynch, a Home Office analyst.

Superintendent Stear reported that after Bridge had been taken to the police station, he returned to the house at Symons Street with Superintendent Howard. They made a thorough search of the premises and found signs that someone had turned out all the drawers in the bedrooms and the kitchen. There was no sign of a forced entry having been made, nor were there any signs of a struggle, meaning that the attack upon Amelia must have been a sudden one. This testimony was confirmed by Superintendent Robert Howard who testified that back at the police station, he had spotted what appeared to be bloodstains on Bridge's clothing and asked him to explain them. Bridge had indicated one of his fingers, which was bandaged, and exclaimed, "It might have come from this." A subsequent examination, however, showed that the wound was an old one and had not bled recently and there was no blood on the bandage itself.

It was Superintendent Howard who asked Bridge to remove his clothing so that it could be examined. As Bridge undressed, Howard asked him how long he had been wearing the clothes and Bridge replied that he had had them on all day. Once the items had been removed, Superintendent Howard made a more careful examination and saw what appeared to be small spots of blood on the right shirt cuff, the left trouser leg and the front of the jacket.

Medical evidence was given by Mr Arnold Renshaw, a Bachelor of Surgery of St John Street, Manchester. He had visited the scene of the crime at 3.30am on April 15th. Amelia's body had still not been moved and he turned the body over to see that there were wounds in the neck. Amelia's hair was heavily matted with blood so at this stage it was impossible to make an accurate examination of the head wounds. There were pools of blood underneath and around the body and spots on a number of locations including the walls, a fireside chair, the skirting board and on a white table cloth. Near the body lay a newspaper dated April 14th. This was also bloodstained and the pattern of staining was consistent with a knife having been wiped upon it.

At 9.30am that same day, Mr Renshaw carried out a post-mortem and determined there were two wounds on Amelia's scalp, both of which penetrated to the bone but had not caused a fracture of the skull. He testified that the scalp wounds had been inflicted before the throat wounds.

There were three distinct cuts on the front of the neck. The first was just below the larynx and went back to the trachea, which was severed. The second wound was slightly less than an inch to the right of the first and was quite superficial, and the third was one inch above the sternum. While it was possible that the second and third wound might have been self inflicted, the first one detailed certainly was not and considerable force must have been used to inflict it. In Mr Renshaw's opinion, the blows to the scalp would have dazed Amelia so that she was unable to put up any degree of a struggle while the throat wounds were inflicted.

Dr Gerald Roche Lynch was the senior official analyst to the Home Office and the director of the department of chemical pathology at St Mary's Hospital in London. He had examined the articles of clothing given to him by the police. Human blood had been found on the clothes and shoes and while some stains were too small to type, others were of the same group as Amelia's, the same group as that held by 40 per cent of the population. Further, Dr Lynch was able to say that the positioning of the stains on the various items was such that they could not have come from a cut finger on Bridge's right hand.

The final medical witness was Dr Howard Shannon, the medical officer of Strangeways prison, who testified that he had interviewed the prisoner a number of times and found no sign of any mental problems. This, of course, closed off any hope that Bridge might be able to claim that he was or had been insane and as such, the jury took just 50 minutes to decide that he was guilty as charged.

The original execution date was set for May 21st, but this was postponed when Bridge applied to appeal against his sentence on May 10th. In the event, nothing came of this, for after discussions with his defence team Bridge withdrew his appeal, preferring to rely on an application for a reprieve. A new execution date was set.

There were other attempts to save Bridge's life. Mrs Van Der Elst, the well-known anti-capital punishment campaigner, travelled up to Manchester to help with the attempts to gain a reprieve for the condemned man. A petition was organised and in due course forwarded to the Home Secretary, Sir John Gilmour. Mr Hinchcliffe, Bridge's barrister, said that he hoped to have a personal interview with the Home Secretary but in the event, none of these avenues proved to be successful.

By 8.30am on Thursday, May 30th, 1935, a large crowd had gathered in Southall Street, outside Strangeways prison. Ten minutes later, Mrs Van Der Elst appeared in her car and attempted to drive through the police barrier, scattering the crowd in the process and causing one woman to faint in front of her car. None of this delayed the execution by one minute and at 9.00am John Harris Bridge was hanged.

Still there was further drama to come. After the notice of execution had been posted on the prison gates, Mrs Van Der Elst became embroiled in an argument with two women, during which she shouted, "Look at the creatures – talk about the French Revolution!" She had to be escorted back to her car by a number of police officers as one of the women cried, "If it was your girl, the boot would be on the other foot."

Olive Bridge, the hanged man's sister, later attended the inquest on her brother and there heard one of the jurors express the opinion that there would certainly be many more murders if there was no death penalty. Another, referring to the antics of Mrs Van Der Elst and her fellow campaigners, stated that there should be some way of preventing such demonstrations. To all these discussions, of course, John Harris Bridge was entirely oblivious.

CHAPTER TWENTY-TWO

A LITTLE FAMILY TROUBLE

CLIFFORD Holmes, a driver in the Royal Engineers and based at the Gibraltar Barracks in Aldershot, had been a married man for some years but had now managed to convince himself that his wife, 23-year-old Irene Holmes, was being unfaithful. In fact, there was no truth in those suspicions but Holmes was adamant.

It was right at the beginning of 1940 that Holmes first wrote to his wife back at the marital home and accused her of committing adultery. The language he used was rather crude and threatening and so disturbed was Irene that she took the letter to Mr Eugene Patrick Lee, a probation officer, who said he would draft a reply to Holmes on her behalf. Alas, that letter, dated January 3rd, 1940, did nothing to mollify Clifford Holmes.

On January 8th, Irene Holmes again visited Mr Lee and just eight days later, on January 16th, she posted him a further letter which Holmes had sent to her. This also contained foul language and threats and was followed by another such letter two days later. This, too, was forwarded to Mr Lee at his office. For some months, the matter continued in much the same vein until finally, in a last attempt to sort out their differences, Irene and Clifford, who had obtained a few days leave, together paid a visit to Mr Lee who pointed out to Holmes that there was no foundation to his suspicions. His letters were full of unnecessary obscenities, said Mr Lee, and in future Clifford should write in a more friendly manner. There was, after all, nothing to his fears. Clifford Holmes reassured Mr Lee that he and Irene had patched things up and everything was now fine between them.

Unfortunately this respite in the troubles that Clifford and Irene Holmes were suffering was only temporary. On August 26th, Irene was back at Mr Lee's office and showed him another letter which she had received from her husband who had by now returned to Aldershot. This letter was as bad as any of the others and Irene told Mr Lee that enough was enough and she wanted a separation order. The wheels of the legal system were put into motion the same day and on September 10th, Irene made her application before the magistrates when the matter was adjourned until October 8th, so that her husband could be given the opportunity to respond. Meanwhile, on September 9th, Irene had moved into a furnished room at 450 Stockport Road, Longsight, at a rent of 10s a week.

The court wrote to Clifford Holmes as soon as the September hearing had taken place and Holmes then went to see his commanding officer, Major Basil Charlton Deacon, to inform him that there was trouble at home. In due course, Major Deacon granted Holmes compassionate leave so that he could return to Manchester to sort things out. So it was that on October 5th, 1940, Clifford Holmes again travelled north from Hampshire to Longsight.

Back in Manchester, Holmes sought his own legal representation and by arrangement, a meeting took place between Holmes and his wife at Mr Eugene Lee's office. Here Holmes admitted that he knew there was no truth in his suspicions of his wife having committed adultery but even this contrition was itself temporary, for later that day, when the adjourned court hearing took place, Holmes was again very defiant.

Frank Ralph Johnson, the solicitor representing Irene Holmes, outlined the details of the application which had been made on the grounds of Holmes' persistent cruelty. The order was duly granted but later, outside the courtroom, Holmes turned to Irene and said, "You won't get a penny out of me. I'll do you in first." This comment was overheard by Mr Johnson who told Holmes to leave Irene alone and 'not be so silly'.

Clifford Holmes was not a man to be to be controlled by a simple court order, however, and the very next day, October 9th, he was again causing trouble for his wife. Irene's new home was a furnished room in a large house owned by Elizabeth Burlinson. There were many other lodgers there and one, Mary Jane Butler, occupied the room next to Irene's. At 11.30am on October 9th, Mary Jane answered a knock at the front door and was greeted by a soldier in uniform who said he knew Irene Holmes, had left a paper in her room and needed it. Mary Butler saw the man enter Irene's room and a few minutes later, heard someone, presumably this visitor, running downstairs.

At 8.20pm the same evening, the man was back but now he was wearing civilian clothing. Without explanation, the man pushed past Mary Butler and again went up to Irene's room. Shortly after the man had entered the room next door to hers, Mary heard what sounded like a scuffle and five minutes later, Irene came into Mary's room sporting a bruise on her face. The visitor, Irene explained, was her estranged husband, Clifford Holmes.

The next morning, Irene was back at Mr Lee's office. By now the bruise had developed into a severe black eye and Irene complained that despite the separation order, her husband had been to her flat to see her and had assaulted her. Mr Lee advised her that further court action might be necessary in order to put a stop to this behaviour once and for all.

Mary Wilson lived at the Plymouth Hotel on Plymouth Grove, Chorlton-upon-Medlock, and worked behind the bar there. It was around noon on Thursday, October 10th, when Clifford Holmes entered and ordered a glass of mild. In order to make polite conversation, Mary asked Holmes how he was. Holmes replied, "Bloody awful." Thinking that he might be dissatisfied with his life in the forces, Mary remarked, "I thought the Army was a good life." Holmes replied, "It is. The Army's all right. It's with the missus everything's wrong." Mary Wilson asked Holmes what he meant and Holmes continued, "You come home on leave to an empty house and find the kids gone and the missus." He went on to complain that his wife was now living somewhere else and he had been forced to trace her. He ended by saying that part of the trouble was carrying around his full kit everywhere he went and asked Mary if he could leave it behind the bar. Mary Wilson said that would be all right but he couldn't leave his rifle there. Cryptically, Holmes replied, "That's what I want to get rid of. I might use it."

Holmes left the bar soon afterwards but was back again at 6.30pm when he had two more pints of mild. He finally left at 7.30pm, telling Mary Wilson that he was going to his mother's house at Clayton. In fact, he walked around to another public house, the Swan Inn on Everton Road, where the landlord, John Stanley, served him with two more pints, and the landlord's wife serving him with a third. Holmes stayed in the Swan for a full hour, during which time he told John Stanley that he had just been discharged from a military hospital after suffering a nervous disorder. Holmes then finished his third pint from the Swan and at around 8.30pm walked out of the pub.

It was not long after 8.30pm that Florence Farrington, who lived with her husband, Ernest, at 450 Stockport Road, heard a knock on her front door. She answered it to be confronted by Clifford Holmes carrying a rifle. Without uttering a word, he pushed Florence out of the way and dashed upstairs to his wife's room. Florence, not one to accept such appalling manners, ran after Holmes and demanded, "What's the big idea, passing me like that?" Without turning around, Holmes shouted back, "Mind your own business."

Florence Farrington saw Holmes stop outside his wife's door and try the handle. The door was locked and Holmes called out, "Will you open the door Irene?"

Florence heard Irene refuse, whereupon Holmes raised his rifle and fired a shot at the lock. Florence ran into one of the other rooms, the one occupied by Mary Jane Butler, and from there, these two women heard the sounds of a scuffle, running footsteps and five more shots fired. Then all fell silent and Florence and Mary Butler ventured downstairs to the kitchen where they found Clifford Holmes kneeling by a couch. On that couch lay the body of Irene Holmes and her husband was crying over her.

By 9.05pm, Constable Henry Fletcher had arrived and Holmes, his mother and Dr Lenten were present in the room where Irene lay. Dr Lenten informed Constable Fletcher that Irene was dead and as he moved to take Holmes in to custody, Fletcher heard him mutter, "I've shot hundreds in France and Palestine but had to miss myself." Holmes was subsequently handed over to Sergeant Samuel Sargeant and Detective Inspector Robert Lennox when they arrived. He was then taken to the police station and charged with the murder of his wife.

Clifford Holmes made his first appearance at the Manchester City police court on October 11th. Two further appearances followed, on October 25th and November 1st, when he was sent for trial. The case finally opened on December 16th, 1940, before Mr Justice Stable. The proceedings lasted two days, during which Holmes was defended by Mr John Caterall Jolly and Mr Percy Butlin while the case for the Crown was led by Mr Neville J. Laski, assisted by Mr T.H. Hinchcliffe.

Mary Jane Butler told the court of Holmes' visit to Stockport Road on October 9th. She then went on to talk of the day that Irene had died. Mary said she had been in her room at around 8.45pm when she heard a loud knock on the door of Irene's room. She heard a man's voice demand that Irene open the door and when she refused, he shouted, "I'll blow the lock off." A shot had been fired almost immediately and Florence Farrington had rushed into her room. After the shooting had stopped, they went downstairs together to see Irene lying on a couch and a man in uniform crying over her. That man was the one who had visited Irene the day before, Clifford Holmes.

Gladys May Burrows was another resident of 450 Stockport Road and at about 8.40pm on October 10th, she was in her room on the second floor when she heard two shots fired, one after the other. Going downstairs to see what was happening, Gladys saw that Irene's door was open and her two children were standing outside, screaming. At first, Gladys thought that there might be an air-raid taking place so she took the children downstairs into the cellar for safety, but on the way she heard two more shots. Later she saw Irene huddled up and crying in a passageway that led to the kitchen. Holmes was bending over her and seeing that this was something more than a domestic dispute, Gladys put the children in Florence Farrington's room and went out of the house to fetch help.

Robert Vaughan lived next door, at 452 Stockport Road and he, too, heard shots fired although at first he was unable to tell from where they originated. Opening his front door, Mr Vaughan saw Gladys Burrows leaving the house next door and she told him that Clifford Holmes was inside, shooting at his wife. Both Robert Vaughan and Gladys Burrows knew the family and also knew that Holmes' mother, Mrs Snowball, lived just a short distance away.

Number 452 was also divided up into rooms for rent and another occupant of that house was Henry Herbert Fraser. Having heard shooting he, too, came out of his front door and spoke to Mr Vaughan and Mrs Burrows. All three then dashed around to 12 Plymouth Avenue, where Catherine Snowball lived, and they told her what was going on at 450 Stockport Road. Then they walked back to that address and entered the kitchen to find Clifford Holmes bending over the still form of his wife.

Holmes was crying bitterly and Fraser heard him remark, "I asked her to let me in and she wouldn't." Vaughan, meanwhile, was handed the rifle and put it into a corner of the room, well out of Holmes' way. They were still in the kitchen when Dr Lenten arrived and began attending to Irene.

Catherine Snowball testified that it was just before 9.00pm when Mr Fraser and the others arrived at her home. She returned with them to 450 Stockport Road and found her son kneeling near the settee, holding Irene in his arms. The rifle was resting against the settee and she told Mr Vaughan to remove it, which he did. Turning to her son, Mrs Snowball asked him what he had done and he replied, "Oh Ma, can you help her because I've shot her." Catherine asked him why he had done this terrible thing and he said, "I have been parted by the Law Court on the Tuesday before and I have waited all day at Ferranti's to make the quarrel up. She has left me and wouldn't see me at all today." Mrs Snowball added that until recently, Irene had worked at Ferranti and Clifford must have waited outside to see her, thinking she still did.

Continuing her evidence, Catherine Snowball said that she told Holmes that she thought Irene had fainted. This was an attempt to reassure him and calm the situation. It appeared to work, for Holmes laid Irene back on the settee. For the first time he noticed a wound close to Irene's heart and, to Catherine's surprise, began poking at this wound with his fingers. She asked him what he was doing and Holmes said, "I'm trying to get the bullet out that I have put there." Soon afterwards, he picked Irene up from the settee and cried out, "Oh Irene, speak to me. I love you so."

Having put Irene back on to the settee, Holmes then half raised her again and put his hand up her skirt. Catherine asked him what he was doing and Holmes replied, "I can love her. She's my own wife." This evidence, of course, indicated that Holmes was not behaving rationally immediately after the attack. Moments later, the doctor arrived and shortly after that, Constable Fletcher took Holmes into custody.

Major Deacon gave evidence about the issuing of ammunition. He pointed out that military regulations stated that a soldier going on leave must take his rifle and bayonet with him but was not issued with any ammunition. On October 2nd, Holmes had been issued with 50 rounds of ball ammunition for guard duty. Records showed that this had been handed back after his duty was completed. No further ammunition had been issued to Holmes and he should not have had any in his possession. For this reason, it was never explained where he had obtained the ammunition he had used to kill his wife.

Dr Jacob Lenten said that it was 9.10pm when he arrived at Stockport Road. Upon examining Irene Holmes, he found that she was already dead. There was a large wound over the region of her heart and her clothing was bloodstained and disarranged, her skirt being pulled up over her knees. As he completed his examination, Holmes had asked, "Is she dead?" Told that she was, Holmes went on to say, "It's a pity I hadn't done myself in. I have one in myself." Asking what he meant, Dr Lenten was shown a wound in Holmes' left arm. It was a superficial flesh wound and as the doctor dressed the arm, Holmes made some remark about killing hundreds of people in France and Palestine. He added that he had shot Irene because she had been unfaithful to him. Finally, Dr Lenten testified that although Holmes had been drinking, he was not drunk.

Dr Reginald Ellis had performed the post-mortem on Irene and he described a bullet wound which had entered the right upper arm, passed through the right breast and emerged at the outer side of the left breast. Another wound on the left wrist had shattered the bones there and in addition there were three stab wounds about the left elbow, and two in the abdomen. One of these had penetrated the liver and in addition, a rib, broken by the passage of a bullet, had perforated the heart. The stab wounds could have been caused by a bayonet found at the scene and the actual cause of death was shock and haemorrhage from the multiple wounds.

Dr Thomas Henry Blench was a police surgeon and he had examined various items including Irene's clothing. All her garments were bloodstained but the upper garments were very heavily stained. In addition, there were cuts in some of the garment consistent with the passage of a bayonet. Another scientific witness was Frank Crawford, a firearms expert who had examined a .303 Enfield pattern 14 service rifle and four spent cartridges. He stated that the rifle had been recently fired and the cartridges had come from it. A live cartridge had also been found at the scene and this was of the same type and markings as the four spent ones.

For the police, Sergeant Samuel Sargeant testified to hearing Holmes say at one point, "I shot her. I only had five. I used the lot. The one I saved for myself didn't work." Later, after Irene's body had been removed, he made a search of the room and found a bloodstained bayonet underneath the settee.

Detective Inspector Robert Lennox told of a statement Holmes had made which read, "I came here and found my wife upstairs. She refused to let me in and I shot once at the door lock. I then forced it open and fired at her but I must have missed. She then ran downstairs and I found her lying behind the back door so I put one in her there. I carried her in the kitchen and put her on the couch and stuck the bayonet in her. I tried to shoot myself but it didn't work." Inspector Lennox told of a search of the premises and of finding bullet holes in the kitchen ceiling, the skirting board upstairs and the floor of Irene's room. He also found a pool of blood behind a door which led to the yard. There were a number of pieces of a glass from a lady's wrist watch in this pool.

The only hope for Holmes was to show that he was unaware of what he was doing when he shot his wife. For the defence, Major Purser of the Royal Army Medical Corps, said that he had examined the prisoner in August and believed that he was suffering from the early stages of schizophrenia and, this being the case, did not appreciate what he was doing when he killed Irene.

Dr Walter Henry Grace was a consulting medical officer at the County Mental Hospital at Chester and he believed that Holmes was suffering from sexual obsessions and these had caused a state of anxiety and neurosis. He thought it was reasonable to assume that Holmes did not know that his actions were wrong. This testimony, though, was largely negated by that of Dr M.R.H. Williams of Strangeways prison who had had five interviews with Holmes and stated that there were no indications of any mental disease and no evidence of sexual depravity.

With so many witnesses, and his own statements at the time, the jury found no difficulty in adjudging Holmes to be guilty as charged and he was sentenced to death. On December 27th, it was announced that an appeal had been lodged and the execution, originally fixed for January 7th, was postponed. That appeal was dismissed on January 27th and just over two weeks later, on Tuesday, February 11th, 1941, 24-year-old Clifford Holmes, who had taken part in the Dunkirk evacuations, was hanged at Manchester.

CHAPTER TWENTY-THREE

DEATH AT THE DOCKS

BURNETT Estill was the third officer on board the *Pacific Shipper*, which docked at Salford on April 1st, 1944. One week later, at some time between 9.00pm and 9.30pm on Saturday, April 8th, Estill went to the bridge to switch off a light which had been left burning. On his way, Estill passed the second radio officer's room and noticed a second light left on there. As he clicked the switch to the off position, Estill noticed a putrid smell and assumed there was some kind of problem with the toilets in that area.

At 11.00pm that same night, Estill went to use the toilet on the deck below. The room he used was directly below the radio officer's cabin. As he entered the toilet, Estill noticed what appeared to be a patch of blood on the floor and directly above it, on the ceiling, a thin pencil of the same crimson liquid. There was something seriously wrong in the radio officer's quarters.

Collecting the keys from the chief officer, Estill entered the radio room a few minutes after 11.00pm. The smell was even more foul and in the radio officer's cabin, Estill recoiled at the sight which met his eyes – the battered and badly decomposed body of the chief radio officer, a 48-year-old Canadian named James William Percey, a native of Montreal. Estill rushed to report his grim discovery to Captain Ledsome, who told him to contact the police.

The first difficulty was deciding precisely when James Percey had met his death. Dr Stanley Hodgson, a police surgeon, arrived on board the ship at 1.50am on April 9th. Going into the room where Percey's body lay, Dr Hodgson noticed that all the portholes of the cabin were closed and the heating was full on. The cabin was still stiflingly hot, even though the doors had now been opened, so it must have been even hotter during the time the body had lain undiscovered. Percey had obviously been battered, but so decomposed was the body that his face was almost black, and his flesh had a dark, bloated appearance. It seemed reasonable to assume, at this early stage, that he had been dead for at least a couple of days, perhaps longer.

This timing also fitted in with the last sightings of Percey. Frank Evans had been supervising the unloading of the *Pacific Shipper* between April 3rd and April 8th. On April 6th, Evans had been on board the ship from 2.00pm and at some time between 3.30pm and 4.00pm he saw Percey walking up the staircase which led from the saloon to the officers' quarters. There was a man with him, who Evans did not know. Further, Evans was able to say that this man had been wearing the uniform of a chief steward of the Merchant Navy.

Stanley Stewart Wheeler was the assistant steward on the *Pacific Shipper*. He, too, had seen Percey come on board at around 3.30pm on April 6th. In fact, Percey spoke to Wheeler and asked for the return of the keys to the radio room, having handed these to Wheeler some time earlier when he had seen him in town. Wheeler handed the keys back to Percey, who then left his cabin, but a few minutes later, a man knocked on the door. He was wearing the uniform of a chief steward and he greeted Wheeler with, "Hello Chief."

Wheeler asked what he wanted and the man said he was looking for 'Sparks'. Knowing that this meant the radio officer, James Percey, Wheeler directed the steward to the cabin next door. A few minutes after that, both Percey and the steward reappeared in Wheeler's cabin and Percey said he wanted some beer. Six bottles were handed over and Percey invited Wheeler to come to his cabin so that he could have a drink. Wheeler said he would call in later, but when he finally did, at 4.45pm, the door to Percey's cabin was locked and there was no reply to Wheeler's knocking.

The inference was that Percey had been killed, probably by his visitor, some time between 3.30pm and 4.45pm on Thursday, April 6th. As for a motive for this terrible crime, the police did not have to look very far because James Percey had recently been in possession of a good deal of money and all that cash was now missing.

The war with the Axis powers was, of course, still raging and early in 1944 James Percey had been on a ship which had been torpedoed. While he survived that experience physically uninjured, he lost some personal effects and there was a system in operation whereby those who had suffered such losses would be reimbursed. On April 3rd, Frank Walker, a cashier at the Mercantile Marine Office in Liverpool, had paid out a number of seamen including Percey. The signature in the book showed that Percey had received a total of £66 13s 4d. Further, Mr Walker said that he had paid Percey from a batch of new banknotes. This was something he did as a matter of course. All large amounts were paid out in new notes when they were available so that the serial numbers would act as an extra check that the recipient had not been paid too much or too little.

Frank Walker also told the police that the new notes he had used were taken from the Castle Street, Liverpool office of the Bank of England. On April 1st, Mr Walker had handed a cheque for £520 to Leonard Rawley who had cashed it and handed the money back to him. The odd £20 he received in silver but the £500 was all in new banknotes. Officers visited the Bank of England in Liverpool and there spoke to Basil Henry Oxenbould, the teller who had served Mr Rawley. He confirmed that the £500 had been paid in new notes and that their serial numbers ran from A88E 514001 to A88E 514500. Somewhere within that bundle were the notes James Percey had received.

In fact, when his visitor had been on the ship with him on April 6th, James Percey had in his possession more than the money for his personal effects. In addition, he had also been entitled to some back pay and on the same day that he drew over £66 from Frank Walker, Percey had also visited the Marconi Marine Company offices in Liverpool. There Harry Jordan Bregazzi had paid Percey £21 11s 10d as his salary up to and including March 31st. This meant that on April 3rd, James Percey had left Liverpool with more than £88 in his pockets.

The police investigation was extremely thorough. Joseph Wallace Bywell was another sailor who was due money from the office in Liverpool, for loss of effects. He had drawn £90 on April 1st, after the cheque had been cashed at the Bank of England. When Bywell was interviewed, the police found that he still had 32 new £1 notes in his possession and the last one was numbered A88E 514199. This, of course, did nothing to help trace the killer of James Percey, but it did narrow down the serial numbers for which the police were looking. Since Percey had been paid after Bywell, the notes he had held must have been numbered after 514199.

By April 9th, the police knew the name of the man they were looking for. Mary Gibbons, who lived at 5 Harold Street, Salford, had known the dead man quite well. On April 4th, she met Percey in the Ship Hotel on Eccles New Road and he repaid her £1 which he had borrowed from her when his ship first docked. Later that night, at around 10.05pm, she had seen Percey again, this time outside the Trafford Hotel. Percey had taken her to a cafe and bought her supper before they went back to her lodgings where they stayed the night together.

The next day, April 5th, Percey and Mary Gibbons went first to the Ship Hotel and then back to the Trafford. At 3.00pm they had something to eat at another cafe before again returning to Harold Street. At 7.00pm they returned to the Ship Hotel and on the way, Percey met Stanley Wheeler, the assistant steward, and handed him some keys. By 9.50pm, Mary and Percey were enjoying a last drink in the Ship Hotel and from there returned to Harold Street, where Percey again spent the night.

A further visit to the public houses followed on April 6th but eventually Percey said he had run out of money and would have to go back to his ship to get some more. He left Mary at 2.00pm, by which time he was already quite drunk, but arranged to meet her in a cafe at 3.00pm. Percey had not kept that appointment. Another witness, Gertrude Tingle, had been in Trafford Road, standing near a bus stop when she had seen two men in naval uniforms walking towards the dock entrance in Aubrey Street. By now it was around 3.00pm and the description of one of the men fitted James Percey. The other man was someone whom Gertrude had known for many years, 26-year-old James Galbraith.

It was when the police made some routine checks on Galbraith, that they discovered some very interesting facts. Galbraith, who was indeed a chief steward and so entitled to wear the uniform, was registered with the employment pool of the Staffing Federation whose offices were in Salford and who found work for sea-going men on cargo ships and the like. A senior official at this pool, Charles Edward Lofthouse, told the police officers investigating the case that Galbraith had been a member of the pool for some years but had not drawn any pay since April 7th, and that had amounted to only £3 11s 8d. About a month earlier, Galbraith had called into the office and said he could not manage financially, asking Lofthouse if he might get him more work. Thus, it was well-known that Galbraith was short of money. This was confirmed by two other witnesses, Eric Houghton and Francis Wilson, both of whom worked for the Federation.

On April 4th, Galbraith had asked Houghton for a loan of £1 and been refused. The next day, at 10.30am, Galbraith did manage to borrow money, but this time he asked Wilson. Francis Wilson refused the request for £1 but handed over 10s. On April 7th, however, Galbraith was back in the office where he asked Houghton if Mr Wilson was in. Told that he was not, Galbraith handed Eric Houghton a 10s note and asked him to pass it on to Wilson.

Further inquiries revealed that from April 6th onwards, the day that Percey was probably killed, James Galbraith had been spending freely. A check was made at Galbraith's mother's house, 32 Cross Road, Stretford, but Margaret Galbraith could only report that her son had slept at her house on the night of April 5th. She had not seen him again until 11.00am on April 7th when he told her that he was going away for the week-end with some friends of his. Her son handed her £2. Mrs Galbraith told police that these had not been new notes.

James Galbraith had told his mother that he intended going away and this he had done. By the time he returned to Salford, on April 11th, details of the police search for him had been published in the newspapers and Galbraith knew he was a wanted man. It was no real surprise to him when, at 11.25pm that evening, Detective Inspector Robert Charles Trevor Settle called at 32 Cross Road and told Galbraith that he would be taken to the Town Hall for questioning. In the car on the way to the police station, Inspector Settle told Galbraith that he was making inquiries into the death of James William Percey, to which Galbraith replied, "I don't know what it's got to do with me. I met him in the road – I showed him the way to 9 Dock, but I didn't go aboard." Galbraith paused for a few seconds before adding, "I'm the chief steward you've been looking for." After another pause, he went on to say, "I had a drink with him on the ship. It looks as though you've found my prints on the glass."

Once he arrived at the Town Hall, Galbraith made a voluntary statement in which he detailed his movements on April 6th. After having a drink in the Salisbury Hotel, he met Percey outside the pub, it then being some time before 3.00pm. Percey was the worse for drink and said he needed to get to 9 Dock where his ship was berthed. Galbraith took him along and to thank him, Percey invited him up to his cabin for a drink. They enjoyed a few bottles of beer and Galbraith shaved Percey before he left. He said that he was on board for about 90 minutes altogether, Percey was alive and well when he left and he had not taken any money.

Galbraith was held while further inquiries were made but at 1.45am on April 12th, he announced that he had been thinking things over and had decided to make another statement. After doing so, Galbraith fell asleep for some hours but when he awoke, he was charged with the murder of James Percey.

On April 14th, Galbraith appeared before the magistrates where he was represented by Mr F. Edwin Monks. A remand until April 18th was granted and on that date a further remand, this time until the 25th, was ordered. By April 25th, the case for the Director of Public Prosecutions had been taken over by Mr J.F. Claxton who pointed out that since there were 42 prosecution witnesses, the evidence would have to be heard over two days.

On the first of those days, it was revealed for the first time that when Percey had been found, he had less than 5s in his pockets. The weapon used to inflict the terrible head injuries from which he had died was an axe which had been found underneath a mattress in a connecting cabin. It was heavily bloodstained and also bore flecks of white paint. This had come from the cabin ceiling and showed that the axe had been raised high before crashing down a number of times on Percey's skull. When all the witnesses had been heard, Galbraith was duly sent for trial.

James Galbraith faced his trial on May 9th, 1944, at Manchester, before Mr Justice Hilbery. The case for the prosecution was led by Mr Neville J. Laski who was assisted by Mr F.J.V. Sandbach. Galbraith was defended by Mr Edward Wooll who was assisted by Mr Percy Butlin. The proceedings lasted until May 11th.

Further details of the discovery of Percey's body were given by John Samuel Ledsome, the acting captain of the *Pacific Shipper*. On April 7th, the day before Percey had been found, Captain Ledsome had spent the morning on the bridge. At some time between 9.00am and 9.30am he had inspected the doors of both the chief radio officer's room and the wireless room and found both to be locked. On the morning of April 8th, the ship was moved from 9 Dock to 8 Dock and that night, at around 11.30pm, Burnett Estill had come to him to report a grim find in the radio officer's quarters. Captain Ledsome had immediately gone to the cabin where he saw Percey's body on the floor. Later he inspected the lavatory and confirmed what Estill had said, that blood had oozed from the room above, which was Percey's cabin. At Captain Ledsome's order, Estill had contacted the police.

Further evidence of Percey's movements were given by Stanley Wheeler, the assistant steward on the *Pacific Shipper*. He stated that the ship had docked at Salford on April 1st. On April 5th, some time after 7.00pm, he had seen Percey between the Ship Hotel and the Trafford Hotel. At the time, Percey was with a woman, Mary Gibbons, and had asked Wheeler for a loan of £1, saying that he did not want to return to the ship to get more cash. When he saw Percey later that night in the Trafford, Wheeler handed over the money and a further 10s. Stanley Wheeler then went on to detail his encounter with Percey and the chief steward on the afternoon of April 6th. Since that time, Wheeler had attended an identification parade at the police station and there he had picked out James Galbraith as the man he had seen with Percey.

Frank Evans, who had seen Percey coming on board on April 6th, had also attended that identification parade and he had also picked Galbraith as the man in the chief steward's uniform. All this had put Galbraith with Percey; now the prosecution had to show that Percey's money had, after this time, been in Galbraith's possession.

One of the most valuable witnesses was Alice Hyde. She had first met Galbraith on April 1st, at a friend's wedding, but they had got on famously with each other and had met up on April 2nd, 3rd and 4th. On that date, an arrangement was made to see each other again on Friday, April 7th.

Galbraith duly called on Alice at her lodgings on April 7th and took her to the Kingsway Hotel for a drink. He suddenly appeared to be flush with money and explained this by saying he had been playing pontoon the previous night and had won quite a bit. Easter was coming up and Galbraith asked her if she would like to go away for the weekend, suggesting first Scotland, then Wales, and then, for some reason, Liverpool. Alice had a small baby from an earlier relationship and said she would have to find someone to look after it. Galbraith returned home with her and they spent that night together.

On the morning of April 8th, Alice, the baby and Galbraith all went to her sister's house and to their delight she agreed to look after the child until the 11th. At 3.00pm

Alice and Galbraith left the house and he took her into Estelles dress shop where he bought her a new red dress for £7 0s 8d. From there they went into a shoe shop where Galbraith bought himself some black boots, which cost more than £1. The spending spree was still incomplete, though, for Galbraith then went into Beswick Stores on Stockport Road, Levenshulme, where he bought a white shirt and two collars. Soon afterwards he bought Alice some flowers and she estimated that the total cost of all these purchases had been close to £11.

That night, Alice and Galbraith enjoyed a drink in the Kingsway Hotel, during which he showed her a wad of new notes in his wallet. Alice estimated that these were a quarter of an inch thick and suggested that he should not be carrying that much cash with him. At her suggestion, Galbraith put some of the notes into a second wallet which he hid in her house.

At 11.30am on April 9th, they left Alice's house and went to the Central Station in Manchester from where they caught the train to Liverpool. There they booked into Hunt's Hotel, as Mr and Mrs Hyde, having been quoted a rate of £2 5s.

On April 10th, Galbraith treated Alice to lunch at the Midland Adelphi. The bill here was 15s and Galbraith paid the bill and then gave the account to Alice as a souvenir. They then went to New Brighton where they spent a good deal of time at the fairground, where again Galbraith spent freely. Later, they returned to the hotel in Liverpool.

At breakfast the next morning, April 11th, Galbraith read a copy of the *Daily Express* and seemed particularly interested in a column on page three headed, 'Murder in Ship's Cabin'. Galbraith told Alice that he recognised the name Percey and admitted that he had had a drink with him. Reading further, Galbraith remarked that the description of the man they were looking for fitted him. Alice suggested that the best thing for him to do was go to see the police at Liverpool but he told her that he would wait until he got back home to Salford.

Galbraith paid the hotel bill and later, on the way to the station, they entered Bunneys store from where Galbraith bought her a handbag for £5 12s 6d. Even Alice was surprised at how much he had spent and jokingly asked if the bank had now been broken. Galbraith replied that he had about £16 left.

Arriving back in Manchester, Alice and Galbraith took a taxi to her house to drop off the luggage. They then went to her sister's house, to pick up the baby and at 4.00pm returned to her home. Galbraith finally left some time before 7.00pm and as he walked out, Alice reminded him to see the police and Galbraith had called back, "All right, I will."

Galbraith had been spending freely and if it were possible to show that some of the notes he had given at the various shops were from that bundle paid out to Percey, then the next link in the chain of evidence would be complete. A large number of witnesses were now called, simply to prove this link.

Alice Hyde had reported that Galbraith had purchased a dress for her at Estelles. Helen Nally, who worked at that establishment, confirmed that a sale had been made at around 4.30pm on April 8th. The gentleman who paid, had given her seven new £1 notes and these, along with the other contents of the till, had later been handed over to the shop proprietor, Mrs Esther Rose.

Esther Rose, as the owner of the shop, could, of course, do what she liked with her own takings and she told the court that some of the money had been kept for her personal use, while other notes had been handed to her husband, Louis. Esther went on to say that when they had been interviewed by the police, she and Louis had checked the money in their possession. Esther had found that she held two new £1 notes numbered A88E 514354 and 514356, while Louis held A88E 514351, 514352 and 514359.

Esther Rose had not kept all the takings that night and now the prosecution called Mr Roy Kirkland, manager of the Levenshulme branch of the Midland Bank. The company account for Estelles was held at that branch and Mr Kirkland confirmed that there had been a credit of £283 to the account on April 11th. Some £230 of that had been in £1 notes and Mr Kirkland discovered that two £100 bundles had been formed from that cash, and marked with the company's name on the back. Those bundles were still untouched when the police visited his bank and Mr Kirkland checked them and found two new notes, A88E 514353 and 514355.

George Edward Lily had known Galbraith for six years and told the court that he had been in the Cattle Market Hotel at 8.00pm on April 6th, when Galbraith had come in wearing his uniform. Galbraith went up to Lily, shook him by the hand and handed him a £1 note to pay off a debt which Galbraith had owed him for four years. Later, Galbraith bought Lily a whisky and two beers. This evidence was of value for two reasons. First, it showed that on the night of April 6th, Galbraith had already started spending money quite freely, but it also showed that he was spending some of that money in the Cattle Market. When Edwin Warwick, the manager of that pub, was called, he was able to say that he had checked his till at the request of the police and had found a single new £1 note, numbered A88E 514375. Another pub landlord, George Henry Pochin, of the New Kingsbury Hotel on Worseley Road, Levenshulme, who testified that Galbraith had been drinking at his hostelry, had also checked his till and he had found the note numbered A88E 514361.

Some of the notes Galbraith had spent took much more tracing than those detailed thus far. One link started with Hellena Cheetham who lived at 73 St James' Street, Salford. On the night of April 6th, Hellena had been in the Clowes Hotel and there saw Galbraith, a man she knew quite well. Galbraith bought her a drink before leaving the

Clowes, but she saw him later that same night, in the Cattle Market Hotel. They had further drinks together before going on to the fairground at Cross Lane, after which Galbraith bought her a chicken supper. Galbraith spent the night with Hellena, giving her £2 the following morning. That £2 was made up of two new £1 notes.

On the evening of April 7th, Hellena handed the same two new notes to her landlady, Mary Baldacchino. When Mary gave evidence, she confirmed that Hellena had given her two new notes on April 7th. That night she had gone to the fairground where she spent one of them but the other she gave to her young daughter, Kathleen, to buy some lemonade at the local off licence.

That off licence was owned by James Aldcroft, and he recalled Kathleen Baldacchino buying lemonade and cakes. She paid with a new £1 note and although James paid some notes over to the brewery on April 11th, he also kept quite a few on the premises. On April 14th, the police had called and asked him to inspect the cash he held. Aldcroft did as he was asked and found a new £1 note numbered A88E 514358.

One of the final witnesses to Galbraith's spending was Samuel Beaumont who was the manager of a seamen's outfitters shop at 195 Trafford Road, Salford, not far from the docks. He testified that Galbraith and a friend of his named Brennan had come into his shop at 4.30pm on April 6th. Galbraith had purchased a bridge coat and a pair of shoulder epaulettes for a chief steward. The total cost was £7 12s 10d and Galbraith paid with eight new £1 notes. None of those notes could now be traced, but this evidence showed that by 4.30pm, Galbraith was in possession of Percey's money.

The post-mortem on Percey had been carried out by Dr Robert William Wyse. He told the court that the features were totally unrecognisable, due to the advanced state of decomposition, and the dead man's clothes had been sodden with blood. A number of wounds were detailed including a compound fracture of the right frontal lobe of the skull, with splintering of the bone. The brain was so damaged that all evidence of the injuries was destroyed. The cause of death was the fractures of the skull which in turn had been caused by heavy blows from some blunt-edged instrument. Having examined the axe found at the scene, Dr Wyse agreed that this weapon could have caused the injuries, if the flat side of the axe head had been used.

On the second day of the trial, the hearing of the evidence had to be adjourned as one of the jurymen had been taken ill. A doctor was called and after inspecting the man, stated that he was unable to continue. The trial resumed with 11 jurors. That same day, Galbraith stepped into the witness box to give his own version of what had taken place in Percey's cabin.

Galbraith had already admitted to the police that he was the man seen with Percey but still denied taking his life. Galbraith said that at one stage, Percey had opened a drawer and he had seen that there was a large amount of money in it. A few minutes later, Percey had had to leave the cabin so Galbraith took the opportunity to steal the £1 notes he had seen. He estimated that he took some £36 in all, but said that Percey was alive when he finally left.

Galbraith had said in his statement to the police that during his stay in Percey's cabin he had shaved him. When the body was found, there was two days' growth of beard on Percey's face and confirmation was now given that the beard does not continue to grow after death. Galbraith had tried to suggest that since Percey was clean shaven when he left, this showed that Percey had, in fact, been killed on April 8th, but the medical testimony proved that this was not the case and implied that Galbraith was simply lying about the shave in order to confuse the time of death. The jury, having heard all the circumstantial evidence against Galbraith, had little difficulty in finding him guilty.

An appeal was heard on July 10th, Mr Wooll for the defence making much of the fact that in such a complex case, the jury had considered their verdict for only a quarter of an hour. He conceded that Galbraith had robbed Percey but robbery was not murder and there was no evidence to link Galbraith directly to that crime. The case, as far as murder was concerned, depended entirely on circumstantial evidence.

Having considered the plea of Mr Wooll, the three appeal court judges ruled that there was more than enough evidence to show that the man who had robbed Percey had also taken his life. It was ludicrous to suggest that after being robbed by one man, another should batter Percey to death in his cabin. The appeal was dismissed.

Galbraith fought hard for his life, now asking the Attorney General for a certificate to make an appeal to the House of Lords. When this was refused, his last hope had gone and Galbraith knew that he would die on the gallows.

Fewer than a dozen people gathered outside the gates of Strangeways prison on the morning of Wednesday, July 26th, 1944, as James Galbraith was hanged. It was the seventh execution for murder in an English prison this year.

CHAPTER TWENTY-FOUR

THE MAN WHO LIKED TO ROMANCE

AT AROUND 2.30pm on Monday, November 26th, 1945, a young man walked into the dingy shop at 57 Great Jackson Street, Manchester, and brandishing a gun at the owner, 72-year-old Henry Dutton, demanded that he hand over all the money in the till. When Dutton did not immediately comply with this order, two shots were fired into him. The assailant made good his escape, only to be followed by Mr Dutton who staggered outside into the street where he collapsed on the pavement.

There had been two witnesses when Mr Dutton emerged from his shop. Harry Dixon was a motor driver and at 2.35pm he and his mate, Frank Laverty, were driving down Great Jackson Street, heading towards the city. As they drew close to number 57, both men saw a man stagger from that shop and try feebly to wave them down. As the lorry stopped the old man fell to the pavement and Dixon and Laverty leapt down and rushed to his aid. By now, Henry Dutton was half sitting and half lying on the flagstones and began to fall backwards as Harry Dixon caught him and supported him. Both Dixon and Laverty stayed with Mr Dutton until the police arrived on the scene.

The first officer to arrive was Constable Frederick William Magerkorth who saw that Dutton was bleeding from two wounds, one in his stomach and one in his thigh. Constable Magerkorth rendered first-aid, waited for the ambulance to arrive and accompanied Mr Dutton to the Manchester Royal Infirmary. Later, the constable returned to the scene of the shooting and inside the shop found two empty cartridge cases which he handed to Inspector Stainton, along with a bullet he had found on the stretcher used to take Henry Dutton into the infirmary. Meanwhile, Mr Dutton's condition was said to be critical and he was visited at the infirmary by his wife and son.

The day after the shooting, November 27th, while Henry Dutton was still fighting for his life, accounts of the shooting appeared in the local newspapers. Many people read those reports and one man who did was 24-year-old Martin Patrick Coffey, who took his meals at the Salvation Army hostel in Francis Street.

It was around 4.00pm when Coffey went over to a friend, John Irvine, who was sitting with another man, William Phelan. The three had known each other for little more than a month but Coffey sat down as Irvine read out details of the shooting of Henry Dutton, from the newspaper he was reading. As he finished the article, Irvine noticed that Coffey was laughing, and asked him what he found so amusing. Coffey replied, "I'm laughing up my sleeve at the description in the paper." Again, Irvine pressed his new friend and asked him what he meant, whereupon Coffey continued, "It was me that done the job." Coffey added that he had gone into the shop at 2.00pm. "I went into the shop and asked the old man in the shop if I could have a look at an overcoat that was hanging up. The old man took the overcoat down and put it on the counter for me to examine. I then pulled out a gun as the old man made to go round the back of the counter. I told him to hand over all the money that was under the counter. He put two or three thousand pounds on the counter. As he was fumbling to pull out some more money, there appeared in his hand a gun. I shot the gun from his hand and wounded him on the wrist. He then pulled a whistle out of his pocket and blew it two or three times. I then fired two or three rounds into his stomach. The old man staggered after me as I made to go out of the shop."

John Irvine found the story difficult to believe but, to humour Coffey, asked him what he had done with the gun. Coffey avoided the question, saying only that he had climbed on to a bus after the shooting, and confirmed that he was alone and not with a partner as the newspaper report suggested. William Phelan did not believe the story either and went to have a wash, leaving Irvine and Coffey alone together.

Ten minutes after this conversation had taken place, Coffey and Irvine left the hostel together but, without explanation, Coffey left his friend standing in the street while he dashed into a bombed out house nearby, reappearing moments later carrying a piece of rag. Unwrapping this small parcel, Coffey revealed a gun which he showed to Irvine who suggested, "You'd better give it to me in case you get into any more trouble." Coffey duly handed the pistol over, warning Irvine to be careful as the magazine was full.

At around 5.00pm the same day, Coffey, Irvine and Phelan were walking up Market Street when they were approached by a plain clothes policeman who said he wished to interview Coffey. This was about a minor matter completely unconnected with the shooting but as Coffey was taken to the police station, John Irvine told Phelan about the gun Coffey had shown him. The two men went to Irvine's lodgings at 3 George Street where they examined the gun together and unloaded the magazine. The weapon was placed on top of a cupboard, for safekeeping.

Back at the police station, Coffey was seen by Detective Chief Inspector Frank Stainton, who noticed that he looked like the description of his assailant given by Henry Dutton. Coffey was asked to give an account of his movements on the day in question and replied, "That's easy. I wasn't in Great Jackson Street and I haven't shot anybody. I stayed at the Salvation Army at Francis Street on Sunday night and occupied bed 290. I left the Salvation Army on Monday morning at half past eleven. I went to London Road station and hung about there until one o'clock. I then went to the amusement arcade in Deansgate and from there to the Salvation Army for dinner, where I stayed until half past two. From there I went up Cheetham Hill Road."

At this stage, of course, there was nothing specific to link Coffey to the shooting and, indeed, there had been another development which seemed to indicate that Coffey could not be the guilty man. While he was in custody, a young man had entered the sub Post Office at Chorlton-on-Medlock and pointed a gun at the two assistants. He had demanded they hand over the cash but had fled empty handed when he was refused. It was possible that this crime was linked to the one in Great Jackson Street and if so, then Martin Coffey could not be the man the police were hunting. Nevertheless, Coffey was held in the cells, pending further inquiries.

Late on the afternoon of Friday, November 30th, Henry Dutton died from his wounds, making this a case of murder. It was that which finally brought John Irvine to the police station where he saw Chief Inspector Stainton and told him of the incident at the hostel and the subsequent handing over of a gun. The chief inspector went back to George Street, Old Trafford with Irvine and there took possession of the gun. He then returned to the police station and faced Coffey with what he had discovered.

When he conducted the second interview with Coffey at the Bootle Street police station, Chief Inspector Stainton was accompanied by Detective Sergeant Crowe and Detective Sergeant Arthur Ormston. The interview began with Coffey being cautioned. The chief inspector then continued, "Since I saw you on Tuesday last, the pawnbroker from Jackson Street has died. I have made further inquiries and I have traced an automatic pistol, which I believe had belonged to you. I am now definitely of the opinion that you are the person who shot the pawnbroker with this pistol."

Coffey paused for a few seconds and then replied, "You're right. That's my pistol. I did it. I would have told you before but I was frightened that the old man would die. Now it doesn't matter. I'll tell you the truth." He went on to make a full statement, admitting his responsibility for the death of Henry Dutton.

The next day, December 1st, Coffey appeared before the magistrates and was remanded until December 10th. On that date, a further remand followed, this time until December 18th. On his third appearance, Coffey was represented by Mr George Hinchcliffe and all the witnesses were called. In addition, Coffey's statement to the police was read out. According to this document, Coffey claimed that Mr Dutton had taken a step towards him when he demanded money and he had become frightened and fired. He said that he had no intention of using the gun when he went into the shop but had ended up firing three times, running out in fear when he saw Mr Dutton fall. Having heard all this evidence, the magistrates sent Coffey for trial at the next Manchester assizes.

The case of the Crown against Martin Coffey took place on March 12th, 1946, before Mr Justice Morris. Coffey was defended by Mr Kenneth Burke while the prosecution case rested in the hands of Mr F.E. Pritchard.

John Irvine gave the details of his discussion with Coffey in the Salvation Army hostel on November 27th and much of his testimony was backed up by William Phelan. In fact, Phelan had seen Coffey earlier that day, again in the hostel, and Coffey had admitted to him that he had 'shot a bloke the day before'. Phelan had not believed Coffey as he knew he liked to invent the occasional tall story, and he had still not accepted that he was telling the truth when Coffey repeated the claim in front of Irvine. There was, however, some discrepancy between the evidence given by Irvine and Phelan, for the latter denied that Coffey had claimed that the pawnbroker had a gun himself.

Brenda Cooke, a nurse at the Royal Infirmary, reported that on the day Henry Dutton died, she had found a bullet on the floor, close to his bed. She handed this to Detective Sergeant Ormston. Further testimony was given by Dr Percy Jewsbury who was in the casualty department of the hospital when Dutton was admitted at 3.10pm on November 26th. Dr Jewsbury found a bullet entry wound in the right lower abdominal wall with a corresponding exit wound in the right buttock. The second entry wound was in the right upper thigh and this bullet had passed through the body, emerging at the back of the leg.

At 5.15pm, an operation was carried out to repair the abdomen and the large bowel. For a time, Mr Dutton's condition remained stable but on November 29th, peritonitis developed and the patient died at 6.45pm on November 30th. The post-mortem was carried out by Dr Charles Evans Jenkins at the Platt Lane mortuary on December 3rd. He traced the path of two bullets and testified that death was due to peritonitis which had been caused by the perforation of the bowel which in turn had allowed faecal matter to escape into the abdominal cavity.

Albert Louis Allen was an Associate of the Royal Institute of Chemistry who worked at the Home Office Forensic Science Laboratory in Preston. On the day after the shooting, he had visited the scene of the crime in Great Jackson Street and he traced the pathways of the various bullets fired. One bullet had penetrated a drawer and, in Mr

Allen's opinion, this had travelled in a downward direction and had been fired from close by the entrance door, just inside the shop.

Mr Allen also examined Henry Dutton's clothing and determined that the shots which penetrated his overall must have been fired from a distance greater than nine inches. He had also examined the pistol, a self-loading 7.55mm calibre weapon which had to be manually cocked before the first shot could be fired. The bullets recovered from the shop and the hospital had been fired from that gun.

In his summing up, Mr Burke, for the defence, said that his client liked to 'romance' and the only real evidence against him was his statements to his friends at the hostel and the police and there were obvious discrepancies between these. At one stage Mr Burke said, "This sort of story is sometimes told by a vainglorious, stupid man, who thinks he is going to achieve some measure of limelight by pretending to have been mixed up in an affair of this kind." Nevertheless, after an absence of almost 45 minutes, the jury came to the conclusion that Coffey was guilty as charged.

Coffey appealed against his sentence, but this was dismissed on April 9th. Just over two weeks later, on Wednesday, April 24th, 1946, Martin Patrick Coffey was hanged at Manchester prison. Only a small knot of people gathered outside the prison at the time but amongst them were the condemned man's father, sister and one of his closest friends.

CHAPTER TWENTY-FIVE

TWICE BEFORE THE GALLOWS

O N MAY 7th, 1934, a murder trial opened at Manchester. The man fighting for his life was 26-year-old Walter Graham Rowland, a casual labourer from Mellor, which was just inside the county of Derbyshire, not far from New Mills.

The facts of the case appeared to be simple enough. Rowland, his wife Annie May, and their two-year-old daughter, Mavis Agnes Rowland, lived at 2 Cheetham Hill Cottages, Mellor, and by the end of February, Rowland was in trouble with the police. The matter was a relatively minor one, Rowland had taken a taxi to Blackpool and avoided paying the £3 fare. As a result, he had been summonsed to appear in court. The initial hearing had taken place, at Stockport, and matters had then been adjourned until the morning of Friday, March 2nd.

For some reason, the idea of returning to court preyed on Rowland's mind and he told his wife that he did not intend to go back and might run away. She tried to reassure him, but Rowland was still apparently deeply disturbed by the ordeal he felt was before him. At one stage he had even been to see his employer, a Mr Renshaw, and borrowed £4 from him to pay off the debt. Rowland had then telephoned the proprietor of the taxi company and said that he was now in a position to pay the money he owed if he would drop the case. The proprietor said that matters were now out of his hands, and would have to be heard in the court.

On the morning of March 2nd, Walter Graham Rowland left his home at 11.30am and did not return until 3.30pm. During the time he was away, Rowland's wife, Annie, busied herself about the house. That afternoon, just moments before her husband returned home, Annie was in the front bedroom when she noticed a pair of Walter's trousers lying on a chair. Annie picked up the trousers, intending to hang them up, but as she did she noticed that there was something in one of his pockets. This turned out to be one of a pair of woman's stockings, almost certainly one of her own. Why would her husband have such a thing in his pocket? Even as these thoughts passed through her mind, Annie heard Walter coming up the stairs. She pushed the stocking back into his pocket and said nothing about it.

At 5.20pm, Annie May left the house to see some relatives at New Mills, leaving her husband to take care of the child. No more was seen of either Rowland or his daughter until some time before 6.30pm when a young boy named Jackson walked past the house. At that time, Walter Rowland was sitting on his front door step and little Mavis was playing in front of him. Rowland called out to Jackson and asked if he had seen the man who delivered the papers. Jackson replied that he had not.

No more than a few minutes passed before Mr Horsfield, the paperman, walked up to the house next door to Rowland's to deliver a newspaper. He walked directly past the windows of number 2, Rowland's home, and noticed that the blinds were up in the front room and the light was on. He knocked on the door of number 3 and when the rather deaf occupant answered, handed over a newspaper. As Mr Horsfield stood at the door, Rowland came out of his house and asked to buy an evening paper. Mr Horsfield then continued on his round.

Walter Rowland never denied why he wanted that newspaper. He scanned the columns quickly until he found a small paragraph which told him that what he most feared, had happened. The report said that a Walter Graham Rowland had failed to appear in court that morning and consequently, a warrant had been issued for his arrest.

Just a few minutes after Rowland had purchased his newspaper, Mr Horsfield walked back past Cheetham Hill Cottages and noticed that the blinds were now pulled down at the front of number 2. Even as he walked on, Mr Horsfield heard what sounded like someone bolting the door from the inside.

At 6.50pm, Mr Hambledon alighted from a bus at the Devonshire Arms pub, situated some 730 yards from Cheetham Hill Cottages. As Mr Hambledon walked off, he saw Rowland, who he knew quite well as he lived close by, running towards the pub to catch the bus which would take him into Stockport. That was the last sighting of Rowland by any of his neighbours.

At 7.45pm, Annie May Rowland returned home to find the house in darkness. She switched on the light and called out for her husband, but Walter did not reply. Looking through the house, Annie found that the electricity meter had been broken open but worse still was to be found in the back bedroom. It was there that Annie found her daughter, Mavis, lying in her cot with a stocking knotted around her throat. Annie ran for help to Mrs Brough, her neighbour, but it was no use. Mavis Rowland was already dead.

Walter Rowland arrived at Stockport and went into the Touchstone Inn, where he saw a friend of his, a man named Henderson. At about 9.15pm, a friend of Henderson's, a woman named Burke, also came into the pub and Mr Henderson introduced her to Rowland. The couple seemed to get on well from the very start and Mrs Burke agreed when Rowland suggested they get a taxi and go to New Brighton for the night. At 10.00pm, Mrs Burke and Rowland climbed into the taxi owned by Mr Grimshaw, and set off.

The cab arrived at New Brighton at 12.15am. Rowland, knowing that he had no money to pay the fare, tried to escape Grimshaw by giving him an address that did not exist, Lime Grove. When Grimshaw failed to find Lime Grove, Rowland announced that he would go to the police station to ask for directions. He strode off, leaving Mrs Burke in the back of the cab.

Rowland did indeed walk into New Brighton police station where he told a strange story about he and three other men bringing a woman to the town and now looking for lodgings. The officer on duty suggested that Rowland speak to Constable Ryan, who was on duty in the street outside. Rowland went to see the officer but on the way, bumped into the taxi-driver, Grimshaw, who had grown tired of waiting.

One thing led to another and soon Constable Ryan was escorting Rowland and Grimshaw back into the police station. Once inside, another officer, Constable Wesley, decided to take Rowland into the back room where the light was better and it was there that Rowland handed over the newspaper he still carried, pointed to the paragraph saying that a warrant had been issued for him and said, "Ring up the police at Mellor, they will tell you something more serious than that."

The upshot of all this was that the Mellor police were contacted and Rowland was taken to Wallasey where he was charged with the murder of his daughter. At his trial, Rowland admitted that he had broken into his own electricity meter and stolen six shillings from it, and this, he said, was the 'more serious' offence to which he had been referring. When he left the house, his daughter was alive and well and he knew that Annie would soon return to take care of her. At one stage, Rowland had even suggested that his wife, who had recovered from a nervous breakdown some months before, might have had a brainstorm and strangled the child herself.

The case of the Crown versus Rowland lasted two days with Mr H. Rhodes representing the prisoner. The case for the prosecution was led by Mr R.K. Chappell, who was assisted by Mr F. Atkinson, and after hearing all the evidence, the jury had no trouble in deciding that Rowland was guilty as charged, although they added a recommendation to mercy.

On June 6th, 1934, Rowland's appeal was heard before Lord Hewart, the Lord Chief Justice, and Justices Humphreys and Macnaghten. The defence claimed that there was nothing to connect him directly to the crime except that the stocking found around his daughter's throat belonged to Annie May. Replying, Lord Hewart said that it was clear that the child had been murdered during the time that Rowland had charge of her. The appeal was lost.

Walter Graham Rowland was due to hang at Manchester on June 21st, but just two days before, on Tuesday, June 19th, the Home Secretary acted on the jury's recommendation and recommended the King to commute the sentence to one of penal servitude for life. Rowland was transferred to the Isle of Wight and the cold walls of Parkhurst prison. That would have been the last that history ever heard of Rowland but for the intervention of World War Two and a tragic incident which took place on a Manchester bomb site.

On the morning of Sunday, October 20th, 1946, a woman's body was discovered on a blitzed site close to the junction of Deansgate and Cumberland Street. The woman had been battered to death and the bloodstained hammer used to inflict the injuries upon her lay close by, as did a piece of brown wrapping paper which bore the impression of the hammer, implying that it might have only recently been purchased. The police had no trouble in identifying the dead woman, for an ID card, found in her pocket confirmed that she was a 40-year-old prostitute named Olive Balchin, a native of Birmingham.

Investigations showed that Olive, who actually used four names and carried two different identity cards, had come to Manchester only 11 days before her death and was registered as a resident of the Ashton House women's hostel in Corporation Street.

The hammer found near the body was of the type used by leather-beaters and the police now began a systematic search of all such workers, and also men who worked with soft metals, in an attempt to trace the ownership of that hammer. Their efforts soon produced three valuable witnesses.

Norman Mercer, the landlord of the Dog and Partridge, a pub on Deansgate, said that he had been walking his dog at around midnight on October 20th when he saw a man and a woman arguing, close to the spot where Olive's body was subsequently discovered. Mr Mercer gave the police a detailed description of the man who was 'aged 30 to 35, 5ft 7ins tall, proportionately built, clean-shaven, round faced, dark hair and wearing a blue suit'.

The next witness was Edward McDonald, a salesman, who told the officers investigating the case that on October 19th he had sold a hammer which might have been the murder weapon. The description he gave of his customer, was very similar to that supplied by Norman Mercer. Further, Mr McDonald said it was his habit to wrap all purchases and the type of paper he used was of the same type as that found at the murder scene.

Finally, the police interviewed Elizabeth Copley, a Lyon's waitress, who said that on the afternoon of the murder she had served two women who were with a man, in her cafe, which was in Market Street. Elizabeth positively identified the younger of the two women as Olive Balchin, and said that the man with her was carrying a parcel which could have been the hammer, wrapped in paper.

On October 22nd, Dr J.B. Firth, the director of the Home Office forensic science laboratory at Preston, visited the bomb site, accompanied by a number of police officers including Superintendent W. Ashcroft, Detective Sergeant W. Trippier and Detective Constable Hesketh. Samples of soil, cement, brick dust and other debris were taken. Before returning to Preston, Dr Firth also spoke to the heads of the recently-formed murder squad, the first in the city of Manchester. Detective Superintendent William Malcolm Page and Detective Chief Inspector Frank Stainton, gave Dr Firth all the details of the case.

On October 24th, a photograph was published of a model wearing Olive's clothes. Although the picture was in black and white, details were given of the blue coat with its distinctive white buttons, the brown beret and the black shoes. Olive had been wearing these items at 8.00pm on Friday, October 18th, in Littlewood's cafe in Piccadilly. A friend of hers had seen her with a man and asked Olive to come away with her. Olive had replied, "No, I'm going with him." Olive had also worn the same outfit the following day, October 19th, when she had been seen in the Lyon's cafe, by Elizabeth Copley, at 5.00pm.

On October 26th, the police announced that they had found a paper money bag amongst Olive's possessions. This bag, from the Midland Bank, had been stamped 'Birchfield Road Depot', together with a date in October. It also bore the initial 'SG' but no sooner had this clue been announced than the police traced the man who had given the bag to Olive. He was able to prove that he had no connection with the crime. That same day, however, the police finally received the breakthrough they needed.

Information had been given to the police about a resident of a service's transit dormitory, in Millgate, who seemed reluctant to venture out of his room during the day. Since this character also fitted the general description of the man wanted in connection with the death of Olive Balchin, two police officers, Detective Sergeant Blakemore and Detective Constable Nimmo, visited the dormitory where they interviewed the man. The officers later claimed that they were greeted with, "You don't want me for the murder of that woman do you?" He went on to admit that he did know Olive, but had not been with her on the night she died, adding, "I'm admitting nothing because it is only a fool's game to do that. I can account for where I was. I was home at New Mills when she was murdered." Nevertheless, the man was taken in for further questioning. His name was Walter Graham Rowland. Although his history was not revealed at the time, Rowland had been released from prison in 1945, providing he joined the Army. This he did, being discharged a year later.

At the police station, Rowland said that he had known Olive for about eight weeks and during that time he had been intimate with her and now suspected that he may have caught a sexually transmitted disease from her. This might have given Rowland a motive for murder, a theory which was reinforced when at one stage during the questioning Rowland remarked that if she had given him a disease, then Olive had 'deserved all she got'. When, on October 27th, Rowland was placed in an identification parade where he was picked out by Edward McDonald, the man who had sold the hammer, the last piece of evidence seemed to fall into place and Rowland was charged with the murder of Olive Balchin.

Rowland appeared at the Manchester City police court on October 28th before the stipendiary magistrate, Mr J. Wellesley Orr. Inspector Stainton said that he had arrived at the murder site at 11.45am on October 20th. Olive had been lying on a heap of rubble, suffering from severe head injuries. The hammer which had been used to kill her lay 26ins away from the body and nearby, the piece of brown paper which bore the impression of the hammer, was discovered.

Inspector Stainton went on to say that he had first interviewed Rowland at 11.15pm on October 26th. After further investigations had been carried out, Rowland had been charged on the night of October 27th, and to that charge, he had replied, "Not guilty." The entire police court hearing lasted only three minutes before Rowland was remanded for a week.

The second hearing, which took place on November 4th, only took one minute. Rowland was now represented by Mr George Hinchcliffe who made no objection to his client being remanded until November 12th. Two days later, on November 6th, the inquest opened and the injuries Olive had sustained were detailed by Dr Charles Evans Jenkins, a pathologist. He reported numerous fractures of the skull and lacerations of the brain and concluded that many blows must have been rained down on Olive's head. After hearing this testimony, the coroner adjourned matters until December 21st.

On November 12th, Rowland was back at the police court, the prosecution case now being put by Mr J.F. Claxton. He stated that Edward McDonald, a licensed broker who operated from premises in Downing Street, had identified the leather worker's hammer as one he had sold to Rowland, for 3s 6d, at 5.40pm on October 19th. The same man testified that he had picked out Rowland at the identification parade, but under cross-examination, Mr McDonald had to admit that his original description to the police had stated that his customer was dark-haired whereas Rowland was blond.

Norman Mercer, the pub landlord who had been out walking his dog, said that it was almost midnight on October 19th when he heard a couple who seemed to be arguing. He, too, had attended the identification parade and had also picked out Rowland. The cafe waitress, Elizabeth Copley, said that she had also picked out Rowland, who she especially recalled as he was 'nowty' at the time. It had to be explained to the magistrate that 'nowty' was a Lancashire dialect word for bad-tempered.

The accused man's mother, Agnes Hall, who lived at 65 Bridge Street, New Mills, said that her son had come home on October 19th, at 7.30pm to change some of his clothing. He left her house at 9.30pm, saying that he was going to catch a bus back to Manchester.

Rowland stated that after arriving back in the city, he went for a drink in the Wellington public house in Stockport, where he stayed until it was quite late. Although he did not know the precise time he entered and left the pub, Rowland had said that at one stage two policemen in uniform entered one of the bars and left through the other. The defence then called Sergeant Jones who testified that he and a constable had done exactly that, at 10.30pm. How could Rowland have known of this event if he had not been in the pub as he said?

After he had left the pub, Rowland said he had caught another bus, this time to Ardwick, where he went into a fish and chip shop for his supper before walking on to a lodging house at 81 Brunswick Street where he signed the register at about 11.00pm. The landlord of the lodging house, produced the register as evidence and this did indeed show that Rowland had registered when he had said. This meant that at the time of the murder, Rowland was apparently miles away from Deansgate, asleep in bed in Ardwick.

There was, however, some very damaging testimony from Dr J.B. Firth. He had carefully examined Rowland's clothing and said that he had found no trace of blood anywhere, except for a small stain on one of his shoes. Dr Firth had, however, discovered some grey hairs on the clothes, which were of the same type as Olive Balchin's hair. In itself, this might not have proved too difficult for the defence to explain. After all, Rowland had admitted being intimate with Olive, but it was the contents of his trouser turn-ups which was the trump card for the prosecution.

Dr Firth had taken samples of five materials from the murder site, brick dust, cement, charcoal, clinker and withered leaf tissue. All five materials had also been found in Rowland's turn-ups, a definite link to the spot where Olive had been found. That, together with the eye-witness accounts proved conclusive and Rowland was sent for trial.

Walter Graham Rowland faced his second trial for murder at Manchester on December 12th, 1946, before Mr Justice Sellers. The jury of three women and nine men heard the evidence detailed by Mr Basil Neild and Mr B.S. Wingate Saul, while Rowland's defence was put by Mr Kenneth Burke and Mr H. Openshaw. The hearing lasted until December 16th.

Much had been made in the police court about the man described by the various witnesses as being dark-haired, while Rowland was blond. An attempt was made to show that under certain circumstances, Rowland's hair might appear much darker, especially if he used grease to keep it in place. The prosecution called Captain Reid, the manager of the Salvation Army Hostel at Chorlton-on-Medlock, in an attempt to prove this point. Rowland had stayed at that establishment for four nights, starting on October 21st, and Captain Reid stated that when the prisoner first arrived, his hair appeared to be dark and greased.

To counter this, Rowland's mother was called. She confirmed that her son had never used grease on his hair. She had bought him some in 1945, when he was on leave from the Army, but he had refused to use it, saying that his friends would think he had 'gone soft', and handed it on to his brother. The most she had ever known Walter to do was use water to keep his hair in place.

On December 16th, Mr Justice Sellers took one hour and 50 minutes to sum up the evidence. The jury retired and in due course returned to court to announce that Rowland was guilty. He was then sentenced to death for the second time. The very next day, the defence team announced that their client would almost certainly appeal.

That appeal was due to be heard on January 27th, 1947, but three days prior to that, the case took a startling turn when David John Ware, a young man serving a sentence for larceny at Walton prison in Liverpool, admitted that he was the man who had killed Olive Balchin. Consequently, when January 27th arrived, the three appeal court judges, Lord Goddard, the Lord Chief Justice, and Justices Humphreys and Lewis, decided to adjourn the matter for two weeks while Ware's astonishing claim could be investigated.

David Ware had made a very detailed statement to the police, claiming that he had been with Olive to a cinema in Belle Vue. He had, he said, met her for the first time on the night he killed her. As for the time of the murder, Ware said it was at 10.00pm on October 19th, and not at midnight as had been stated at Rowland's trial.

Rowland's appeal was reconvened on February 10th and the defence were allowed to call two new witnesses. Henry Somerville testified that he had been in the Wellington Hotel, some time after 10.15pm on the night of October 19th. A man he now identified as Rowland, had sold him some cigarettes.

The other witness was Walter Haydn Elwood, manager of the Plaza Cinema which was just up the road from the Wellington. Rowland had claimed that when he finally left the pub, there were crowds of people coming out of a cinema. Mr Elwood said that on October 19th, the main film finished at around 10.12pm and that there would have been crowds around the Plaza after that time. Mr Elwood also said that to get from the area of the Wellington to Deansgate would take at least 25 minutes by bus.

For the Crown, Mr Neild admitted that all this evidence negated the testimony of Elizabeth Copley but there remained the evidence of two others who had picked Rowland out as the man seen arguing with Olive and buying a hammer. The Lord Chief Justice announced that the appeal would be dismissed and the reasons would be put in writing.

Rowland, who was present in the court, did not accept this judgement lightly. Grasping the rail of the dock he shouted, "I am an innocent man. This is the greatest injustice that has ever been offered in an English court."

Four warders tried to remove Rowland but he continued to call out, "Why did you not have the man here who has made the confession? I'm not allowed justice because of my past." The warders finally managed to prise Rowland's fingers away from the dock but as he was taken down to the cells, he screamed, "It would have knocked the bottom out of British law if you had acquitted me and had proved me innocent. I say I am an innocent man before God."

The written judgement of the appeal court was given on February 17th, when it was read out by Mr Justice Humphreys. According to that document, the reason why Ware had not been heard was that the appeal court was not the proper place. The judge said, "It is no light matter to reverse the finding of a jury which has convicted a person of murder." He could just as well have said that it was a light matter to allow a man to hang for a crime he may not have committed. The judgement continued, "If we had allowed Ware to give evidence and he had persisted in his confession, the court would have been compelled to form some conclusion of his guilt or innocence and express that opinion in open court. The court would have been engaged in trying not only Rowland, but also Ware."

An inquiry into Ware's confession had been announced by the Home Office and this was put into the hands of Mr John Catterall Jolly, a noted barrister. That report was sent to the Home Secretary on February 25th, and its conclusions made public on the following day. It was an astounding document.

Mr Jolly said that Ware had now admitted that his statement to the police had been false. On February 22nd, Ware had written, 'I have never seen the woman Balchin, who was murdered in Manchester, in my life. I did not murder her and had nothing whatsoever to do with the murder.

'I made the statements out of swank more than anything, but I had a feeling all along that I wouldn't get very far with them. My health has not been, too, good since the outbreak of war, and I really do feel I want some treatment.

'I also thought I was putting myself in the position of a hero ...I wanted to get myself in the headlines. In the past I wanted to be hung. It was worth while being hung to be a hero, seeing that life was not really worth living.'

Mr Jolly had come to the conclusion that Ware had gleaned the details of the crime from press reports and other such sources. There were no points in his 'confession' which could not have been obtained from the newspapers and Ware had even referred to his victim as Olive Balshaw, an error made in early newspaper reports. Further, he had been forced to alter the actual time of the attack from the correct time of midnight on October 19th to 10.00pm since a lodging house register had been produced showing that Ware was asleep in bed at midnight. Ware had even gone so far as to prick his fingers and put spots of blood on his coat sleeves so that forensic evidence would be found to back up his fake story.

Rowland's defence team pointed out many of the inaccuracies in Mr Jolly's report. They found 13 separate items in Ware's original confession which could not have been obtained from any press articles. For instance, Ware had said the woman wore a double-breasted coat and this was not revealed by any newspaper. Further, Mr Jolly had said that a lodging house register had proved Ware could not have been with Olive at midnight and yet exactly the same type of evidence had been produced for Rowland but the report had concluded this had been forged.

Rowland's last chance was a recommendation for a reprieve from the Home Secretary, Mr Chuter Ede. This never came and at 9.00am on Thursday, February 27th, 1947, Walter Graham Rowland was hanged at Strangeways, by Albert Pierrepoint as a crowd of 100 people gathered outside the prison gates.

Some days after Rowland's body had been laid in an unmarked prison grave, the text of his last letter to his parents was published. It read, 'Dear Mother and Dad, I understand just how you must have been feeling today when you came to see me for the last time in this world.

'I ask you to forgive me for trying to cheer you up in the way I did. I just had to keep you up, for I would have broken down myself. I am sure you will understand, Mother and Dad. You know I have told you the truth all along, and you have promised never to doubt or cease from seeking the truth of my total innocence. The truth will out in God's own time, so just go on with this firm belief in your hearts. Please do not mourn my passing.

'I am going into God's hands and into His keeping. I shall walk beside you until we meet again. I am just going on before, away from the injustices and the strain of all the past long days.

'When you receive this letter I shall be at my rest, so do not grieve my passing. Hold up your heads, for I die innocently. I die for another's crime ...Before my Maker, I swear that I am completely innocent of the death of that poor woman. May God bless you and comfort you until we meet again ...Goodbye in this world. Your innocent and grateful son, Walter."

In time, the disquiet expressed in some circles over the execution of Walter Rowland disappeared, until that is another trial, at Bristol, on November 22nd, 1951. It was on that date that David Ware was found guilty but insane of trying to kill a woman named Phyllis Fuidge by hitting her repeatedly, on the head with a hammer. Ware had surrendered himself to the police on July 13th and while being interviewed by the police had once again admitted that he had been responsible for the death of Olive Balchin in Manchester in 1946.

At the time of writing, Rowland's conviction has not been declared unsafe, he has received no pardon and as such, he may hold the 'distinction' of being the only man reprieved for a murder he did commit and hanged for one he possibly did not.

CHAPTER TWENTY-SIX

THE MAN WHO
KEPT A DIARY

ELIZA Wood lived at 33 Knott Street, Oldham, but as a good and dutiful daughter she called almost every day on her mother, Mrs Clark, at 58 Union Street West, also in Oldham. Mrs Clark ran a lodging house from that address and among her residents was 37-year-old James Henry Corbitt. He and Eliza Wood became friendly towards each other and although Corbitt left Union Street West at the end of July 1950, his relationship with Eliza was maintained.

There did, however, appear to be some problems between James Corbitt and Eliza Wood. They began in early July, before Corbitt had moved out of Mrs Clark's house. She had gone on holiday, leaving her daughter, Eliza, in charge. Eliza had moved into number 58 to look after things while her mother was away and one day in the middle of the month, another lodger, Ann Barrett, had seen Corbitt go out at about 8.00pm. Eliza had gone out soon afterwards and Ann Barrett saw neither of them again that night. She did hear a man, whom she presumed was Corbitt, return at some time between 1.00am and 2.00am. He was followed by Eliza a couple of hours later.

Ann was up and about by 7.00am the next morning and to her surprise found that Eliza was already downstairs, sitting in the kitchen with a cloth over her head. There was a great deal of blood on Eliza's clothing and when Ann asked her what had happened, Eliza had said that there had been some trouble between her and Corbitt. Ann saw a deep cut on Eliza's head and poured some cold water over the wound to staunch the bleeding. At this, Eliza Wood fainted but she soon recovered and Ann left her in the care of yet another lodger, Mrs Mary Chorley.

That evening, at around 6.00pm, Ann Barrett returned from work and found Eliza still in the kitchen. Soon afterwards, Corbitt came in and Ann asked him what had taken place between him and Eliza. He took her to one side and whispered, "I'll have to tell you on the quiet." He then went into the kitchen to have his dinner, after which he asked Ann if she would darn a pair of socks for him. Ann realised that this was a ploy so that she and Corbitt could be alone together and he could tell her what had happened, so she went up to his room. There, Corbitt told her that he believed Eliza had been keeping company with another man, Tommy, who also lodged at the house. Corbitt went on to admit that he was jealous and for good measure added that if he could not have Eliza, the other man certainly would not as he would 'finish her off'.

Once Corbitt had moved out of Union Street West, on July 22nd, he took new lodgings at 212 Portland Street, Ashton-under-Lyne, a house owned by Martha Ann Shaw. Corbitt proved to be a good tenant, causing no problems for Martha until, on August 19th, he told her that he was expecting his wife to call and asked Martha if she might stay. This was the first time Martha had ever heard of a wife and, somewhat suspicious, told Corbitt that his 'wife' would not be able to stay with him overnight in her house. That night, Corbitt did not return home to Portland Street.

Alfred Egan was the landlord of the Prince of Wales Hotel in Stamford Street, Ashton-under-Lyne, and he was busy in his bar when, at 8.30pm on Saturday, August 19th, Corbitt walked in and asked if he could book a room for the night for himself and his wife. Mr Egan agreed and handed over the key to room number seven. Corbitt, who was alone at the time, said that his wife would be coming along later, and left the pub.

At 11.30pm Corbitt and his 'wife', who was, of course Eliza Wood, were back at the Prince of Wales. Both seemed to be under the influence of drink but if anything, Eliza appeared to be the more inebriated of the two. Corbitt saw that Alfred Egan had noticed her condition and said, "Take no notice, she's had a drink." The couple then went up to room seven.

Soon after midnight, Mr Egan, who was still downstairs in the bar, heard a series of eight loud thumps from upstairs. His only guests were Corbitt and Eliza, so Alfred Egan dashed upstairs, knocked on their door and called out, "Is everything all right?" From within the room, Corbitt called back, "We've just fallen out of bed." Mr Egan told his guests to make less noise and returned to the paperwork he had been doing in the bar.

Alfred Egan was still working at 1.30am on August 20th when he suddenly saw Corbitt coming downstairs, wearing his trousers and shirt. Corbitt had not noticed Mr Egan and was just making for the side door when Alfred, believing that his guest must be looking for the lavatory, told him that he would find one upstairs. Corbitt, somewhat startled, hurried back upstairs after proffering his thanks.

By 2.30am Alfred Egan had been joined by his wife and both were now sitting downstairs in the bar area when Corbitt again appeared and made towards the side door. This time it was Mrs Egan who called out to him before he again scurried back upstairs. For Mr and Mrs Egan, that was, thankfully, their last sighting of James Corbitt that night.

Margaret Bailey, a cleaner at the Prince of Wales, arrived for work at a few minutes after 7.30am on Sunday, August 20th. She noticed that the side door was open, something which was quite unusual, although she did not think anything of it at the time and walked straight into the kitchen where she started to make herself some tea. It was 7.45am when Corbitt, who was already fully dressed, appeared at the bottom of the stairs strolled into the kitchen, and almost bumped into Margaret.

Corbitt explained that he was a resident, having booked in with his wife the night before, and asked Margaret what time breakfast was served. She replied that he could have it at once if he so wished, but Corbitt told her, " Don't want it now. I'm going for a walk until 8.30." Margaret, still wishing to be helpful, offered to take a cup of tea up to the room for Corbitt's wife but he replied, "You needn't bother. I'll do it when I come back." With that, Corbitt left the premises by the side door. He was never to return.

Despite what Corbitt had said, Margaret Bailey did indeed take a cup of tea to room seven, knocked on the door and walked in and placed the cup on a small table between the two beds. She noticed a woman lying in one of the beds and assumed that she was still asleep. Leaving the room quietly, she saw the landlord, Alfred Egan, and told him that she had just seen his male guest leaving, ostensibly for a stroll. At Egan's suggestion, she returned to room seven to wake the woman.

Margaret Bailey, though, found that she was unable to rouse 'Mrs Corbitt'. After gently shaking her a couple of times, she pulled the bedclothes down and discovered why the guest was not responding. The woman was completely naked, the word 'Whore' was written on her forehead in capital letters, and she appeared to be dead. Margaret rushed to tell Mr Egan, who checked for himself and then telephoned the police.

Sergeant Arthur Bradley arrived at the Prince of Wales at 8.40am. One of the first things he found was a bead from a necklace on the landing carpet outside room number seven. Inside the bedroom, on a mantelpiece, he found a broken string of beads of the same type. Soon afterwards, Detective Chief Inspector Colin Campbell, the officer in charge of the fingerprint bureau at Hutton, dusted the room and discovered a set of palm prints on the head of the bed in which the body lay, and also on the head and foot of the other bed. When the man who had shared the room with the dead woman had been traced, it would be possible to confirm that these prints belonged to him.

Personal items found in the room identified the dead woman as Eliza Wood and once her family had been contacted, the police had the name of James Henry Corbitt. At

8.29am on August 21st, Sergeant Bradley called at 212 Portland Street where he found Corbitt lying on his bed. Corbitt was taken into custody and at an identification parade was picked out by both Alfred Egan and Margaret Bailey. The same day, Chief Inspector Campbell received a print of Corbitt's hand and confirmed that it matched those found in room seven at the Prince of Wales. Corbitt was then charged with murder.

James Corbitt made his first appearance before the magistrates on the day he was charged but only the most basic details of arrest were given before the proceedings were adjourned until August 28th. By that date he had obtained legal representation in the form of Mr George Furniss, who made no objection to a further remand, this time until September 4th. On that date, all the evidence having been considered, Corbitt was sent for trial. That trial took place at Liverpool on November 6th, 1950, before Mr Justice Lynskey. Corbitt was defended by Mr E. Rowson while the case for the prosecution rested in the hands of Mr Edward Wooll.

Mr Wooll began by saying that the jury would hear a story of 'a morbid, squalid and repugnant tragedy'. He went on to refer to one of the most important pieces of evidence in the case. When Corbitt had been arrested, a diary had been found on him. This went into great detail about his relationship with the dead woman and excerpts were read out.

The entry for July 31st, for instance, indicated that Corbitt was perhaps bored with his relationship with Eliza Wood. It read, 'Undecided what to do tonight. Should see Liza but will give her a miss. Liza waited from 7.15 to 9.00 she said.' The very next entry, for August 1st, read, 'Expected some letter or word off Liza. Will make no mistakes next time.' By August 7th, Corbitt was writing, 'Have got tired of Liza. She is just a whore and the world's biggest liar.' And a few days later he referred to an insulting letter he had sent to her, asking her to stay away from him and his place of work. This desire that the relationship should end was not, however, lasting. Corbitt had written as his next diary entry, 'Waiting for next move from Liza.'

Liza did make her move, for she and Corbitt started going out together again and his diary referred to various meetings, some of which ended with them having sex. There were, though, still sinister undertones and on August 12th, Corbitt wrote, 'Booked a room for Lisa and I tonight. She should have met me at 5.30pm. She did not turn up. Will finish with her. I would have finished her last night. She must be born under a lucky star. A miracle saved her before.' These threats continued until August 17th when Corbitt had scribbled, 'Praying for one more chance to get Liza in a position to finish her off. Have lost a few opportunitys (sic).'

The prosecution then began to call their witnesses which, of course, included Alfred Egan, Margaret Bailey and Ann Barrett. Mary Chorley, who now lived at 2 Garlick Street, Oldham, but who had once lodged at Union Street West, was also called. She, too, referred to the night that Corbitt had attacked Eliza over his belief that she was seeing another man. It had been in the early hours of July 21st that she had seen Eliza with her face smeared with blood. A few hours later, at 6.30am, she had seen Corbitt when he got up for work and asked him why he had injured Eliza. He had replied, "I don't really know what came over me. I am sorry that I have done it. I was jealous."

Dr Walter Henry Grace had visited the scene of the crime at 12.30pm on August 20th. He determined that Eliza was dead and there were clear signs of strangulation, including a large amount of urine which the dying woman had passed in the bed. He performed the post-mortem and said that he found marks of violence around Eliza's neck, chiefly on the front. These marks had been caused by the bead necklace she wore and the application of some kind of ligature. Eliza's upper arms were both bruised, which was consistent with a struggle having taken place, and a small bruise on her upper lip showed that she might also have been struck by a fist. The cause of death was confirmed as manual strangulation.

Alan Thompson was the staff chemist at the North-Western Forensic Science Laboratory at Preston. He had attended the post-mortem and had seen Dr Grace remove the skin from Eliza Wood's forehead so that he could examine the writing inscribed upon it. The word 'Whore' had been written with ink from a ball-point pen and the ink had the same chemical composition as that in a pen found in Corbitt's possession. Mr Thompson had also examined four pieces of shoelace found close to the Prince of Wales. He was able to confirm that they had once formed two laces and might account for some of the marks found on Eliza Wood's throat.

Corbitt had made a full written statement to the police. In this he admitted that he had known Eliza for a year and a half but at Christmas 1949, he had grown suspicious of a man named Tommy who lodged at Union Street West. Eliza had first told him that this man was her brother but had later changed her story and said he was her cousin. Corbitt had come to suspect that he was actually no relation at all, and was in fact her lover.

Corbitt went on to say that he had tried to break off the relationship a number of times between Christmas 1949 and February 1950 but finally he agreed to go back with her, providing she gave up Tommy. Corbitt and Eliza then started seeing each other again but she, too, was jealous and had often remarked that if she ever saw him with another woman, she would gas herself. Eliza had also spoken of wanting to kill herself at other times, the last occasion being Saturday, August 19th.

Referring to the events which followed, Corbitt said he and Eliza had enjoyed several drinks together on that Saturday afternoon, during which she had again said that if she ever saw him with another woman, she would kill herself. They parted for a short time but arranged to meet up again at 6.45pm at the Railway pub. Corbitt tried to book a room at the Railway, but the landlord there said they were full so he went over to the Prince of Wales and took a room there. By the time he and Eliza returned to the Prince of Wales, both were very drunk and he barely remembered going up to the room.

After getting undressed, Corbitt and Eliza made love, during which she suddenly shouted, "I want my dad." Within seconds, this changed to, "I want Tommy." At hearing this, Corbitt said his brain had 'snapped' and he could recall nothing else until the following morning when he woke and saw what he had done. Corbitt said he then left the pub, walked to his lodgings and along the way discarded his bootlaces by tearing them apart and throwing away the pieces. These laces had been around Eliza's throat until he cut them off her at 6.00am. The statement ended with the words, "I must have been temporarily insane at the time as I could not have done this thing if I had been sane."

Relying on that statement, Mr Rowson, for the defence, called no witnesses and asked the jury to return a verdict of murder, but implored them to find that at the time he committed the crime, Corbitt was insane. In the event, the jury decided that this was indeed a case of murder, but that Corbitt had carefully planned the death of Eliza Wood, knew exactly what he was doing and was guilty as charged.

There was no appeal against the death sentence and on Tuesday, November 28th, 1950, James Henry Corbitt was hanged at Manchester prison by Albert Pierrepoint. There was one final twist. Corbitt had died at the hands of a man well-known to him. Pierrepoint ran a public house which Corbitt sometimes visited, even playing the piano there on occasion. From a popular song at the time, they had nicknamed each other 'Tish' and 'Tosh'. As Pierrepoint entered the condemned cell, Corbitt stood and said, "Hello Tosh." Pierrepoint replied, "Hello Tish" and then ended the life of a man he might have called a friend.

CHAPTER TWENTY-SEVEN

CONFESSION

GEORGE CAMP was a one-eyed night-watchman who worked on a building site at the Crossacres Estate, Wythenshawe. Much of his time there he spent in a small hut which he shared with his dog, a brindle whippet named Peggy.

On the morning of Sunday, August 12th, 1951, George Camp was found lying dead in his hut, suffering from appalling injuries. He appeared to have been brutally beaten during the early hours of Sunday. His ribs and jaw had been fractured and his wounds were consistent with the 48lbs plank which was close by his body having been dropped on to him from a height of a few feet. It seemed, though, that a bloodstained axe, lying nearby, had also been used. The police officer in charge of the case was Detective Chief Superintendent Dan Timpany and after making inquiries in the immediate area, he discovered that the dead man had been seen in the Red Lion Hotel at Gatley on the night of Friday, August 10th. At that time he had been in the company of a young man who other drinkers there were able to describe, in some detail.

By August 13th, the police had issued his description to the newspapers. According to the reports, they were looking for a young man, aged about 26, who had fair hair, rather large hands and a fresh complexion. The newspaper reports, seeking perhaps to pander to the British public's fondness for animals, ended with confirmation that Camp's dog, Peggy, who had vanished from the building site, had now been found and was being cared for at Rose Hill Farm which was about 100 yards from where George Camp had met his death.

On August 14th, the police team investigating the matter visited a number of cafes, hostels and pubs which George Camp had been known to frequent. No fresh information was forthcoming but the next day, August 15th, the police in Hanley reported that they were holding a man fitting the description released by the Manchester police. Detective Sergeant Nimmo travelled down to the Potteries but this lead proved fruitless. The young man held there was able to prove that he had not been anywhere near Wythenshawe on the night George Camp had been murdered.

Further inquiries brought forward other people who might have seen something of significance, but many of these 'leads' proved to be dead-ends. One such report was of a thin-faced Irishman who had been seen boarding a bus at Crossacres some time around 12.40am on August 12th. Details of this Irishman were published on August 16th and the next day, a man came forward and told the police that he thought he was the person witnesses had seen. He was eliminated from the inquiry and since he did not actually fit the description given by the witness, officers now suggested that there must have been two Irishmen, not one. The one with the thin face had been wearing gumboots and the man who had come forward wore shoes. The second Irishman, if indeed he existed, was never traced.

The investigation seemed to be getting nowhere, even though hundreds of statements had been taken. So, on August 21st, a door-to-door inquiry was started in and around Wythenshawe. Finally, on August 24th, the young fresh-faced man who had been in the Red Lion with George Camp on August 10th was traced. The same day, Chief Superintendent Timpany made a statement to the press: "We have interviewed him and he is now eliminated from the inquiry." With the last real lead gone, the investigation into the death of George Camp came to a halt. Officers still tried to find new leads but no one seemed able to offer further help.

It was not until October 8th that a new development brought fresh information to the police. It was on that day that 24-year-old Alfred Bradley, an inmate at Strangeways prison, saw the governor, Mr Gilbert Hair. Bradley had already spoken to the Church Army chaplain at the prison and a report of their conversation was passed on to Mr Hair, who asked for Bradley to be brought to him. Bradley repeated what he had told the chaplain, which was that he and two others were responsible for the death of George Camp.

Bradley went on to say that it had been the other two men who had struck Camp. He added, "I didn't hit him but I was there when he was killed." Mr Hair asked Bradley to clarify exactly who he was talking about and Bradley replied, "The night-watchman at Wythenshawe." Mr Hair had a wide experience of inmates, for one reason or another, confessing to crimes they had not committed and he warned Bradley of the consequences of wasting police time. Bradley, though, was not to be swayed. He continued, "I was there with two other men. I hit him with a piece of wood and the other two finished him off. I can take the police to the scene of the crime."

Bradley was, of course, already contradicting himself. At first he had said he did not struck Camp. Now he was admitting that he had attacked him, but was still saying that he was not responsible for the night-watchman's death. Mr Hair had no option but to take the matter further and the same day, he contacted Chief Superintendent Timpany.

On a number of occasions over the next few days, Bradley was questioned by both the police and the governor of the prison. At one stage, on October 9th, he was driven around the streets of Wythenshawe in a police car and correctly located the spot where George Camp had been killed. He even pointed out to the police that some sewer shafts had not been there at the time of the crime.

On October 12th, Bradley made a second statement. The details were much the same as those in his first, but now he said that there was no one else with him when Camp was murdered. Then, almost immediately, he changed his mind once more and said that there had been one other person present at the time. Later that day, he was seen again by Mr Hair, Chief Superintendent Timpany and Chief Inspector Green. As he was speaking, Bradley suddenly burst into tears, pointed towards Mr Timpany and said, "I told him there were two men present, but it is not true. I killed him." Bradley went on to make a full statement claiming that Camp had made homosexual advances to him on more than one occasion. Bradley continued, "I didn't want my father to know the type of life I have been leading. I have been indecent with Camp regularly, for which he paid me. That night he gave me beer – about ten pints. I am not used to beer. I was so disgusted with myself I killed him with the axe. I have been doing this thing for many years since I was taught to do so by a rich man who paid me." Bradley said that after Camp was dead, he had taken £16 from his body.

There were a number of conflicting statements to consider and, of course, the only hard evidence against Bradley was his own confession, detailed though it was.

It was for that reason that on October 15th, all the documents relating to the case were sent to the Home Office and the police then waited for instructions on what action to take next. Eventually, the documents were sent back to Manchester with a recommendation that Bradley should face the court. On November 6th, 86 days after George Camp had been killed, 24-year-old Alfred Bradley was charged with his murder.

That day, Bradley appeared before the stipendiary magistrate, Mr F. Bancroft Turner. The hearing was adjourned for 45 minutes while Mr Turner read over Bradley's final statement. Having done so, he ruled that there was a case to answer and Bradley was remanded until November 13th.

On November 13th, Bradley was back in court where the case for the Director of Public Prosecutions was presented by Mr R.L.D. Thomas. The circumstances of the crime were recalled and the timetable of Bradley's interviews with the prison governor and the police was given. His various statements were read out, including the final one in which he admitted that he and he alone had been present when George Camp met his death. As a result, Bradley was duly sent for trial.

On November 29th, just 16 days after he had been committed, Alfred Bradley appeared at Manchester before Mr Justice Lynskey. Mr A.D. Gerrard appeared for the prosecution while Bradley was defended by Mr Kenneth Burke. From the very outset, there was drama.

When Bradley was handed a copy of the New Testament and asked to swear the oath, his words were not very audible and Mr Justice Lynskey told him to speak up, pointing out that it was very important that everyone should be able to hear him. Bradley made no reply, so the judge asked, "Do you understand?" At this, Bradley threw the book at the judge crying, "I've finished." A glass of water was knocked over and as Bradley was removed by the police, the judge ordered an adjournment so that the accused could compose himself.

Although all the evidence was heard that day, Mr Justice Lynskey, wishing to be scrupulously fair to a man on trial for his life, refused to allow the jury to retire, believing that they might be influenced by Bradley's outburst in court. He ordered that a second trial must take place.

Mr Justice Stable had been hearing civil cases at the same sessions and he was now asked to take charge of Bradley's second trial. There was very little delay and on December 6th, Bradley stood in court at Manchester again, with the same prosecution and defence teams, giving the same evidence as before. This second trial lasted for two days.

The main evidence against Bradley was, of course, his own statement. This was read out in court and ended, "I had no intention of hitting to kill. I just wanted to get away. I am sorry for what I have done. I did not intend to kill. This thing has been preying on my mind and I could not sleep. Money can get people into trouble. Money and drink done it."

Post-mortem evidence was given by Dr G.B. Manning. He had determined that the injuries had been inflicted in two separate attacks. In the first attack, Camp had received a number of head wounds, almost certainly inflicted with the axe found at the scene. The other injuries, which included fractured ribs at both the front and back of the body, were consistent with the heavy plank found nearby being thrown or dropped on to the body. Dr Manning confirmed that the first set of injuries would not have proved fatal. It was the plank which had caused George Camp to die.

For the defence, Mr Burke said that there were two separate arguments. In the first place, there was the possibility that Camp had died as the result of an accident. It was true that Bradley had struck him with the axe but it was arguable that after this, the plank had fallen on Camp's still body, inflicting the injuries which killed him. When asked to clarify this point, by the trial judge, Dr Manning agreed that the injuries could have been caused by the plank falling on Camp. As for the fact that the plank was not found on top of Camp, Mr Burke suggested that someone might have gone into the hut, found the body, moved the plank and then panicked and left.

Mr Burke's second line of defence was the severe provocation that his client had suffered, having been forced to engage in unnatural sexual acts for payment. If Bradley had killed Camp, then that provocation was so great that it should reduce the murder charge to one of manslaughter.

In the event, on December 7th, the jury took 50 minutes to decide that Bradley was guilty as charged. One of the two women on the jury wept bitterly as the foreman announced the verdict and Bradley was sentenced to death.

Six days later, on December 13th, Bradley's legal advisors announced that they. were to lodge an application with the Home Secretary for an inquiry into Bradley's sanity. Just over a week later, on December 22nd, that application had been considered and the Home Office announced that after reading a medical report on Bradley's mental condition, the Home Secretary had decided not to recommend a reprieve. A new execution date was now set.

On Tuesday, January 15th, 1952, Alfred Bradley, a native of Macclesfield, was hanged at Manchester. It was to prove a busy year for the hangman, with no fewer than 23 men dying on the gallows of England and Wales.

CHAPTER TWENTY-SIX

A JIGSAW PUZZLE

O N THE afternoon of Friday, May 4th, 1962, at around 3.50pm, Maureen Lang went into the sweet shop run by 57-year-old Sarah Isabella Cross and purchased three sixpenny ice-creams for her children. Sarah Cross was in a happy mood at the time. She was a supporter of Burnley Football Club and she and her husband, David, also a life-long fan, had tickets for the FA Cup Final against Tottenham Hotspur, which was to take place the following day. Although now living in Manchester, Sarah and her husband were both natives of Burnley and had remained faithful to their home-town team. Sarah was certain they would prove victorious at Wembley and said as much to Mrs Lang during the few minutes she was in her shop.

About an hour later, at around 4.50pm, nine-year-old Stephanie Howarth popped into the same shop on Hulme Hall Lane, Miles Platting, to buy herself a bar of chocolate. There was no one in the shop and after calling out for 'Aunt Belle', as all the children knew Sarah, young Stephanie looked behind the counter, where she found Sarah Cross lying on the floor.

Thinking that 'Aunt Belle' had fainted or fallen ill, Stephanie ran to her married sister, Doreen Kenyon, who had a hairdressing shop nearby. After listening to Stephanie's story, Doreen dashed straight round to the sweetshop, went behind the counter and the first thing she noticed was that there were some scratches on Sarah Cross' arms. At the time, Doreen could not see Sarah's head because it was covered with an overall. She tried to pull this off but for some reason could not budge it and felt she might do more harm than good, especially when she thought she heard Sarah Cross make a strange gurgling noise. Only now did Doreen Kenyon see that the floor behind the counter was littered with broken glass.

In fact, if Sarah Cross had made any noise, it was an involuntary one because she was already dead when little Stephanie Howarth found her. Detective Inspector Thomas Butcher, the first senior police officer to attend the scene, soon discovered that Sarah had been hit about the head by means of several mineral water bottles which had been smashed to pieces in the process. The motive was easy to see, for the till behind the shop counter had been rifled. Someone had robbed Sarah and battered her to death in the most brutal fashion.

A murder squad was organised, led by Detective Chief Superintendent Cunningham. Initially there were suggestions that the crime might be linked to two others. In August 1957, Alice Moran, aged 65, had been battered and stabbed to death in the kitchen behind her sweetshop in Collyhurst Road. Soon afterwards, another shopkeeper, 80-year-old Emily Pye, had also been battered to death. Neither crime had been solved.

Hundreds of shopkeepers and householders were interviewed and people were asked if they had seen anything or anyone strange, perhaps running away from Hulme Hall Lane, at around 4.10pm to 4.30pm on May 4th. Alternatively, perhaps some man might have been missing from work on that Friday afternoon. Many reports came in, but all the lines of inquiry soon petered out.

On Friday, May 18th, the possibility that the man the police were hunting might be responsible for a series of crimes was reinforced by another, very similar attack. Lilian Hayes ran a Temperance bar and herbal shop in Downing Street, Ardwick. On this particular Friday, Lilian was about to close the shop when a young man came in and without warning, vaulted over the counter, grabbed a bottle from a display and brought it crashing into Lilian Hayes' face. The man then forced her back into her living room at the back of the shop and there continued beating her about the head. She would almost certainly have died but for the intervention of a lorry driver, John Dawson.

Mr Dawson, seeing that the door of the shop was unlocked, went in to buy some cigarettes. The shop was empty and so Dawson tapped on the counter. From the back somewhere a man's voice shouted, "Sorry Jack, we're closed." Just as he was about to leave, Dawson heard a cry for help. This time it was a woman's voice and luckily, at that moment, John Dawson saw a policeman walking past the shop.

He called to the officer, told him what he had heard and the constable ran into the living quarters at the back of the shop. He was in time to save Lilian Hayes' life but was unable to catch the man who had attacked her, for he dashed out of the back door and escaped over the gate.

The similarities were obvious. Both Lilian Hayes and Sarah Cross had been attacked on a Friday. Both had been beaten by the same type of weapon, a mineral water bottle, and both women had been alone in their shops at the time. Detectives investigating the murder of Sarah Cross took a keen interest in the attack upon Mrs Hayes. Perhaps best of all, the officers working on the latter case had a description, albeit very scant. Lilian Hayes had said her attacker was 'aged about 38, 5ft 9ins tall, wearing a dark-coloured jacket.'

Chief Superintendent Cunningham had one clue, though, which he had not revealed to journalists. David Cross, the dead woman's husband, was an ordnance worker and had left home early on the morning his wife had been attacked. When he was interviewed by the police, Mr Cross explained that the back door of the shop was always kept locked when Sarah was alone on the premises. When the police arrived at the scene, that door was wide open and it was reasonable to assume that the killer, whoever he was, had made good his escape that way. The back door had only recently been painted and on the sticky surface a clear fingerprint had been found. Since that print did not belong to either Sarah or her husband, and Mr Cross had reported no visitors of late, it seemed certain that it must have belonged to the man who had killed Sarah Cross. When police records were checked, the breakthrough came. The print was on file and its owner was 26-year-old James Smith who lived in Corfe Street, Beswick.

At 8.00am on May 27th, Chief Superintendent Cunningham and Inspector Butcher called on Smith at his home and took him to the police station. Asked to make a statement, Smith had very little to say, giving only the briefest details of his movements. He claimed that on the day Mrs Cross was attacked, he had been in the Sun Inn until 3.10pm, and by 4.30pm was at home. On no fewer than three occasions he said that, although he knew where Mrs Cross' shop was, he had never set foot inside it. His answers did not satisfy the police and Smith was charged with murder, although he was never linked with any of the other crimes the police had also been investigating.

Smith appeared before the stipendiary magistrate on May 28th. After details of the arrest were given, the magistrate asked what evidence there was to link the prisoner to the crime. Inspector Butcher replied, "Fingerprints on the premises," and Smith was remanded in custody.

The final magistrates hearing took place on June 27th, with Mr John Wood acting for the Director of Public Prosecutions. He stated that it had been estimated that the till on the premises would have contained somewhere between £70 and £80 on the afternoon of May 4th, but only 3s remained when the police arrived. The last customer known to have entered the shop was Mrs Lang, who was there at 3.50pm, but Sarah Cross was still alive at 4.25pm because a tobacconist's driver had made a delivery then.

Smith had claimed that he was at home at 4.30pm, talking to an insurance man who called every Friday. When this man had been interviewed, he stated that he could not recall whether he saw Smith on that date but added that if he had, it would have been after 4.45pm

Mr Wood went on to detail some magnificent detective work by Chief Inspector Allen, a fingerprint expert who worked on the case. He had lifted one whole fingerprint and two partial prints from the recently-painted door at the shop, and these matched Smith's. Further, Inspector

Allen had collected all the broken glass found at the scene of the crime and painstakingly pieced the four bottles back together. None of the bottles was quite complete, with small gaps here and there where fragments of glass were missing. When Smith had been arrested, his home had been searched, as had his clothing. The police had found three minute pieces of glass in an armchair, one in his carpet sweeper and one in his jacket pocket. All these five were handed to Inspector Allen who found that they fitted precisely into gaps left in the bottles.

Smith was sent for trial and his case opened at Liverpool, on October 15th, 1962, before Mr Justice Stable. The proceedings lasted until October 18th, and Smith was defended by Mr Godfrey Heilpern and Mr W.F.N. Perry, while the case for the Crown was led by Mr Glyn Burrell.

Little Stephanie Howarth told the court how she had found Mrs Cross' body. The shop had appeared to be empty when she first went in and after tapping on the counter, she walked around the side and saw a pair of legs, wearing slippers, sticking out from the side. Stephanie said that the only other thing she saw was a bottle lying near the door at the back. She estimated that she was only in the shop for a minute or so before running to fetch her sister.

Smith had claimed that he spent most of the afternoon in question in the Sun Inn. A workmate of his, named Wrigley, now testified that he and Smith had left their factory at Failsworth together at noon. They first called at a hairdresser's in Oldham Road and then went on to the Sun Inn which was at the corner of Oldham Road and Cheetham Street. They had a few drinks together before Wrigley left at some time between 2.00pm and 2.30pm. This testimony was important to the prosecution for the Sun Inn was only a few minutes walk from the scene of the attack upon Sarah Cross and Smith had been left alone in the area some two hours before that attack took place.

In the witness box, Smith maintained that after leaving the Sun Inn, he had gone straight home by bus and had never been inside Mrs Cross' shop. The evidence of his fingerprints being found at the scene, together with the glass discovered at his home which fitted into the broken bottles, was more than enough to convict him. An appeal was heard on November 5th but the judges ruled that there could be no criticism of Mr Justice Stables' summing up and the evidence showed conclusively that Smith was guilty as charged.

On the day before he was due to die, Smith was visited by his wife, Mary, and told her that nothing had changed between them. She forgave him for whatever he had done and said that she were still very much in love with him. At 8.00am the next morning, Wednesday, November 28th, 1962, James Smith was hanged at Strangeways prison. Mary Smith was outside the jail at the time and was weeping as the moment of execution arrived. Only a handful of other people kept that vigil with her.

The execution of James Smith was the first hanging at Manchester in more than eight years, and only one more man would ever face his death on the gallows there.

APPENDIX

There have been many more executions at Manchester than are covered in the pages of this volume. I have tried to include only those who were hanged for crimes committed within Manchester itself, or cases which have a strong Manchester connection. However, those who study true crime will find this list of all the 71 executions at Strangeways since 1900, a useful addition to their knowledge.

Joseph Holden, 4th December, 1900.
Patrick McKenna, 3rd December, 1901.
Henry McWiggins (Harry Mack), 2nd December, 1902.
William George Hudson, 12th May, 1903.
Charles Whittaker, 2nd December, 1903.
John Griffiths, 27th February, 1906.
John Ramsbottom, 12th May, 1908.
Frederick Ballington, 28th July, 1908.
Mark Shawcross, 3rd August, 1909.
Joseph Wren, 22nd February, 1910.
Walter Martyn, 12th December, 1911.
John Edward Tarkenter, 12th December, 1911.
Arthur Birkett, 23rd July, 1912.
James Ryder, 13th August, 1913.
Ernest Edward Kelly, 17th December, 1913.
Frederick Holmes, 8th March, 1916.
Reginald Haslam, 29th March, 1916.
James Howarth Hargreaves, 19th December, 1916.
Thomas Clinton, 21st March, 1917.
William Rooney, 17th December, 1918.
Hyman Perdovitch, 6th January, 1920.
David Caplan, 6th January, 1920.
Frederick Rothwell Holt, 13th April, 1920.
William Thomas Aldred, 22nd June, 1920.
Charles Colclough, 31st December, 1920.
Frederick Quarmby, 5th May, 1921.
Thomas Wilson, 24th May, 1921.
Hiram Thompson, 30th May, 1922.
George Frederick Edisbury, 3rd January, 1923.

George Perry, 28th March, 1923.

Francis Wilson Booker, 8th April, 1924.

John Charles Horner, 13th August, 1924.

Patrick Power, 26th May, 1925.

James Makin, 11th August, 1925.

Samuel Johnson, 15th December, 1925.

William Thorpe, 16th March, 1926.

Louie Calvert, 24th June, 1926.

Frederick Fielding, 3rd January, 1928.

Walter Brooks, 28th June, 1928.

Chung Yi Miao, 6th December, 1928.

George Cartledge, 4th April, 1929.

Francis Land, 16th April, 1931.

Solomon Stein, 15th December, 1931.

George Alfred Rice, 3rd February, 1932.

Charles James Cowle, 18th May, 1932.

William Burtoft, 19th December, 1933.

John Harris Bridge, 30th May, 1935.

Buck Ruxton, 12th May, 1936.

Max Mayer Haslam, 5th February, 1937.

Horace William Brant, 12th August, 1937.

Charles James Caldwell, 20th April, 1938.

Clifford Holmes, 11th February, 1941.

John Smith, 4th September, 1941.

James Galbraith, 26th July, 1944.

Harold Berry, 9th April, 1946.

Martin Patrick Coffey, 24th April, 1946.

Walter Graham Rowland, 27th February, 1947.

Margaret Allen, 12th January, 1949.

James Henry Corbitt, 28th November, 1950.

Nicholas Persoulious Crosby, 19th December, 1950.

Nenad Kovacevic, 26th January, 1951.

James Inglis, 8th May, 1951.

John Dand, 12th June, 1951.

Jack Wright, 3rd July, 1951.

Alfred Bradley, 15th January, 1952.

Herbert Roy Harris, 26th February, 1952.

Louisa May Merrifield, 18th September, 1953.

Stanislaw Juras, 17th December, 1953.

Czelslaw Kowalewski, 8th January, 1954.

James Smith, 28th November, 1962.

Gwynne Owen Evans, 13th August, 1964.